'Dip Kapoor and Steven Jordan have gathered a powerful set of writers who live and work, write and imagine, at the intersection of critical inquiry and radical action in the Americas and Asia. The complex and compelling chapters remind us of the academic obligation to engage the class struggle; calling for research that can historicize injustice and resistance movements; make visible capillaries of global capital and land grabs; connect campaigns and struggles across groups and place; articulating unapologetically the "need for research that contributes to the critical and rigorous analysis of reality".'

Michelle Fine, The Graduate Centre, CUNY, and author of
Just Research in Contentious Times

'The relationship between research and social movements is fraught with many potential pitfalls. Kapoor and Jordan's collection offer strategies for politically engaged, useful research. Activist researchers, working in solidarity with struggles around the world share their experiences using various forms of Participatory Action Research, ethnography, and oral history to do public sociology. This book is both a critical resource for evaluating research methods, and for thinking about the power and politics of struggle.'

Lesley Wood, York University, Toronto

RESEARCH, POLITICAL ENGAGEMENT AND DISPOSSESSION

RESEARCH, POLITICAL ENGAGEMENT AND DISPOSSESSION

INDIGENOUS, PEASANT AND URBAN POOR ACTIVISMS IN THE AMERICAS AND ASIA

Edited by Dip Kapoor and Steven Jordan

ZED

ZED BOOKS
Bloomsbury Publishing Plc
50 Bedford Square, London, WC1B 3DP, UK
1385 Broadway, New York, NY 10018, USA
29 Earlsfort Terrace, Dublin 2, Ireland

BLOOMSBURY, ZED BOOKS and the Zed Books logo
are trademarks of Bloomsbury Publishing Plc

First published in Great Britain by Zed Books 2019
Paperback edition published 2021

Cover design: Burgess and Beech
Cover photo © Robert Wallis, Panos Pictures

A catalogue record for this book is available from the British Library.

A catalog record for this book is available from the Library of Congress.

ISBN: HB: 978-1-7869-9440-0
PB: 978-1-7869-9441-7
ePDF: 978-1-7869-9442-4
eBook: 978-1-7869-9443-1

Typeset by Swales and Willis Ltd, Exeter, Devon

To find out more about our authors and books visit
www.bloomsbury.com and sign up for our newsletters.

CONTENTS

ILLUSTRATIONS

Figures

Tables

CONTRIBUTORS

Bijoy P. Barua (PhD, OISE/Toronto) is currently honorary fellow of Asian Center for Development. He is a former professor of East West University, Dhaka, Bangladesh. He also served as honorary visiting professor at the International School of Advanced Studies/Mid Western University, Nepal/University of Pavia (Italy) Kathmandu Campus in Spring 2014. He has published in scholarly journals such as *International Education* (USA), *Canadian Journal of Development Studies* and *Development Review* (Bangladesh). He has also contributed book chapters in several edited collections. He is a member of the Advisory Board of the Indian Association of Journalism and Communication, Delhi, India and former associate fellow of the Centre for Developing Area Studies (CDAS), McGill University, Canada. He has co-edited *Globalization, Culture, and Education in South Asia: Critical Excursions* (2012). Currently, he is conducting research with Adivasi and other rural communities pertaining to education, indigenous knowledge, social mobilization, and development in Bangladesh and Northern Thailand.

Hsiao-Chuan Hsia is professor at the Graduate Institute for Social Transformation Studies of Shih Hsin University, Taipei, Taiwan. She was part of the institute's founding faculty and served as the director from August 2010 to July 2016. Her many publications analyze issues of immigrants, migrant workers, citizenship, empowerment, and social movements. Her publications in English include: *For Better or For Worse: Comparative Research on Equity and Access for Marriage Migrants*, the result of collaborating with member organizations of Alliance of Marriage Migrants Organizations for Rights and Empowerment (AMMORE) to address issues of marriage migrants in the Asia Pacific region; "The Making of a Transnational Grassroots Migrant Movement: A Case Study of Hong Kong's Asian Migrants' Coordinating Body"; and *Multiculturalism in East Asia: A Transnational Exploration of Japan, South Korea and Taiwan* (co-edited with Koichi Iwabuchi and Hyun Mee Kim). Hsia is also an activist striving for the empowerment of immigrant women and the making of im/migrant movement in Taiwan. She initiated the Chinese programs for marriage migrants in 1995, leading to the establishment of TransAsia Sisters Association, Taiwan (TASAT). She is also the co-founder of the Alliance for the Human Rights Legislation for Immigrants and Migrants (AHRLIM) in Taiwan. Internationally, she has been instrumental in forming AMMORE. She serves as a board member of Asia Pacific Mission for Migrants (APMM) and was elected as the member of the Regional Council of Asia Pacific Women, Law and Development (APWLD), and a member of the international coordinating body of the International Migrants Alliance (IMA).

Steven Jordan is chair and associate professor in the Department of Integrated Studies in Education (DISE), Faculty of Education, McGill University. He has worked with indigenous peoples and immigrant workers in Canada over the past 20 years using forms of participatory action research/evaluation (PAR/PE) and critical ethnography. He currently serves on the editorial board of the *Canadian Journal of Action Research* and will co-chair and chair the organization committee of the Action Research Network of the Americas conferences to be held in San Diego and Montreal in 2018 and 2019.

Dip Kapoor is professor in international development education in the Department of Educational Policy Studies, University of Alberta, Canada and volunteer research associate and board member, Center for Research and Development Solidarity (CRDS), an Adivasi-Dalit popular indigenous and small/landless peasant rural organization in South Odisha, eastern India. His research and applied engagements in Odisha and with the CRDS have been funded by the Social Sciences and Humanities Research Council (SSHRC) of Canada, facilitating prior non-funded Popular Participatory Action Research (PPAR) going back two decades. He is co/editor of several book collections including *Against Colonization and Rural Dispossession: Local Resistance in South and East Asia, the Pacific and Africa* (2017) and *NGOization: Complicity, Contradictions and Prospects* (2014).

Ligaya Lindio-McGovern is a professor of sociology and the major co-founder of the Office for Sustainability at Indiana University Kokomo. A recipient of a Fulbright Research Award in 2017, she conducted research on the impacts of extractive corporate mining on indigenous communities in the Philippines and its implications towards an integrated framing of human rights and sustainability. With research and teaching interests on women/gender and globalization, Third World development, social movements and social change, and sustainability she is author of *Filipino Peasant Women: Exploitation and Resistance* and *Globalization, Labor Export and Resistance: A Study of Filipino Migrant Domestic Workers in Global Cities.* A former director of women's studies, she is co-editor of *Globalization and Third World Women: Exploitation, Coping and Resistance,* and *Gender and Globalization: Patterns of Women's Resistance.* She received her doctoral degree at Loyola University Chicago in sociology of development and gender, race, and class. Her activism centers on Philippine national liberation, human rights, and women's movements.

Alessandro Mariano grew up in MST encampments and settlements in the state of Paraná and obtained a high school degree with a specialization in teaching (2003) from the Josué de Castro Institute, a school in Rio Grande do Sul administered by the MST leadership. In terms of higher education, he received a Bachelor degree from the State University of Western Paraná (UNIOESTE) (2008), a graduate specialization in Human and Social Sciences from the Federal University of Santa Catarina (UFSC) (2011), and a graduate specialization in *Educação do Campo* (Education of the Countryside) also from UNIOESTE (2015). All of these university degree programs were administered through a partnership between the universities and the MST, with funding through the federal program PRONERA (National Program for Education in Areas of Agrarian Reform). Alessandro also has a Master's in education from the State University of Central-West Paraná. Through his activism with the MST, Alessandro has coordinated Freirean literacy programs (2000–2003) and has participated in the pedagogical coordination of the MST's Itinerant Schools in Paraná (2003–2014). Alessandro is currently a member of the national MST education sector, national coordinator of the MST's LGBT collective, and a doctoral student at the University of Campinas (UNICAMP), and part of a research group on social movements and education at UNICENTRO. He can be contacted at alessandromstpr@gmail.com (in Portuguese or Spanish).

Hasriadi Masalam has a doctorate in the sociology of adult education and development from the University of Alberta, Canada and is a co-founder of ININNAWA Community, a federation of popular social action NGOs in South Sulawesi, Indonesia. His current research concerns a Third-Worldist PAR engagement pertaining to learning in social action and resistance to capitalist development dispossession (palm oil and coconut plantations) in rural Indonesia.

David Meek is an assistant professor in the Department of International Studies, University of Oregon, where he teaches courses surrounding food systems and Latin America. Dr. Meek theoretically grounds his research in a synthesis of political ecology, critical pedagogy, and place-based education. His interests include: sustainable agriculture, social movements, and critical pedagogy. Dr. Meek's research has been funded by the National Science Foundation, Social Science Research Council, and Fulbright Foundation. He has published in *Studies in the Education of Adults*; *Environmental Education Research*; *Antipode*; *Journal of Sustainability Education*; *Environment and Society: Advances in Research*; *Global Environmental Politics*, and the *Journal of Peasant Studies* among other journals.

Patrick O'Hare is an Economic and Social Research Council (ESRC) post-doctoral research fellow in the Department of Social Anthropology at the University of Manchester. He received his PhD in Social Anthropology from the University of Cambridge in 2017, and subsequently worked as a research assistant on the Arts and Humanities Research Council (AHRC) project "Precarious Publishing in Latin America". He has conducted ethnographic research in Argentina, Mexico, and Uruguay with both informal and formal sector waste-pickers and "waste-picker publishers" and studies the politics and economics of waste and recycling. He is interested in the study of nonconventional labor organization, post-neoliberalism, waste and landfill economies and his work has been published in various edited volumes and journals. Patrick has long been involved in radical activism, including pro-independence Scottish politics, solidarity activity with Palestinian and Arab peoples, and the student movement, including a spell as president of the University of St. Andrews Students' Association.

Pablo Pozzi received his PhD in history from the State University of New York at Stony Brook in 1989. He is a plenary full professor in the History Department of the University of Buenos Aires, where he holds the chair in United States History and teaches the dissertation seminar on Argentine labor. He specializes in contemporary social history, specifically post-1945 labor, both in Argentina and in the United States. He is a class I (one) national researcher, and has published numerous articles and books on Argentina and on the United States. His most recent book is *Historia oral e historia política: Izquierda y lucha armada en América Latina 1960–1990* (2012) [Oral History and Political History: The Left and Armed Struggle in Latin America, 1960–1990]. In addition, he is on the Advisory Board of the National Memory Archive (Argentina), was a member of the International Committee of the Organization of American Historians, a former contributing editor to the *Journal of American History*, and a current editor of *Latin American Perspectives*. He heads the Oral History Program at the University of Buenos Aires. He was also the elected representative for South America to the International Oral History Association (IOHA) Board (2008–2010), is on the Scientific Board of the Brazilian Oral History Association, and is the current president of the Argentine Oral History Association (AHORA), as well as one of the administrators of the Latin America Oral History Network (www.relaho.org).

Robyn Magalit Rodriguez is a sociologist (University of California, Berkeley) and currently an associate professor of Asian American studies at the University of California, Davis. She is an Asian migration expert. The key topics her research explores are the political economy and governance of labor migration, the question of migrants' rights and citizenship and migrant workers' transnational activism. She is the author of *In Lady Liberty's Shadow: Race and Immigration after 9/11* (2017). Her scholarly work has been critically informed by her activist engagements. Organizations she has worked with include Migrante Northern California, the Critical Filipino/Filipina Scholars Collective, and the National Alliance for Filipino Concerns.

Eurig Scandrett is a senior lecturer in public sociology at Queen Margaret University, Edinburgh, with research interests in environmental justice struggles, especially in Scotland, India, and Palestine. After an initial career as an environmental scientist, he spent 15 years in adult education and community development. For eight years he was head of community action at Friends of the

Earth Scotland. He was principal investigator for Bhopal Survivors' Movement Study and has been active in Bhopal solidarity groups in Britain. A trade union activist, Eurig is currently vice president of University and College Union Scotland.

Shalini Sharma is Fulbright Fellow at Princeton University studying smart cities and climate justice. She helped set up the Remember Bhopal Museum as researcher and oral historian, and remains a trustee. Her work links environmental studies, cultural studies and community development largely in context of social/environmental changes in cities. This includes her work with the International Campaign for Justice in Bhopal, her PhD on Media, Memory and Social Movements from SOAS, her work as Visiting Fellow at UNESCO C2C for Natural Heritage Management, teaching at the Tata Institute of Social Sciences in Northeast India where the majority of students came from indigenous communities, and most recently, her postdoctoral research on indigenous urbanism and climate justice as Commonwealth Rutherford Fellow at the University of East Anglia.

Santiago Sorroche holds a doctorate in social anthropology from the University of Buenos Aires (UBA). He currently holds an Argentine National Scientific and Technical Research Council (CONICET) post-doctoral position in UBA's department of social anthropology. He coordinates the program Filo Recupera: Trabajo y Residuos. He has been researching on and with Argentine waste-picker (*cartonero*) cooperatives for over ten years. He is working with the Federación Argentina de Cartoneros, Carreros y Recicladores (Argentine Federation of Waste-Pickers and Recyclers). He is interested in the political organization of waste-pickers and their process of unionization. His most recent publications include "Replicable Experiences: Analysis of the Relationships between Recycler Co-operatives, Agencies of the State and NGOs in the Greater Buenos Aires" (*Estudios Sociales* 61: 58–68, 2017) and "Neither 'Lazy' nor 'Thieves': Cartonero Organisations and the Struggle for Recognition" (*Épocas*. Revista de Ciencias Sociales y Crítica Cultural Dossier no. 3).

Rebecca Tarlau attended public school in the United States and went to college at the University of Michigan (2006), where she majored in anthropology and Latin American studies. She received a doctoral degree in social and cultural studies in education from the University of California, Berkeley (2014), focusing her studies on the MST's attempt to implement its educational proposal in public schools throughout Brazil. Between 2009 and 2015, Rebecca spent 20 months collecting ethnographic data on the movement's educational initiatives in four regions of the country, conducting more than 200 interviews with MST activists and state officials, observing dozens of MST teacher trainings, and participating in other educational activities. Her book *Occupying Schools, Occupying Land* (2019) is about the MST's 30-year struggle to transform education in the Brazilian countryside. Rebecca is currently part of the national coordinating collective of the Friends of the MST-U.S. and an assistant professor in education and labor and employment relations at the Pennsylvania State University. She can be contacted at rtarlau@psu.edu.

Irene Vélez-Torres holds a PhD in human and political geography from University of Copenhagen, has an MsA in cultural studies and a BA in philosophy from Universidad Nacional de Colombia. She is associate professor at the Universidad del Valle and her work aims to contribute to the academic challenge of creating science with communities. The focus of her research is on environmental conflicts that have relation to the access and control over natural resources, and racial and ethnic inequalities, utilizing participatory and action methodologies. Maintaining an activist academic approach, she is also engaged in the analysis of social, political, and environmental transitions that occur in the context of current peace-building processes in Colombia.

ACRONYMS AND ABBREVIATIONS

AAAS	Association for Asian American Studies
ABD	accumulation by dispossession
ADB	Asian Development Bank
AHRLIM	Alliance of Human Rights Legislation for Immigrants and Migrants
AMAN	Indigenous Peoples Alliance of the Archipelago
AMM♀RE	Action Network for Marriage Migrants' Rights and Empowerment
AMMORE	Alliance of Marriage Migrants' Organizations for Rights and Empowerment
APAR	anticolonial participatory action research
APMM	Asia Pacific Mission for Migrants
APMMF	Asia Pacific Mission for Migrant Filipinos
ATSA	Aviation Transportation Security Act
BAYAN	Bagong Alyansang Makabayan
BGPMUS	Bhopal Gas Peedit Mahila Udyog Sangathan
BPL	Below the Poverty Line
BSMS	Bhopal Survivors' Movement Study
BWDA	Bangladesh Water Development Authority
CBNRM	Community Based Natural Resource Management
CEP	Coastal Embankment Project
CFFSC	Critical Filipino and Filipina Scholars Collective
CFR	Community Forest Rights
CMC	Paraguayan Peasant Women's Coalition
COFECA	Cooperative Felipe Cardoso
CONICET	National Science Council
CONTEND	Congress of Teachers/Educators for Nationalism and Democracy
CPO	crude palm oil
CRDS	Center for Research and Development Solidarity
CRI	International Relations Collective
CTEP	Popular Economy Workers Confederation
CUNY	City University of New York

DD	development dispossession
DDP	development-displaced persons
DNR	Department of Environment and Natural Resources
EA	Ektha Abhijan
EBA	Enabling the Business of Agriculture
EJC	Evolução da Juventude Camponsea
FACCyR	Argentine Federation of Waste-Pickers, Carters, and Recyclers (Federación Argentina de Cartoneros, Carreros y Recicladores)
FCC	Filipino Community Center
FOCUS	Forwarding Opportunities through Community Upliftment and Service
FRA	Forest Rights Act (2006)
FRC	Forest Rights Committees
GMO	genetically modified organism
HGU	Indonesian land concession
HPH	Indonesian forest concession
HYV	high-yielding variety
IALA-Amazonia	Agroecological Institute of Latin America-Amazonia
IAMR	International Assembly of Migrants and Refugees
ICDP	Integrated Conservation and Development Project
ICJB	International Campaign for Justice in Bhopal
IFR	Individual Forest Rights
IMA	International Migrants Alliance
IMF	International Monetary Fund
INCRA	National Institute of Colonization and Agrarian Reform
INSIST	Indonesian Society for Social Transformation
IWC	Immigrant Worker's Center
JFM	Joint Forest Management
KATRIBU	National Alliance of Indigenous People in the Philippines
KCERP	Khulna Coastal Embankment Rehabilitation Project
KJDRP	Khulna-Jessore Drainage Rehabilitation Project
KSNP	Kerinci Seblat National Park
LAM	Lok Adhikar Manch
MASTRO	West Paraná Farmers' Movement
MFI	microfinance institution
MIDES	Ministry of Social Development

MRA	Microcredit Regulatory Authority
MRF	Movement of Recovered Factories (Movimiento de Fábricas Recuperadas)
MST	Brazilian Landless Workers Movement (O Movimento dos Trabalhadores Rurais Sem Terras)
MTE	Movement of Excluded Workers (Movimiento de Trabajdores Excluidos)
NAFCON	National Alliance for Filipino Concerns
NBA	Narmada Bachao Andolan
NGO	non-governmental organization
NTFP	non-timber forest product
PACE	Pilipino American Collegiate Endeavor
PAR	participatory action research
PDC	Public Distribution Center
PKSF	Palli Karma-Sahayak Foundation
PMA	Philippine Mining Act (1995)
PR	participatory research
PRA	participatory rapid appraisal
PRONERA	National Program of Education in Agrarian Reform
RA	Research Assistants
RBM	Remember Bhopal Museum
RBT	Remember Bhopal Trust
SC	Scheduled Castes
SEZ	Special Economic Zones
SFAU	San Francisco State University
SRI	Secretariat for International Relations
ST	Scheduled Tribes
TAN	transnational advocacy network
TASAT	TransAsia Sisters Association, Taiwan
TRM	tidal river management
TWLF	Third World Liberation Front
UC	Union Carbide
UCR	Radical Civic Union
UDR	Rural Democratic Union
UFW	United Farm Workers
UN	United Nations
UNDP	United Nations Development Programme
UNDRIP	UN Declaration for the Rights of Indigenous People
UNICAMP	State University of São Paulo in Campinas

UNIFESSPA	Federal University of South and Southeastern Pará
UOM	Unión Obrera Metalúrgica
US	United States
USAID	United States Agency for International Development
UWTL	Unggul Widya Teknologi Lestari
WAPDA	Water and Power Development Authority
WTO	World Trade Organization
WWF	World Wildlife Fund

1 | RESEARCH FOR INDIGENOUS, PEASANT, AND URBAN POOR ACTIVISM: CAPITAL, DISPOSSESSION, AND EXPLOITATION IN THE AMERICAS AND ASIA

Dip Kapoor and Steven Jordan

Introduction

Dispossession, pauperization and the exploitation of labor by a historical process of colonial capitalism continues to be met with resistance by indigenous peoples, small/landless peasants/workers, development-displaced persons (DDPs) and semi/urban poor and (racialized-gendered) forced migrant and labor/working classes in the neo/colonies. Praxis and the production of movement-relevant knowledge as research are central to the work of their organic intellectuals and organizational leaders, including local and trans/national activists working with(in) these struggles and movements (Fanon 1963; Gramsci 1971; Kelley 2002). Academic researchers located in post-secondary institutions also engage with these struggles. This collection seeks to contribute in this vein as engaged academic researchers draw on their respective research relationships with and for these struggles and movements in the neo/colonial regions of the Americas and Asia. It is our intention that this contribution is of use to researchers in academia as faculty and graduate students alike and to organic movement intellectuals, activists, and researchers. We extend our initial international perspectives on participatory action research (PAR) collaboration (Kapoor and Jordan 2009) but now in relation to *engaged academic research* broadly defined (including variants of PAR) and specifically in contexts of neo/colonial capitalist dispossession, pauperization and urban poor labor/working-class exploitation (Jordan 2013; Jordan and Kapoor 2016; Kapoor 2017).

Kapoor's anticolonial PAR work over two decades with Adivasi (Scheduled Tribes or *original dwellers*) and Dalits (Scheduled Castes or *outcastes/avarnas*) in rural eastern India in the state of Odisha and Jordan's engagements with the James Bay Cree in northern

Quebec (Canada) (2013) and Immigrant Worker's Center or IWC (Montreal) (2009) have prompted this conversation with other similarly engaged academics. Contributors to this collection were included based on our long-term relationships with some of them and from related networks of academics selected via personal familiarity with their work or based on referrals from those known to us and acquainted with our engaged research contributions.

The collection is informed by the interdisciplinary social sciences and includes engaged academic research methodologies (and methods) variously labeled as: comparative (historical-dialectical) ethnographic approaches; critical oral histories; participatory research (PR); anticolonial participatory action research (APAR); "Third-Worldist" PAR and PAR; grassroots-oriented (insurgent) research; waste-picker ethnography; guerrilla history (class struggle); public sociology and scholar-activism; activist ethnography; and praxis-oriented research. All approaches are informed by (depending on the politics of social groups and/or classes being engaged) an anticolonial, anti-capitalist, anti-dispossession, anti-proletarianization, anarchist, labor/socialist and/or an (indigenist) environmental politics addressing colonial "racial capitalism" (Robinson 2000) in select locations of ongoing contributor research in the Americas and Asia.

As editors we sought to include the work of those academics who were engaged with struggles variously addressing the historical continuity of the coloniality of Euro-American capitalism and power including a comprador national bourgeoisie and growing transnational capitalist and consumer class. These struggles continue to address a political-economic and cultural system of racial (gendered) social domination created by colonial conquest and the emergent system of capitalist accumulation and exploitation connecting all forms of control of work (slavery, servitude, simple commodity production, reciprocity, capital) to produce (through a racialized-gendered division of labor) initially for Europe and then the capitalist world market. The process is centered around the hegemony of a system of states wherein populations classified as inferior in racial terms (indigenous peoples, small/landless peasants, pastoralists, nomads) are excluded from the formation and control of this system (Quijano 2000; 2005) or are simply *in the way of* if not deemed superfluous for the reproduction of colonial (racial) capitalism.

Hence the struggles against (or to replace) colonial capital and the related research relationships are variously located (in terms of politics) in these chapter contributions. For instance, where capitalist relations are relatively established, struggles defined by the labor–capital dialectic (accumulation as expanded reproduction) or a class politics are paramount. Where such relations are still emergent (contexts of colonial accumulation by dispossession from land) "a dialectics of colonial domination and anticolonial resistance (internally penetrative and mutually constitutive of each other)" (Kapoor 2017: 21) or land-based territorial politics takes precedence. The uneven development of capitalist social relations also ensures the prospects and possibilities for contradictory responses and resistance, if not other historical projects which pre-date capital.

This collection *shares experiences of how* and *what is entailed* in engaged academic research *with and for these struggles* and movements understood as "sustained challenges to powerholders in the name of disadvantaged populations living under the jurisdiction or influence of those powerholders" (Tarrow 1996: 874), while demonstrating the many ways in which academic research engagements *can be productive for movements*, despite the potential contradictions and challenges of such cross-locational socio-political work. The emphasis is on political solidarity through relationship with organized groups engaged in struggle which in turn demands significant changes in conventional academic research *methods* given the recognition that to be (critically) aligned with the politics of subjects in struggle is to recognize that knowledge is situated, intersubjective, and produced through a continuous praxis between movement actors and engaged academic researchers. The primary emphasis is on yielding political processes and outcomes that are of use to the struggle, as research-education/pedagogy-organizing and mobilization are often, methodologically speaking, indiscrete and in relation to political action addressing the structures and conditions of colonial (racial) capitalism.

What counts as *academic research contributions* to struggle in this volume is mutually defined (movements and academics) and largely dependent on the politics of the agents of struggle themselves. While knowledge production is central to any form of research engagement and is a primary contribution, academic research relations with social struggles can also include a much wider set of possible contributions determined through ongoing dialogue with movement actors.

These non-discrete possibilities, at the risk of over-simplification, could include for instance:

a. resource support via academic grants/other sources when deemed politically appropriate by all concerned including related deliberations around means and ends;
b. stimulating trans/local networks, coalition building and social mobilization (existing and/or encouraging new socio-political relations);
c. helping establish movement (research/other) organizations with a long-term commitment to knowledge for movements;
d. pedagogical engagements (e.g. social movement memory/ historical projects for movement development);
e. formalized (specific) research inclusions in movements (e.g. around MST schools and rural education in Brazil);
f. pedagogical work with movement activists (with potential multiplier effects over time) and movement constituencies in strengthening research–organizing–education and mobilization depth/width (e.g. stimulating activist reflections on their own movements or engaging in tactical knowledge contributions);
g. international/regional linkages and public education/advocacy and the potential amplification of movement politics by public intellectuals in the context of engagement and beyond; and
h. using academic researcher social, cultural, political, and economic capital to legitimate movement claims or engage with hegemonic social groups and classes, institutions, and actors.

These potential examples regarding academic contributions (always mutually constitutive with movement actors) are intended to be illustrative as opposed to exhaustive.

Engaged academic research(ers) and fault lines of academic contention

Engaged academic research(ers) seeking to work *with* and *for* movements occupy a contentious location in academic–movement relations as such work is subject to a variety of possible questions and criticisms from within academia and movement circles alike for different reasons. Traditional intellectuals (Gramsci 1971) claiming objectivity and the ability to transcend or stand outside class locations (otherwise equated with bias and sectoral interests) thereby seeking scientific legitimacy and authority for their prognostications on movements for academic knowledge production predictably take issue with engaged academic research as being partisan, biased, and sectoral and therefore beneath the necessary level of scientificity (legitimacy) to qualify as being anything but trivial (illegitimate) knowledge.

Traditional intellectuals in turn have been scrutinized by activists and engaged academic researchers alike (Bevington and Dixon 2005; Choudry 2015; Choudry and Kapoor 2010/2013; Jordan 2003). These criticisms range from parasitic knowledge appropriation and claims to expertise thereof based on an alleged disengaged observation and objectification, to an elitist class-defined preoccupation with theoretical innovation for academic consumption (of little relevance for movements) and hegemonic knowledge production in the interests of maintaining and enhancing dominant and ruling ideologies and social relations. This could potentially include misrepresentation and distortions of movement (*real*) politics for the purposes of reproducing these dominant interests. Associated claims around asserting scientific (ill)legitimacy amount to little more than attempts to insulate knowledge production for dominance (=bias), while simultaneously sealing out and delegitimating knowledge(s) informing social action that is potentially disruptive, if not structurally destabilizing in terms of the status quo of unequal and oppressive social relations of colonial (racial) capital.

Oppositional research in academia takes on both divergent and convergent possibilities. For instance, various post-isms advancing "cultural criticism" (Hale 2006; 2008) define their critical and/or oppositional work and potential (qualified) alignment with the politics of movements/struggles primarily if not exclusively in terms of their political commitments to academic institutional space. This is expressed through a penchant for the continuous production of theory and theoretically innovative *emancipatory knowledge* or "luxury production" for "individual careerism", according to Gilmore (1993: 73) often characterized by a demand for analytical complexity, erudition, and appeals for nuance. There is a preoccupation with deconstructive scrutiny of all knowledge categories, including movement-produced/relevant categories; movements which are characterized as being susceptible to resorting to a politics which reproduces what the movement claims to be against for instance. Cultural critics/theorists also give undue attention to horizontal power relations and schisms, given that "there is always another level, another twist or turn in the analysis, another irony or unintended consequence" (Hale 2006: 114).

The attendant and acute concerns with academic research(er) positionality and situatedness, voice (ventriloquism), re/presentation and/or appropriation of situated subaltern perspectives, demands a political-ethical vigilance if not a heavy dose of necessary research(er) reflexivity "embodying familiar progressive desires to champion subaltern peoples and to deconstruct the powerful; yet it neither proposes nor requires substantive transformation in conventional research methods to achieve these goals". It assumes political alignment with the oppositional politics of movements as being exercised through the *emancipatory content of the knowledge produced* and "not through the relationship established with an organized group of people in struggle" (Hale 2006: 98). For all its "epistemological radicalism, cultural critique introduces very little change in the material relations of anthropological knowledge production" making such contributions "theoretically important but methodologically limited projects" (100–101). Furthermore,

> simply critiquing hegemony (and dominance) or adamantly disassociating the research from the dominant discourse might be right in the intellectual sense ... but may also be utterly irrelevant to the struggle at hand ... [T]hose who have only cultural critique to offer will often disappoint the people with whom they are aligned. (Hale 2006: 113)

The methodology (and methods) of what we are calling engaged academic research (or "activist research" in Charles Hale's terms) in contexts of struggle on the other hand, is usually unconventional out of political necessity and given the dual (though not necessarily equivalent) political commitments (social struggles and academia) at play. This is potentially incompatible with rigorous academic analysis (hence intellectually suspect to "cultural critique/theorists"), as *commitments to practical politics* transform research methods (*including use of contradictory means like using the master's tools out of strategic necessity*) and at times prioritize politically-induced analytical closure (*objectionable to cultural criticism*) over further complexity driven by the search for ever greater analytical complexity and sophistication [potentially leading to] simplistic, unproblematized, and undertheorized [research]. (Hale 2006: 101)

Subsequently, there is a tendency towards "ethnographic refusal/thin ethnographies" (Ortner 2006) if not "romantic particularism" (Gilmore 1993: 70) or a reluctance to present the *marginalized* in all their complexity or in terms of their internal politics. This is often done in the interests of necessary political expediency (even immediacy), the calls for building (even temporary and problematic) horizontal political unity to address what are overwhelming vertical struggles against colonial racial capitalist hegemony and dominance, if not encouraged by a strong inclination to produce (expedient) movement-relevant knowledge that movement actors might need, if not ask for.

While some (engaged) academic traditions continue to develop more nuanced understandings and analyses of colonial capitalist domination and power while doing little to enable collective efforts to address these social-structural impositions, those whom they analyze with increasing sophistication and complexity (dealing in sandpits of abstraction in the name of academic/theoretical rigor) persist with colonizing, pauperizing, and exploiting. This is not an option (political nor ethical) for engaged academic researchers developing methods/ways to work with and for struggles and who may be well aware of the (theoretical) contradictions and problematic reproductions of such involvements but remain critically and reflexively politically aligned nonetheless, given the compelling social-structural impositions and dislocations which demand such engagement.

Contexts of struggle and colonial capitalist dispossession, ejection (pauperization) and the exploitation of urban poor labor in the Americas and Asia

Engaged academic researchers in this collection address their work with struggles and movements in the Americas and Asia as they pertain to neo/colonial capitalist dispossession or what is being referenced today as "land grabbing" (see www.grain.org or www.oak landinstitute.org) from indigenous peoples, small/landless peasants/ workers, and DDPs and related semi/urban poor slum-dwellers and (racialized-gendered) migrant/labor class struggles and movements.

While Marx coined the term "land grabbing" (*Capital* Vol. 1: 470) in relation to European capital's relentless search for markets and accumulation in Europe and beyond, a continuous process of "accumulation by dispossession" (Harvey 2003), indigenous schol- ars and activists recognize this process as an

> ongoing [as opposed to formerly] colonial relationship between
> ourselves and those who want to control us and our resources
> … We are surrounded by other, more powerful nations that
> desperately want our lands and resources and for whom we
> pose an irritating problem. This is as true for the Indians of the
> Americas as it is for the tribal people of India and the aborigines
> of the Pacific. (Trask 1993/1999: 102–103)

In the latest round of neo/colonial capitalist globalization some observers have noted that the "contemporary period has witnessed a vast expansion of bourgeois land rights … through a global land grab unprecedented since colonial times … as speculative investors now regard 'food as gold' and are acquiring millions of hectares of land in the global South"[1] (Araghi and Karides 2012: 3); a process that has explicitly targeted racially marginalized (emergent) social classes, groups, and ethnicities in Africa, Asia, and the Americas (Borras et al. 2012; GRAIN 2012; Oakland Institute 2019; War on Want 2012). "Once again, such a project exalts white bodies, capitalist investment and private property and while simultaneously condemn- ing brown and black bodies, subsistence production and collective and customary property arrangements" (Mollett 2015: 425) echoing Frantz Fanon's (1963) observation that,

> Europe [*and America*] is literally the creation of the Third
> World … an opulence that has been fueled by the dead bodies
> of Negroes, Arabs, Indians and the yellow races (76) … When
> you examine at close quarters the (*neo*)colonial context, it is
> evident that what parcels out the world is to begin with the fact
> that of belonging to or not belonging to a given race, a given

species. In the (*neo*)colonies, the economic sub-structure is also a superstructure and the cause is a consequence. (32)

Drivers of neo/colonial rural/semi-urban capitalist dispossession initiating and repeating processes of accumulation in the Americas and Asia (and Africa) include: mining and agribusiness (food/ export commodities) plantations (including cattle farming land purchases); non-food agri-commodities and biofuels; nature reserves, conservation zones, and eco-tourism and tourist complexes; Special Economic Zones (SEZs), urban extensions, and large-scale infrastructure development (e.g. dams); and retirement and residential real estate migrations and remittance-based purchases.

While 70 percent of the global land grab today is taking place in Africa, at least as much money and more projects are in operation in Latin America, including intra-Latin American land grabs for food and non-food items (e.g. biofuel) (Borras et al. 2012; GRAIN 2010) aided and abetted by multi-lateral agencies including the World Bank via its latest push under the Enabling the Business of Agriculture (EBA) project (Oakland Institute: 2019). Today's invaders are not the *finqueros* (estate owners) of the 19th and 20th centuries who relied on "indebted servitude" (slave-like conditions) and the carving up of indigenous territories for vast plantations for export production (sugar cane, coffee, cacao, banana, gum, rubber, and hardwoods) nor the descendants of European conquistadores who plundered colonial domains but big corporations and joint ventures. Millions of hectares of farmland in Latin America have been taken over by these distant foreign investors and by corporatized neoliberal states in Latin America over the past few years for the production of food crops and agrofuels for export.

> The state, instead or protecting its people, protects the investments of foreign companies and governments by criminalizing and repressing the communities who defend their territories. The structures of the host state serve the interests of their new foreign "bosses", not in the manner of the old colonial system of tribute, but through the new neoliberal commercial system, where laws and regulations are dictated by free trade agreements and investment treaties instead of national constitutions or even international law … [O]ver the last fifty

years, corporations have constructed the framework that
facilitates today's land grab, and now they are moving in to reap
the harvest. (GRAIN 2010: 3)

In the Americas the struggles of 210 million indigenous and
Afrodescendent peoples over two decades and more pertaining to
ancestral territorial claims have by some estimates gained legal recognition to over 200 million hectares (Bryan 2012: 215) although such
arrangements (especially titling funded by the World Bank) require
continuous struggle to ensure that "extra-legal" (land systems that
operate outside the state system/institutions) (Mollett 2015: 422)
indigenous lands (including *de facto* systems of land commonly used
by small-scale *campesinos*) remain inalienable, collective, and un-
individuated and cannot be sold or used as collateral, i.e. remain as
"dead capital" (Hernando de Soto 2000, quoted in Mollett 2015:
423). These ongoing struggles of indigenous land tenure systems of
the Inka (*Ayllu*), Aztec (*Kalpulli*), Taino (*Conuco*), Guarani (*Chaco*),
and others continue to contest the homogenizing (neo)colonial *terra
nullius* intrusions of the *hacienda* and the plantation (Ross 2014).
      In India, the colonial Land Acquisition Act of 1894 continues to
facilitate the violent acquisition of land in the post-independence
period from peasants and Adivasis (tribals) and hand it over to private speculators, real estate corporations, mining companies, and
industry, now abetted by the neoliberal turn and the introduction
of Special Economic Zones (SEZs) which number well over 600
zones. In west Kalimantan, Indonesia, of a total territory of 40 million hectares, 5 million is under oil palm, 1.5 million is allocated for
mining, and 3.7 million hectares is for timber, making a total of
70 percent of the land licensed to some 529 companies. Meanwhile
3.7 million hectares are protected, leaving just 0.7 million hectares
for 4.3 million family farmers (Hall 2015: 2).
      Dispossession and displacement in turn lead to scales of land-
lessness and *pauperization*, a term used by Marxist analysts along
with the concept of *absolute surplus populations* for those colonized
by processes of *primitive accumulation* who are *ejected* from *expanded
reproduction* (industrial absorption and waged-employment), i.e. a
process of primary accumulation without proletarianization in the
global South (Harvey 2003). One global estimate of those considered to be surplus to the needs of capital places this number at

2.4 billion (a third of the world's population) with 1.4 billion as the total active army of labor (Foster and McChesney 2012).

Samir Amin (2003) suggests that even with an annual GDP growth rate of above 7 percent for the next 50 years, only up to a third of the existing populations of former peasants and the indigenous and simple commodity producers could be absorbed into industry in the global South, setting aside (if at all possible) the matter of the coloniality of such prognostications of course. In relation to South Asia alone, an estimate suggests that roughly 250 million or a fifth of the population qualify as paupers (Breman 2016), thereby contributing towards a burgeoning "Planet of Slums" (Davis 2007) and the making of "migrant (gendered) labor brokerage states" out of Southern nations like the Philippines (Rodriguez 2010). Given the population density of these regions, this is probably hardly unsurprising but remains socially, politically, and ethically disturbing nonetheless.

Rural and semi/urban land wars and in/formal (migrant) labor organizing in the South (Asia Pacific Mission for Migrants 2016; Kabeer, Sudarshan, and Milward 2013; Kapoor 2017; Ness 2015; Perry 2013; Ross 2014) are part of the growing response to these usurpations and dislocations being engendered by a globalizing colonial (racial-gendered) capitalism. According to Raul Zibechi (2005: 17–18), with reference to the *seringueiros* or rubber tappers in Brazil's Amazon forests, "new subjects emerge by instituting new territorialities, as Indians and landless peasants engage in prolonged struggles to create or broaden their spaces by seizing millions of hectares from estates or landowners or consolidating the spaces they already had (as in the case of the Indigenous)". He also suggests that,

> new urban poor movements are in tune with the indigenous and landless movements (and are in fact living through what rural movements have already experienced), operating with a very different logic from that of the narrow interest-based worker associations. Their political subjectivity is determined by its subordination to capital as new urban occupants (*asentados*), i.e., they create forms of organization closely tied to territory while relying on assemblies of all the people in the urban settlement (*asentameinto*) to decide on the most important

issues. The anti-systemic disposition and militancy of these movements is made possible by their partial control over the re/production of their living conditions. (Zibechi 2005: 18)

Speaking in terms of "dispersed space" or "non-state space" (Andrej Grubacic in Ross 2014: 163) where capital has a limited and distant presence, people are moving to (or are forced to) these spaces and "creating new forms of sociability and resistance" (Zibechi 2012: 50) with a new autonomous urban economy where "the popular sectors have erected for the first time in an urban space a set of independently controlled forms of production" which "although connected to and dependent on the market ... are no longer dominated by the rhythms of capital and its division of labor" (2012: 203).

As men have migrated in search of wages, there has been an increasing "feminization of the rural areas" too wherein women have strategically expanded subsistence farming, including in urban areas. Peasant women's organizations, like the Paraguayan Peasant Women's Coalition (CMC), the Asian Peasant's Coalition (initiated in the Philippines), the Landless Women's Association of Bangladesh (and the occupation of "chars" or low-lying islands/soil deposits in rivers), the National Alliance for Women's Food Rights in India or women's mobilization against Japanese Eucalyptus plantations in Northern Thailand – it is rural/urban poor women's organizing that has had to take on industrial development and agribusiness, real estate, and landed interests (Silvia Fedirici in Ross 2014: 115–123).

It is with these historical-geographical, political-economic, and cultural contexts and connectivity's that engaged academic researchers in this collection address their work with related movements and struggles in their respective locations of engagement in the Americas and Asia.

Organization of the collection and chapter overviews

The book is divided into two sections. "Part I" focuses primarily on engaged research with indigenous and peasant activisms in contexts of dispossession, while "Part II" addresses research with exploited/marginalized labor and urban poor/informal labor struggles. Each chapter explores, describes, and details the relationship between academic research/ers and these activisms in their respective political-geographical contexts in the Americas and Asia with an emphasis on questions of how, where, why, with whom, and to what end(s). As has been suggested, engaged research methodologies in this collection have been variously labeled, including: historical-dialectical comparative ethnographic approaches (Chapter 2); critical oral histories (Chapter 3); participatory research (PR) (Chapter 4); anticolonial participatory action research (APAR) (Chapter 5); "Third-Worldist" PAR (Chapter 6) and PAR (Chapter 7); grassroots-oriented (insurgent) research (Chapter 8); waste-picker ethnography (Chapter 9); guerrilla history (class struggle) (Chapter 10); public sociology and scholar-activism (Chapter 11); activist ethnography (Chapter 12); and praxis-oriented research (Chapter 13).

Social groups/classes and rural contexts of dispossession and exploitation in this collection include: landless workers/small peasants and land dispossession (by hydroelectric plants, landowning classes, and agribusiness), including reclaiming education and public services (*Brazil*); indigenous and Afrodescendant communities and mining (gold) and agribusiness (sugarcane) (*Colombia*); Adivasi (original dwellers) and Dalit ("untouchable castes") and land-forest dispossession by state–corporate ventures in Scheduled (protected) Areas (*India*); indigenous and small peasants and conservation zones and palm oil plantations respectively (*Indonesia*); small peasants and coastal embankment (river diversion/management) projects (*Bangladesh*); and indigenous peoples and gold/mining (*Philippines*). Social groups/classes in urban poor contexts of exploitation and/or dispossession include: waste-pickers/cooperatives (*Argentina and Uruguay*); labor unions/metal workers (*Argentina*); im/migrant workers and undocumented caregivers (*Philippines/USA*); urban poor/plant workers (chemical disaster-dispossessed) (*India*); and forced (marriage/women) migrants and migrations (*Taipei/East Asia*).

What follows is an overview of each chapter, demonstrating engaged research and its contributions and wider implications for these struggles.

Part I: Research and indigenous and peasant activisms

Mariano and Tarlau's chapter is embedded in the flagship Brazilian Landless Workers Movement or "MST" that consists of 1.5 million landless farmers who fight for land reform and social transformation in the countryside. As they note, the MST is "among those resistance movements that prioritizes research and knowledge production, always searching for ways to appropriate research in the service of the organization of landless families and class struggle". After providing the history of the MST and its current struggles against transnational agribusiness, they elaborate on the central role of research in the movement including the role for "research-activist engagement in the context of conservative resurgence" in the country under Jair Bolsonaro who has specifically targeted the MST.

Commencing in the late 1970s, the MST has been at the fore-front of land occupations in Brazil. A diverse organization in terms of its leadership and composition, it has evolved in recent decades as a rural social movement representing the interests of the landless poor (peasants), agricultural workers, and small farmers against the intensification of land concentration and agribusiness development in Brazil. For example, the MST has had some success in challenging the introduction of genetically modified crops by conglomerates such as Bayer, Monsanto, and Cargill. However, it has also developed an autonomous system of cooperatives, agro-industries, schools, and partnerships with higher education institutions "as well as initiatives pertaining to women, youth, communication, political formation, human rights, and international relations".

Of significance for this volume is its relationship to research and how the MST understands the purpose of research (and research-ers) in contexts of rapid neoliberal accumulation and dispossession. Mariano and Tarlau point out that the overall orientation of the MST is towards forms of critical research, including historical-dialectical-oriented comparative ethnography undertaken by the second author with/for the MST. In other words, forms of research that "contributes to a critical and rigorous analysis of reality" and which is "directly connected to the organizational challenges of workers struggle to help inform the future actions of movements". To this end the MST has identified three types of researchers: (i) the "activist researcher" who in essence is an organic intellectual of the MST; (ii) the "external researcher" (i.e. from a university) who is committed to the MST; (iii) the "uncommitted researcher" conducting research on secondary sources and who has little or no relationship to the MST. Needless to say, it is the first and second type of researcher that are central to the MST, "as they understand that there is no neutrality in knowledge production". Mariano and Tarlau extend this analysis by noting that understanding the "*state-society relational*" (i.e. how and in what ways a social movement is embedded in history and social context) is critical to its overall trajectory; researchers who work with social movements must respect and abide by their internal collective decision-making processes; and last, "political engagement" often means producing knowledge for the movement to inform its actions, not necessarily academic publications and journals. With the election of neo-fascist President Jair Bolsonaro in Brazil they argue that the need for politically engaged research has never been more urgent.

Meek's chapter also focuses on the Brazilian MST. With Mariano and Tarlau, Meek emphasizes that for the MST education is central to the creation of a politically engaged and ethical research process which trains "its members as activist scholars". To this end it projects an alternative vision of education (derived from Paulo Freire's philosophy) that consists of: free universal education based on social justice; "agricultural cooperation"; "environmental respect"; and the "valuing of rural culture". Further, this vision "consists of a series of teaching practices that explicitly value the knowledge systems of rural agricultural communities". Integral to this is the idea of an "alternating pedagogy" where students are expected to conduct critical research in their home communities. Through oral history work with MST students, Meek notes that "perpetual movement has long defined their lives". He then explores this collective memory and experience of perpetual movement through an oral history of a young MST activist, "Maria", whose life has been "characterized by movement, and shaped by migrations in search of education". Through interviews conducted over seven years with Maria, Meek traces her development as an organic intellectual within the MST and her evolving understanding of the "political economy of dispossession" in the Brazilian countryside. This understanding stems from her educational work for the MST, conducting oral histories with miners, running workshops for peasants and the rural poor, writing booklets, and public presentations in communities where she is sent. Eventually, these experiences lead her to a critique of accumulation by dispossession (ABD), a counter-hegemonic standpoint, that she calls a "pedagogy of the land" that involves: decolonizing formal education; stemming the processes of depeasantization and reconnecting peasants with the land or "repeasantization"; revaluing traditional forms of agrarian knowledge and knowledge production; and ultimately "promulgating an alternative vision of the relation between nature and society". The boundaries between academic and popular research and knowledge production for the movement are porous and the contributions of one or the other to the MST, multifarious.

Torres' chapter on the relationship between academic knowledge and social change pursues a number of themes and issues explored later by Lindio-McGovern in her chapter as well. Like Lindio-McGovern, Torres focuses on the role of research and the researcher in contexts where neoliberal accumulation has disrupted and degraded traditional rights of land tenure, in this case in relation to gold mining and sugar cane production in Colombia. As she points out, the historical shifts in economic policy from "National Development" in the 1950s, to the articulation of the Colombian economy with a globalized neoliberal capitalism from the 1990s, has led to geographies of extractivism and dispossession in Colombia which have had severe consequences for indigenous and Afrodescendant communities. Large-scale agro-industry and corporate mining have not only displaced entire communities, but forced them to contend with violence, and poisoned land and water through the use of mercury, glysophosphate (Roundup), and other chemical contaminants in the pursuit of profits. As was the case in the Philippines, forms of ABD are legitimated by the state through legal measures and quasi-private militia hired by corporations. Torres response to this is to adopt the stance of an "activist researcher" or "politically engaged research". This involves research that has: (i) a critical predisposition towards the contexts to be researched; (ii) a participatory approach that is also interdisciplinary; (iii) a commitment to social change. As Torres notes, these three moments are essential in research in contexts where ABD is prevalent to ensure that *action* is placed at the center of PAR "to overcome the instrumental use of social participation and to return the transformative strength of the PAR approach".

Drawing on non/funded academic research over the past two decades, Kapoor elaborates on the prospects and possibilities of conducting anticolonial participatory action research (APAR) with Adivasi (indigenous original dwellers) and Dalit (untouchable or outcaste) peoples in the Indian state of Odisha. Informed by locally generated Adivasi-Dalit "oppositional politics addressing colonial continuities" and the theoretical work of Fals-Borda, Fanon, Freire, and Gramsci, APAR aims to simultaneously build solidarity (*ektha*) among subalterns, as well as "enhance the material and cultural prospects of projects for communal-collective economic relations" that can challenge and confront capitalist social relations as lands under traditional forms of tenure while negotiating the contradictions of working with/through Constitutional guarantees in Scheduled Areas. Kapoor is also concerned with detailing how the work of academic researchers located in institutional contexts (universities) can be harnessed to these struggles without being subordinated to the stipulations and exigencies of the state agencies that fund research. The chapter demonstrates how APAR in contexts entangled in ABD and following Gramsci or Freire's aphorism that all social (research) relations are also educational in nature, has to be methodically anchored within forms of popular organizing and education that "provide the conceptual analytics for political reflection concerning colonial capitalist and feudal dispossession and exploitation" in relation to Adivasi and Dalit struggles. The chapter details how APAR is used to address land-forest dispossession and exploitation of Adivasis-Dalits, including how APAR is built on local (including indigenous) knowledge to reveal how and in what ways the social relations of capitalist accumulation and dispossession can be systematically challenged and contested. This APAR contestation has been enabled by: (a) stimulating the emergence of an Adivasi-Dalit movement or Ektha Abhijan (EA), currently including some 350,000 constituents in 500 villages; (b) helping develop popular research organizations like the Adivasi-Dalit Center for Research and Development Solidarity (CRDS) which is engaged in APAR work with the EA (e.g. in asserting land-forest claims via Individual and Community Forest Rights claims now exceeding some 110,000 acres); and (c) initiating trans-local networking (scaling up) between 15 Adivasi-Dalit anti-dispossession movements in the region addressing development dispossession by state-corporate mining, agribusiness, dam, military installation, conservation zones, etc.

Masalam's chapter focuses on what he terms a "Third-Worldist-PAR praxis" in Indonesia. His work focuses on two instances of PAR in contexts of ABD, the first being in relation to "conservation dispossession" of indigenous peoples in the Serampas Highlands of Sumatra. As Masalam shows, a combination of state-sponsored development (backed by the World Bank and non-governmental organizations [NGOs]) and increasing exposure to the international markets for agricultural produce has led to their ongoing expropriation. In the contemporary era this has led to 40–65 million people being made homeless through measures introduced by the state that have effectively redefined the indigenous Serampas as "forest-encroachers" on ancestral lands that they settled from the 11th century. A similar process has been enacted in the development of lands for the purposes of palm oil production in the province of West Sulawesi. The state in conjunction with the corporate sector has systematically used a combination of legal and bureaucratic processes, paramilitary police, and "corporate thugs" to demoralize, intimidate, and harass people opposing their eviction (or return) to the land. However, despite these tactics, he shows how a "praxis of resistance" within a Third-Worldist-PAR is emerging to "reclaim" the land for traditional and sustainable farming. These range from simply re-building homes and meeting places on expropriated land to blockading roads on which palm fruit is transported. Significantly, he notes that "direct action" in combination with "historical learning" have proven to be the most effective strategies for resistance and Third-Worldist-PAR contributions to resistance in the face of these types of dispossession.

Barua's chapter explores development dispossession in Bangladesh that has masqueraded as enlightened, scientific-rational progress for the rural poor and peasants. As he points out, this has largely been achieved through a process of "NGOization" that has seen a plethora of small, medium, and large-scale NGOs that have in many instances constituted "neoliberalism from below" in reconfiguring local and community relationships so that they work in the interests of capital accumulation and metropolitan elites. In this context, "bigger NGOs often act as parallel to the state for investment and profit-making business instead of collective mobilization". Indeed, Barua's exposé is that the activities of microfinance NGOs, such as the Grameen Bank, systematically work to "demobilize, depoliticize and de-radicalize grassroots-based people's organizations and subalterns in the country", thus clearing the way for forms of neoliberal accumulation sanctioned by the state and Western development

agencies led by the World Bank. His response to this as an activist who has worked in the field for over two decades is to call for a
resurgent PAR, free of entanglement with NGOs, aimed at generating "indigeneous ecological knowledge" that is "people-centered"
in promoting "biodiversity and ecological balance" in the country.

Concluding the section on indigenous and peasant activisms,
Lindio-McGovern's chapter on "grassroots-oriented" (insurgent)
research raises a number of questions about doing academic research in contexts where neoliberal accumulation is severing indigenous
populations from their traditional relationship with the land. As she
makes clear, dispossessing indigenous people of their ancestral lands
for mining development in the Philippines is not just simply a matter of physical displacement, but also involves the destruction of
an entire way of life, a culture, language, identity, and ultimately
indigenous knowledge systems that have been in place for millen-
nia. In such circumstances, research she argues cannot be anything
but politically engaged in focusing on supporting struggles around
social justice and liberation. As she shows in her research with
indigenous groups confronting mining by transnational corporations such as Oceana Gold (a Canadian-Australian corporation),
ABD is something that has to be forcibly imposed through coercive and often violent measures that involves the "militarization of
research". Militarization is a strategy used to isolate and marginalize indigenous communities, thereby making them vulnerable to
intimidation by the state (police, armed forces), paramilitary groups,
illegal arrests, and in some instances, extra-judicial killings. It is
in this context that research is militarized in the sense that grassroots researchers become the focus of these tactics in a quest by
the state–corporate complex to maintain a grip on the production
and flow of knowledge about the devastating impacts of mining on
people, their land, waterways, air, and environment. In this respect
Lindio-McGovern's notion of grassroots or "insurgent research" is
a "methodological and epistemological choice" aimed at supporting
indigenous peoples struggles against neoliberal accumulation, the
state, and militarization in the Philippines.

Part II: Research and urban poor activisms
Until relatively recently, research has invariably been viewed
as something that has been the preserve of institutions of higher

learning, primarily universities. Unlike research conducted by inter-governmental organizations (e.g. World Bank) or corporations (e.g. Rand), university research still tends to be viewed as "neutral", "independent", "objective", and "scientific" and is regarded with a high degree of trust by many social groups within civil society. However, in the last two decades this aura of objectivity/truth that has characterized research conducted by universities (and other institutions of higher learning) has come increasingly into question. This has been for a complex of reasons that are internal to the academy which we cannot explore here (see Kapoor and Jordan 2009). However, of equal importance are social movements outside the academy that have not only questioned the premises on which research has traditionally been founded, but have asked questions that are radically different from those posed by academics. As is evident in the chapters by Pozzi, Scandrett and Sharma, and Hsiao, the role of the researcher and his/her relationship to knowledge production is radically shorn from its traditional disciplinary and institutional moorings from within the university.

Working closely with waste-picker cooperatives in Buenos Aires and Montevideo, O'Hare and Sorroche adopt a critical reflexive stance on the traditional role of anthropology and anthropologists working with marginalized people under conditions of neoliberal dispossession. As they note, after a decade of field work, "becoming part of the social world of waste-pickers, the 'objective' relations of classical anthropology came undone". This did not only imply a re-evaluation of the knowledge producing practices of conventional anthropology, but a reversal of the traditional role of anthropologists collecting data and information on behalf of the state – as in ethnography, from the Greek *ethnikos* and *graphos*, "mapping the other". In contexts of dispossession, such as Argentinian and Uruguayan waste-pickers, an "engaged ethnography" can reveal how "anthropologists can conduct research within state bodies on behalf of the marginalized rather than with the marginalized on behalf of the state". Sorroche captures this kind of ethnographic work in his notion of "*Walking with them*" in his work with a waste-picker cooperative in Buenos Aires. He notes that after some hesitation on their part (they thought he was a spy), he came to be accepted as a member of the cooperative planning team for city waste disposal. Also, by virtue of his position as a university researcher he was able to establish close working relationships with city councilors – as the cooperative's "assessor" – who worked with him to change city regulations that improved the working conditions of waste-pickers. O'Hare and Sorroche also point out that the method of the traditional ethnographic workshop can be used "as a space" and is "not just about research". Using this method he goes on to describe how he created workshops in popular education for the unemployed, as a means to dispel the idea that unemployment was their fault and to build solidarity. O'Hare and Sorroche describe a similar, but in some ways more contradictory situation in Montevideo, where some waste-pickers have been collectivized, but at the same time others have faced eviction and displacement by the state through measures such as "hygienic enclosure" and the widespread use of "anti-vandal" containers that have effectively given the state a monopoly over waste collection, recycling, and processing. In this context, state-sponsored collectivization of waste-pickers has heralded dispossession from what should be considered a common good. Although they conclude their chapter by noting that the question of the state and one's relationship to it as a researcher remains contradictory, they also argue that "ethnography is a key methodology that lets us immerse ourselves not only in the lives of waste-pickers but also in their struggles".

We have already seen that history and the idea of making history was a theme that emerged in Part I of the book (e.g. Meek's chapter). This theme also emerges in Part II. Pozzi's account of "guerrilla" or "militant history" ultimately leads him to ask the question, "Am I still an historian?" As he puts it, "I liked History [but] not historians who tended to encase themselves in the marble halls of academe". In contrast to "traditional history", he situates himself as an "activist historian" whose focus is to "break through the methodological impasse of being an observer" by "going out into society" and engaging with people in their everyday lives and struggles. Through his reflections over 40 years of direct involvement with an illegal radio station (The Voice of the South), a steelworker's history group, popular education in poor/urban neighborhoods with the unemployed, and a newspaper (*Our Struggle*), he discusses how and in what ways these experiences changed his understanding of what constituted history and his practices as an historian. This transformation is summed up in the idea of "guerrilla" or "militant history", where the activist historian understands herself as deeply embedded within society, has a social and political commitment that aims at fostering "civility", "democratic tendencies", and "critical thinking" with the poor and marginalized. In particular, training people in the methods of oral history, sharing anecdotes, poems, songs, and humor allows the activist historian to tap into a "subaltern subjectivity" that reconfigures the past and challenges how the present can be understood. The history that emerges is, therefore, subversive, relevant, and, through its popular methods, productive of organic intellectuals who will lead later struggles.

Pozzi's reflections on how his involvement with popular struggles changed his understanding of his relationship to research (in his case, historiography) is also taken up in Rodriquez's chapter on migrant Filipino workers in the San Francisco Bay area. Rodriquez's research explores the establishment of the Critical Filipino/Filipina Studies Collective and work that she and a former doctoral student (Valerie Franscisco) conducted with Filipino caregivers. In relation to the Critical Filipino/Filipina Studies Collective, Rodriquez focuses on the ways in which Filipino scholars began to organize against deportations of Filipino workers (and other migrants) in the wake of the 9/11 attacks in New York and the rise of the "homeland security state" and increased levels of surveillance. As she notes, "distinctions between legal and 'illegal' immigrants have become practically meaningless" as the "war on terror" redefined who and what was illegal (as witnessed most recently in state-sponsored kidnapping of children at the US/Mexican border). Among other things, deportations of Filipinos (and other migrants) became the focal point of activist-scholars who became deeply involved in community struggles against the worst effects of increased surveillance. The Filipino caregivers project that Rodriquez discusses focuses on undocumented caregivers and their experiences of work in the informal labor market. As she points out, "wage theft" among this group was of particular concern given their undocumented status. Using PAR and Freirian methods, such as "theatre of the oppressed", to organize these workers, Rodriquez discusses how despite the intention to "decentering our roles as academics [and] challenge the hierarchies between researcher and researched" caregivers nevertheless became involved *because* of Rodriquez's connection with a university. Second, she notes that "PAR was seen as a tool for organizing, not for data collection" during the life of the project. In other words, the research process orchestrated through PAR was key, not research findings per se. However, she questions if this emphasis attenuated the impact of the project as data was not adequately analyzed and findings not discussed with caregivers. If it had been, she speculates, organizing efforts might have been transferable to "different policy reform efforts".

Scandrett and Sharma's "activist ethnography" on community responses to the Bhopal disaster (1984) shows how local, grass-roots leaders, activists, and "mostly poor, village-born uneducated women" spearheaded the development of the "Remember Bhopal Trust and Museum". As they point out, the "cultural-epistemological achievements of the movement as a locus of cognitive resistance to the wider trends towards neoliberal orthodoxy have been significant". Among these achievements has been employing a "blend of ethnography with participatory action and activist research in solidarity with the survivors" of the Bhopal disaster. This blend of research methodologies relies on Freire's notion of coding/decoding and dialectical knowledge production in stark contrast, for example, to academic nostrums that insist on the use of positivist versions of the constant comparative method. The avoidance of orthodox conceptual frameworks adapted from the academy has meant that an "anti-history" of the Bhopal disaster could be constructed from survivors lived experience and memories that challenged and sub-verted state-sponsored narratives that construed it as simply an unfortunate tragedy. This also implied that the Bhopal Survivor's Museum, established in 2014, was founded on principles that were open access, free of corporate or state sponsorship, and has no entry charges, thus making it accessible to those most affected by the disaster.

In similar vein, Hsia's study of migrant women as foreign brides in Taiwan also attempts to confront apparently commonsense notions of doing research that challenges theory, methodology, and conceptual practices that are taken for granted within the academy, as well as some NGOs. Her chapter looks at the way in which cross-border marriages in East Asian countries can be understood as a form of labor migration generated by neoliberal globalization. As Hsia points out, while the issue of migrant workers has attracted a great deal of attention, the study of marriage migrants has not only been less scrutinized by researchers, but tends to situate women who are involved in it as victims of sex trafficking. This is not so in Taiwan where, she argues, marriage migrants have "been transformed from being isolated 'foreign brides' to migrant activists" who have been able to change laws and policies affecting migrant brides. This transformation she attributes to what she calls "praxis-oriented research". That is, in contradistinction to action research, which Hsia argues does not involve personal transformation and is most often coopted by policy makers "who want efficient – rather than fair – outcomes", praxis-oriented research focuses on participation, as well as engagement with "the material world, analyzing the contradictions in societies, and pinpointing the possibilities of changing them". For example, Hsia employs the concept of the "conscientious wolf-man" as a metaphor to remind researchers that they are not the leaders of social movements but are essentially there to fulfil a service role in empowering the collective and individuals within it. In this respect, although the concept of a "conscientious wolf-man" may seem curious, it nevertheless draws on a complex reservoir of activist theory and lived experience that reflexively aims at instilling critical consciousness in marginalized populations (in this case, migrant brides) through literacy programs designed to allow these women to engage in meaningful public discourse on their predicament.

Note

1   An Oxfam study (2011) suggests that some 227 million hectares – an area the size of Western Europe – has been sold or leased mostly to international investors since 2001, the bulk of these taking place in the last two years alone (125 million hectares of which are in Africa alone grabbed by rich countries for outsourcing agricultural production). GRAIN's recent study (2016), building on research from 2008, documents 500 current land grab deals across 78 countries (around US$94 billion in farmland investments) and over 30 million hectares (the size of Finland). Also see www.oaklandinstitute.org or www.farmlandgrab.org and www.foodfirst.org for current developments in the global South.

References

Amin, S. (2003). World poverty, pauperization and capital accumulation. *Monthly Review*, 55(5): 1–9.

Araghi, F. and Karides, M. (2012). Land dispossession and global crisis: introduction to the special edition on land rights in the world system.

Journal of World Systems Research, 18(1): 1–5.

Asia Pacific Mission for Migrants. (2016). Migrant unionism in Hong Kong: a case study of experiences of foreign domestic workers in union organizing. In Aziz Choudry and Mondli Hlatshwayo (Eds.), *Just Work?: Migrant Workers' Struggles Today*. London: Pluto.

Bevington, D. and Dixon, C. (2005). Movement-relevant theory: rethinking social movement scholarship and activism. *Social Movement Studies*, 4(3): 185–208.

Borras, S., Franco, J.C., Gómez, S , Kay, C., and Spoor, M. (2012). Land grabbing in Latin America and the Caribbean. *Journal of Peasant Studies*, 39(3–4): 845–872.

Breman, J. (2016). *On Pauperism in Present and Past*. New Delhi: Oxford University Press.

Bryan, J. (2012). Re-thinking territory: social justice and neoliberalism in Latin America's territorial turn. *Geography Compass*, 6(4): 215–226.

Choudry, A. (2015). Activist research. In *Learning Activism: The Intellectual Life of Contemporary Social Movements*. Toronto: University of Toronto Press.

Choudry, A. and Kapoor, D. (Eds.). (2010/2013). *Learning from the Ground-Up: Global Perspectives on Social Movements and Knowledge Production*. New York and London: Palgrave Macmillan.

Davis, M. (2007). *Planet of Slums*. London: Verso.

Fanon, F. (1963). *Wretched of the Earth*. Boston, MA: Grove Press.

Foster, J. and McChesney, R. (2012). *The Endless Crisis*. New York: Monthly Review Press.

Gilmore, R. (1993). Public enemies and private intellectuals: apartheid USA. *Race and Class*, 35(1): 69–78.

GRAIN. (2010). Land grabbing in Latin America. Against the Grain (March). Available at: www.grain.org/atg/ [Accessed November 8, 2018].

GRAIN. (2012). *The Great Food Robbery: How Corporations Control Food, Grab Land and Destroy the Climate*. Cape Town: Pambazuka Press.

GRAIN. (2016). *The Global Farmland Grab in 2016: How Big? How Bad?* Barcelona: GRAIN.

Gramsci, A. (1971). *Selections from the Prison Notebooks of Antonio Gramsci*. London: Lawrence and Wishart.

Hale, C. (2006). Activist research v. culture critique: indigenous land rights and the contradictions of politically engaged anthropology. *Cultural Anthropology*, 21(1): 96–120.

Hale, C. (Ed.). (2008). *Engaging Contradictions: Theory, Politics, and Methods of Activist Scholarship*. Berkeley, CA: University of California Press.

Hall, R. (2015). Landgrabbing in South East Asia: what can Africa Learn? In *Another Countryside: Policy Options for Land and Agrarian Reform in South Africa*. Cape Town: Institute for Poverty, Land and Agrarian Studies.

Harvey, D. (2003). *The New Imperialism*. Oxford and New York: Oxford University Press.

Jordan, S. (2003). Who stole my methodology? Co-opting PAR. *Globalisation, Societies and Education*, 1(2): 185–200.

Jordan, S. (2013). New approaches to governance and decision-making: Quebec's Plan Nord and integrating indigenous knowledge into social science research. In *The World Social Science Report 2013: Changing Global Environments*. Paris: UNESCO/OECD.

Jordan, S. and Kapoor, D. (2016). Re-politicizing PAR: unmasking neoliberalism and the illusion of participation. *Educational Action Research*, 24(1): 139–149.

Kabeer, N., Sudarshan, R., and Milward, K. (2013). *Organizing Women Workers in the Informal Economy: Beyond the Weapons of the Weak.* London: Zed Books.

Kapoor, D. (Ed.). (2017). *Against Colonization and Rural Dispossession: Local Resistance in South and East Asia, the Pacific and Africa.* London: Zed Publishers.

Kapoor, D. and Jordan, S. (Eds.). (2009). *Education, Participatory Action Research and Social Change.* London and New York: Palgrave Macmillan.

Kelley, R. (2002). *Freedom Dreams: The Black Radical Imagination.* Boston, MA: Beacon Press.

Marx, K. (1977 [1867]). *Capital.* Vol. 1. London: Lawrence and Wishart.

Mollett, S. (2015). The power to plunder: rethinking land grabbing in Latin America. *Antipode*, 48(2): 412–432.

Ness, I. (2015). *Southern Insurgency: The Coming of the Global Working Class.* London: Pluto.

Oakland Institute. (2019). The highest bidder takes it all: the World Bank's scheme to privatize the commons. Available at: www.oaklandinstitute. org [Accessed February 1, 2019].

Ortner, S. (2006). *Anthropology and Social Theory: Culture, Power and the Acting Subject.* Durham, NC: Duke University Press.

Oxfam. (2011). Land and power: the growing scandal surrounding the new wave of investments in land. Available at: www.oxfam.org/ en/grow/policy/land [Accessed October 5, 2018].

Perry, K. (2013). *Black Women against the Land Grab: The Fight for the Racial Justice in Brazil.* Minneapolis, MN: University of Minnesota Press.

Quijano, A. (2000). Coloniality of power and eurocentrism in Latin America. *International Sociology*, 15(2): 215–232.

Quijano, A. (2005). The challenge of the "indigenous movement" in Latin America. *Socialism and Democracy*, 19(3): 55–78.

Robinson, C. (2000). *Black Marxism.* London and New York: Zed Books.

Rodriguez, R. (2010). *Migrants for Export: How the Philippines State Brokers Labor to the World.* Minneapolis, MN: University of Minnesota Press.

Ross, A. (Ed.). (2014). *Grabbing Back: Essays against the Global Land Grab.* Oakland, CA: AK Press.

Tarrow, S. (1996). Social movements in contentious politics: a review article. *American Political Science Review*, 90(4): 874–883.

Trask, H.-K. (1993/1999). *From a Native Daughter: Colonialism and Sovereignty in Hawai'i*, revised edition. Honolulu, HI: University of Hawai'i Press.

War on Want. (2012). *The Hunger Games: How DFID Support for Agribusiness Is Fuelling Poverty in Africa.* London: War on Want.

Zibechi, R. (2005). Subterranean echos: resistance and politics "desde el Sotano". *Socialism and Democracy*, 19(3): 13–39.

Zibechi, R. (2012). *Territories in Resistance: Cartography of Latin American Social Movements.* Oakland, CA: AK Press.

PART I

RESEARCH AND INDIGENOUS AND PEASANT ACTIVISMS

2 | THE MST AND RESEARCH WITH AND FOR LANDLESS PEASANT-WORKER STRUGGLES IN BRAZIL

Alessandro Mariano and Rebecca Tarlau

Introduction

Scientific investigation is directly influenced by class struggle. Research is always in the service of someone, and the majority of times it is in the service of the dominant class. As Marx and Engels write in the *German Ideology*, "the ideas of the dominant class are in every period the dominant ideas" (Marx and Engels 1986: 72). These ideas shape people and influence their actions to be consistent with the dominant class. These ideas also construct an ideology in the service of capital, or in other words, in the service of the exploitation of workers' labor power.

In modern society, scientific research initially gained relevance in order to increase the "efficiency" of commodity production. Research, the pursuit of knowledge, and technological innovation all led to huge transformations in industrial production and an unprecedented era of economic growth and also extreme inequality. Although a countless number of intellectual pursuits emerged in the 19th and 20th centuries, especially with the expansion of formal educational institutions around the world, the research agendas that gained power and economic investment were almost always the ones aligned with the needs of capital.

Nonetheless, grassroots social movements have also attempted to employ research to support working-class movements. Karl Marx's *Capital* includes hundreds of pages of analysis of the internal workings of the capitalist system, helping workers understand this system and resist it. Other scholars and intellectuals, both within and outside of grassroots movements, have attempted to employ research on behalf of marginalized classes and groups.

The Brazilian Landless Workers Movement, also known as the MST, is a social movement of more than 1.5 million landless

farmers who fight for land reform, agrarian reform, and social transformation in the Brazilian countryside. The MST is among those
resistance movements that prioritizes research and knowledge production, always searching for ways to appropriate research in service
of the organization of landless families and class struggle. How do
we produce knowledge that speaks to the questions that are vital to
a social movement? How do we offer immediate and medium-term
answers to the challenges that movements face? How do we organize
production and social relations in agrarian reform settlements? How
do we produce technologies suitable for agroecology?

These questions have become even more important since the
MST began "occupying" the formal educational sphere, helping to
co-govern dozens of high school, university, and graduate programs
across the country in partnership with over 100 Brazilian universities. Research has been a central component of these courses. In this
chapter, we draw on these movement experiences as well as our own
research engagements to address how, when, and where research
can be in the service of social movements.

The first author of this text, Alessandro Mariano, is an MST
leader who has participated in the movement since his parents first
occupied land in 1995 in the state of Paraná when he was only 11
years old. Since then, Alessandro has become a leader in the MST
education sector, coordinating dozens of the MST's educational initiatives, including a network of public "Itinerant Schools" located in
MST occupied camps in the state of Paraná (Mariano, Hilário, and
Tarlau 2016). Alessandro also participated in the coordination of
the MST's National School Florestan Fernandes between 2015 and
2018. Currently, he is pursuing a doctoral degree in education at
the State University of São Paulo in Campinas (UNICAMP). The
second author, Rebecca Tarlau, is engaged in activism in the US
context. She has also been doing research on the MST's educational
initiatives since the mid-2000s. She has written dozens of articles
about the MST's educational program, both single-authored and co-
authored with MST activists. Currently, she is an assistant professor
of education and labor studies at Pennsylvania State University.

The following chapter is the synthesis of an extended dialogue
between the two authors about the political engagement of researchers within social movements, and in particular, with and for the
MST. The first section briefly describes the history of the Brazilian

Landless Workers Movement and its current struggle against trans-national agribusinesses. It is followed by a section about the role of research in the movement and the leadership's current position on research and researchers. These first two sections are written primarily by Alessandro, often in the voice of the movement. The next section, written by Rebecca, offers some lessons on effective methods of research and how these research-political engagements can contribute to social movements. Finally, we end by summarizing some of the major lessons that emerged in this chapter as well as a call for more research-activist engagement in the context of conservative resurgence.

The Brazilian Landless Workers Movement: a brief history

The MST has consolidated in Brazil as an important social actor, a space of struggle where workers demand the realization of their rights. The peasant-workers who participate in the movement are struggling to survive because they have been deprived of their main means of production – land.

As Stédile (2012) writes, the Portuguese who arrived in Brazil in the early 1500s financed their invasion by the nascent European commercial capitalism. The Portuguese seized the territory for its economic and military supremacy, imposing the law and political will of the Portuguese monarchy. Ribeiro (1995) states that from the point of view of the indigenous peoples who lived in Brazil, the arrival of the Portuguese meant true genocide. The native population included approximately seven million people; today that number is less than one million. In addition, during a period of slavery that lasted from 1530 to 1888, four million enslaved people from Africa were brought to Brazil to work on agricultural-export plantations in what was the largest slave trade in the Americas.

Brazil is still among the countries with the highest concentration of land in the world, due to these histories of land expropriation and labor exploitation of indigenous and Black populations. In addition, many of the Italian, German, and Polish immigrants that traveled to Brazil in the late 1900s either received land plots that were too small to sustain their family, or in many cases, have always been landless. The concentration of land only increased over the course of the 20th century, with Brazil becoming a major agricultural exporter through green revolution technologies and the mechanization of farming that displaced many rural laborers from the countryside. Bernardo Fernandes (2008), one of the principle researchers of the agrarian question in Brazil, states that land concentration is

> a structural problem of the capitalist mode of production. This problem is created by the logic of the expanded reproduction of capital, which causes unequal development, and the concentration of power expressed in different forms, for example: land ownership, money and technology … capital needs to be territorialized without limits. For its territorialization [expansion], capital must destroy other territories, such as peasant and indigenous territories. (Fernandes 2008: 43–44)

According to Fernandes, there have been many moments of conflict between landowners and landless people in Brazil, including between the Portuguese colonizers and Indians, the masters of the sugar mills and enslaved Africans, and the regional landowners known as Colonels and the peasants. The current conflicts between the landless people who make up the MST and the landowning class is a contemporary manifestation of these historical conflicts.

The first land occupations that led to the formation of the MST began taking place in 1979. There were soon dozens more occupations across the southern region. One of the most important factors driving these occupations was the construction of hydroelectric plants, which resulted in the expropriation of land from thousands of families. In Paraná, these displaced families organized camps in front of a hydroelectric plant for 17 days in 1980 and during 57 days in 1981. From these mobilizations, the West Paraná Farmers' Movement (MASTRO) formed (Morissawa 2001). Other land occupations took place in diverse organizational forms during this period, most often with the help of Catholic nuns and priests practicing liberation theology. In January 1984, the leaders of these diverse land occupations came together to found a new national autonomous organization, which would not be linked to the Church, a labor union, or a political party – the Landless Rural Workers Movement (MST).

The MST defines itself as a social movement with a popular, union, and political character. Since its foundation, it has expressed three main objectives: the struggle for land, agrarian reform, and social transformation. The MST combines the immediate struggle for access to land as a condition for the survival of the landless people, to the broader and more general struggles of workers in the countryside. The movement identifies as part of a larger working-class struggle and realizes that access to land for landless families cannot take place without altering the land structure of the entire country through broader reforms.

In the 1990s, MST leaders traveled throughout the country, organizing in more than 20 states and mobilizing thousands of landless families to occupy large land estates. At the same time, the agrarian bourgeoisie began to organize as well, founding the Rural Democratic Union (UDR) in 1985, in conjunction with right-wing governments, the judiciary, and the police force. The UDR is a group of violent and conservative farmers, whose fundamental principle is the preservation of property rights and the maintenance of "order". These conservative organizing efforts triggered many conflicts over the next decade, including the Corumbiara massacre in Rondônia during which two police officers and nine landless activists were killed, and the Eldorado do Carajás Massacre in Pará in 1996, when police murdered 19 MST activists. Other casualties of this rural violence have been religious and trade union leaders, such as Chico Mendes who died in 1988.

Despite this violence, during the 1990s, the MST continued to improve the organization of its camps and settlements, transforming many of these territories into spaces of cooperative agricultural production. The movement also began to take on other struggles, most significantly the fight for education, as well as initiatives pertaining to women, youth, communication, political formation, human rights, and international relations.

The MST continues to be the main movement fighting for agrarian reform in Brazil. In 2018, the MST had helped 400,000 families achieve lands on agrarian reform settlements. The movement also has 100 cooperatives, more than 1,900 associations and 96 agro-industries, 2,000 primary schools, and partnerships with more than 100 universities to provide higher education to students living in areas of agrarian reform (MST 2014).

The fight against agribusiness and its genetic research

Since the 1980s, world capitalism has entered a new phase of development, with the hegemony of financial capital, banks, and transnational companies increasingly controlling the world commodity market. This dominant form of global capital has brought structural changes in the control and production of agricultural commodities. As a result of this reorganization of capitalist agriculture, we have agribusinesses with large-scale monoculture production that use large volumes of chemical and industrial fertilizers. They also depend on scientific studies that optimize machines, control seed genes, among other interventions. This agricultural research is often funded through public money. The first objective of agribusiness is to control the entire production chain: from the seed to the industrialized product. The second objective is to produce commodities, or agricultural products that are accepted in the world market (MST 2014).

In the last ten years, there has been an accelerated process of land concentration. According to the National Institute of Colonization and Agrarian Reform (INCRA), between 2003 and 2010 the average size of land properties increased (MST 2014: 25). Agribusinesses have become even more powerful since the 2008 global crisis, as a huge amount of fictitious, speculative capital came to Brazil to buy land and natural resources. An increase in foreign ownership of Brazilian land has also raised the average prices of agricultural commodities, as well as the price of land, constituting an additional barrier to the democratization of land access.

This agricultural model, besides increasing the concentration of land, drives small farmers to leave the countryside and move to the city. The MST has contested this model of agriculture, and in recent years has organized direct actions in experimental fields of transgenics owned by Bayer, Monsanto, and Cargill. The landless women within the movement have been the leaders of these protests. For example, on August 8, 2008 2,000 peasant women wrested thousands of transgenic eucalyptus seedlings at the Aracruz Celulose forest garden, in Barra do Ribeiro in Rio Grande do Sul. Another protest took place on May 3, 2015, with 1,000 women who destroyed thousands of transgenic tree seedlings that were the subject of 15 years of research by the company FutureGene, part of a larger group Suzano Papel e Celulose, in Itapetininga, São Paulo. The movement also organizes annual actions to destroy genetically modified organisms (GMOs) maize planting in experimental fields throughout the country.

When the MST destroys an experimentation field funded by agribusiness, this is not an action against technology or scientific research, as the media claims. Rather, it is an act of denunciation that questions the morality of research in the service of capital and profit. This research destroys biodiversity by turning seeds, plants, and animals into commodities. When landless activists destroy the seedlings, they are defending life, biodiversity, and the planet.

The MST and the role for research and external researchers

Ever since the MST's founding in 1984, research has been a central and dynamic part of the MST's struggle. For example, it is through research that the movement is able to organize the necessary actions for a land occupation: choosing the land to be occupied, organizing the families to enter the land, and determining how to produce food collectively on the land with hundreds or thousands of people. These are actions that all require investigation, the defining of actions and strategies, and of course, a particular conception of the world.

The MST leaders, through their decades of experiences, understand that research itself is not sufficient for the success of an occupation; however, research increases the possibilities for success. As both agrarian capitalism and the MST's own agrarian reform struggle have expanded in Brazil, the number of questions that the MST has had to explore increased. Some of these questions are internal. For example, in order to organize the camps and settlements the movement has had to research self-governance, agroecological production, the collective organization of social and cultural activities. Other research questions are external, such as the role of agribusinesses in global food production, the production of GMOs, and the alliances between agribusinesses and banks. The other challenge is to understand the links between these two spheres, or in other words, how these external conditions shape the internal challenges of the movement. Through research, the MST seeks to better understand its reality and the transformations that the movement inspires – in order to determine the appropriate paths towards a more just and egalitarian society.

A formal discussion of the role of research within the movement began in the early 1990s. In 1993, the MST organized a seminar on "Research and Popular Movements" in the Três Passos, Rio Grande do Sul. The goal of the seminar was to answer the following question: What does it mean to do research committed to popular movements? One of the most important conclusions of the seminar was the need for research that contributes to a critical and rigorous analysis of reality. This led to the prioritizing of research in the movement's formal educational programs. At this point, in the early 1990s, MST leaders were already overseeing multiple high school degree programs in teacher training and cooperative administration. The movement decided to organize these programs through an "alternating pedagogy", which brought students together for several "study periods" over the course of three years, with "community periods" in between. During the community period students were tasked with investigating their local realities, based on the theories they had studied. The priority was both research and action. For example, some students would lead agricultural trainings in their communities or educational courses about student self-governance. The goal was to analyze and systematize the contributions and challenges of these efforts, thus informing their future action. This internal research practice continues to guide the movement's educational efforts today.

In 1998, the MST organized a National Meeting of Articulation of Researchers of the MST in the city of São Paulo. The major product of this meeting was a booklet on "The MST and Research", the movement's first official publication on the topic (MST 2001). This booklet has guidelines about research methods, including concrete steps, procedures, and processes that researchers should follow. The booklet also describes research as something that is not spontaneous, but rather, takes discipline and extensive study, and appropriate mentorship from experts in the disciplinary area. The booklet also addresses other questions: What method or methods are we talking about? What is our comprehension of science? Is research only about the production of scientific knowledge? The MST's principle conclusion is that the purpose of research is to produce knowledge that is directly connected to the organizational challenges of workers' struggle to help inform the future actions of movements.

In 2005, the MST helped to organize the National Meeting for Research in Education of the Countryside, with financial support from the federal government. This meeting brought together dozens of different social movements to discuss the challenges of developing a research agenda for the field of Education of the Countryside.[1]

During this seminar, the movement took the emphatic conclusion that research involved both a rigorous study of reality (understanding the essence of social phenomena) as well as an intervention, which directly contests capitalist exploitation. The movement referred to this as research-action, whereby researchers study reality, and at the same time, intervene in that reality.

It is important to note that these discussions about research within the movement have involved not only MST educational activists, but also the university professors that have worked in the movement's different formal educational courses. Over the past two decades, the MST has developed a network of more than 200 university professors who are allies to the movement, and who help to coordinate both the movement's formal courses and teach classes in the non-formal political training programs. These university professors have mentored hundreds of students in these courses as they carry out research committed to the MST's struggles.

The MST and external research(ers)

Researchers from diverse academic fields have always studied popular movements. In these studies, landless peasants are often treated only as research objects. Researchers document their histories of struggle and their experiences of collective organization, extract these life experiences, record their interviews and their dreams. This research then turns into dead words, which sit on the shelves of the universities, serving only to confer degrees. Many researchers develop their monographs, dissertations, theses, reports, and other documents about the MST not as committed allies of the movement, but as neutral bystanders. Even worse, many of these researchers do not even return the results of their research to the communities.

This posture represents a lack of professional ethics. Moving beyond this way of doing research is necessary. Researchers should be in dialogue with the movement, from the initial elaboration of their projects until their execution and final products. This process of dialogue should be seen as an initial step of respect and consideration for the movement.

Another limit of much of the research on the MST is the generalization of the results. The MST is a large organization that intervenes in several spheres of struggle with a huge diversity of actions, depending on the local socio-political conjunctures. By assuming that the results of a particular research project apply generally to the entire movement, the researcher distorts reality. When doing a case study about one camp, settlement, or region, the researcher should respect the scale of the project and not universalize the results to other contexts and local realities.

The MST leadership agrees that it is important to study the historical, social, economic, and political realities of the movements' occupations, camps, settlements, and other processes of struggles. However, beyond simply documenting these realities, research should contribute to the political, human, and intellectual formation of the community. Therefore, it is critical that the researchers provide the results of their research to the settlements and the camps that are studied, as well as to the MST's organizational bodies.

There is a huge potential for conducting research across a range of areas that are important to the movement: agricultural production, education, culture, health, gender, race, and sexual diversity. The MST has identified three types of researchers who study its movement. First, the activist-researcher, who is a member of the MST and enters a formal educational program, often at the university level, and develops a research project on the movement's organization, following the advice and needs of the community. The second type of researcher is the external researcher, who is committed to the MST's struggle. In this case, the researcher presents a proposal to study one of the MST's many areas of struggles, but is open to adjust this focus based on the needs of the movements. For example, historians have researched the history of the MST's land occupations in a particular state, thus expanding the movement's own historical record. There are also researchers of the public health effects of pesticides and the form of organization of large landowners, which also contributes to the movement. The third type of researcher is the uncommitted researcher, often doing research based on secondary sources, re-writing what has already been written with very little relationship to practice. From the MST's perspective, the first and second type of researchers are important to class struggle, as they understand that there is no neutrality in knowledge production.

Another central issue is the theoretical perspective and methodological approach of a research project. Again, since the MST leadership believes that science is always political, the clear identification of a theoretical perspective is necessary. Likewise, methodological rigor is a way of preserving the seriousness and quality of research. Without these two elements, research loses all of its potential to rigorously analyze reality. It is important that there is coherence among the different currents of thought in the research project. Over the course of its struggle, the MST has decided to privilege historical-dialectical materialism as a method of interpreting reality and analyzing history. The MST sees historical-dialectical materialism as a method that seeks not only to understand reality but to transform it.

The methodological question refers to the procedures for executing the research, which are directly related to the theoretical basis of the project. The MST has identified several types of research, which align with the movement's own strategic objectives. One of them is applied research that aims to analyze a certain reality in order to make short-term interventions in this reality. In contrast, theoretical research is focused on understanding a particular issue and proposing new policies. This type of research requires a lot of study of previous theoretical discussions and debates. When engaging in a theoretical research project, the movement suggests that the researcher be familiar with the texts of the movement itself on a particular topic (MST 2001). Another form of research is participatory research. This is an important methodology as it allows researchers to be integrated into the organizational structure of the community. For example, participatory research involves a constant dialogue with the organizational bodies of the movement, whether that is the local settlement coordinating committee or the leadership of a thematic sector. In participatory research, these collective organizational bodies should be central to the process of reflection on the topic of study. The decision to carry out research in these formats recommended by the movement depends on the researcher's objectives and whether her interests are in harmony with the movement, the community, or the thematic sector.

In summary, the MST believes that research is a critical part of the struggle for popular agrarian reform. First, research can help to make a radical critique of capitalist agriculture, illustrating the problems with the use of pesticides. A theoretical, scientific debate about the different projects for the countryside (peasant agriculture versus agribusiness) is necessary in order to illustrate the concrete agricultural alternatives. Second, research can also illustrate the importance of healthy and environmentally sustainable food for the population as a whole, questioning the dominant paradigm of treating food as a commodity, and instead, promoting food sovereignty as a fundamental right of all people around the world throughout history. Third, research can document the attempts to implement agrarian reform – both the successes and the challenges. Fourth, research can advance in the development of technologies that preserve biodiversity and modernize work in the field, with the development of small agricultural machinery for small-scale family farming and cooperative relationships in agricultural production. Finally, the MST also believes in training its own researchers, by universalizing access to higher education as well as technical and professional training that can support the implementation of popular agrarian reform.

Doing external research as comparative ethnography for the MST: process and contributions towards educational programs

It is unusual for a researcher from the "North" to embark on a study of a social movement from the "South" that has such clarity on the role of research and researchers within its ranks. The Brazilian Landless Workers Movement's immense organizational capacity and three decades of accumulated experience has led it to create a formal, structured process for vetting and engaging researchers. Typically, research with community-based movements emerges from informal contacts. In contrast, the MST requires that all people who want to "study" its movement make a formal request to one of their official decision-making bodies. For Brazilian researches, this means contacting the state leadership collective. For international researchers, all requests must go through the International Relations Collective (CRI), a group of activists within the movement that is responsible for developing relationships with other social movements from around the world and cultivating internationalism.

This process of vetting research proposals through the CRI is important, in part because the MST leadership is very intentional and careful about the connections it develops globally. For example, the movement only aligns with organizations that share its core values, and refuses to work with anyone who could potentially threaten the movement's autonomy or undermine the movement's international solidarity, for example, in Palestine or Haiti. Similarly, the CRI is unlikely to accept a proposal for research that is funded from what the movement perceives as a questionable source. For local activists who are not part of these ongoing conversations within the CRI, it is difficult for them to assess whether a researcher is aligned with the movement's international commitments. This is why the CRI vets all international research requests. Another consideration, of course, is the movement's time and capacity to invest in hosting a researcher versus the relative benefits of the study for the movement or other global struggles.

The focus of this section is on this latter question: how research can contribute, directly or indirectly, to global social movement struggles. I will speak to a few possibilities, based on my experiences and ongoing conversations with the MST. In June 2009 I embarked on my first research trip in Brazil, with a plan to study the MST's educational initiatives. In particular, I was interested in the content and pedagogical approach of the movement's educational programs and how the movement has been able to implement its pedagogical approach in schools across the country. My first day in Brazil I met with the CRI coordinators to explain my project. I wanted to spend the summer in Brazil collecting "pre-dissertation research" and then return for a longer, ethnographic study in several different communities across the country. I emphasized my dedication to political organizing in the United States and my interest in sharing the MST's educational experiences with US social movements. Thus, from the very beginning, I expressed my intention to engage in activist-research, with the hope of intervening in my own US context. In my experience, the MST values this contribution just as much as direct research contributions to its own struggles. In other words, MST leaders realize that strengthening US social movements is critical to combating the hegemony of transnational agribusinesses and the various forms of US imperialism that impede their own fight for food sovereignty in Brazil.

The MST eventually approved my project, which meant I could travel to diverse parts of the country under the official sponsorship of the movement. In every location I visited, I had a contact person in the local educational sector who was in charge of "accompanying" my research – and often hosting me in their home. Without these local MST contacts, it would have been impossible to carry out my research. In terms of the typology of "types of researchers" described above, I was clearly put in the category of "external researcher committed to the movement's struggle". Now, I had to make sure my research lived up to that ideal.

As we also describe in the previous section, one of the big concerns of the movement is the generalization of research results, or in other words, the tendency of researchers to take a small slice of reality and apply that to the whole movement. Before beginning this research, I had an acute sense of the diverse social, economic, and political contexts in which the MST organizes, and as Wolford (2010) beautifully documents, the different understandings and meaning of land itself. I wanted to draw out some general lessons about how social movements can promote their educational programs within the public school system, but I did not want to extrapolate from one particular case. Therefore, I decided to design my research project as a comparative ethnography, embedding myself in four different regions in order to understand the difference that difference makes. I sought out both locations that were exemplars of the MST's educational program, and regions where local activists had never been able to move forward with these educational initiatives. In some of these locations there were deep divides between the MST leadership and the local community. I sought to understand these conflicts, not to discredit the MST, but to highlight the organizational challenges that the movement faces and – as the movement itself articulates – how these challenges are shaped by the broader political economy.

For example, in the sugar cane region of Pernambuco, while the sugar cane economy was in crisis the MST leadership organized dozens of land occupations and convinced hundreds of families to begin producing a diversity of food products through agroecological methods. However, when the sugar prices skyrocketed a decade later, many families returned to sugar cane production, as the short-term monetary benefits of growing sugar cane were more enticing than the long-term project of constructing a new agrarian society. This directly affected the school system, as families that no longer supported the movement's economic initiatives also mobilized against activists' influence in their local schools. Again, the point is not to "prove" the movement's "failure". Rather, the goals are to document the real challenges that the movement faces, which are often outside of local activists' control, and to think about effective social movement strategy in these diverse contexts.

Another component of my research proposal was its relational state–society approach. I proposed not only to study the MST but also the interconnections between activists and the Brazilian state. My intention, and what I think turned out to be the major contribution of the project, was to use my privilege as a white US citizen from a prestigious academic institution to access information from spheres of the state that might be difficult for activists themselves to enter. Studying the state and not only the movement became a central component of my research approach, as I interviewed mayors, city council members, municipal and state secretaries of education, and Ministry of Education officials across the country. Some of the data I gathered was very time sensitive: temporary configurations of state officials and internal alliances that offered particular strategic openings for the MST to promote its educational program. Given that Brazilian politics is a moving target, it became evident that I had to find more efficient ways to share these findings with the movement than the typical journal article, which could take years to publish.

My "research dissemination" strategy began while I was still in the field, through oral presentations with different collectives of MST leaders. The National MST Educator Sector identified seven local leadership bodies that they thought could benefit from listening to my research findings – a clear indication of the value that the movement places on politically aligned research. Again, the content of these presentations was the relational aspects of the movement's educational program, or how activists in particular geographical contexts negotiated and contested power in the public school system, and the diverse reactions, responses, and concessions of ideologically inconsistent state actors. Movement leaders who I spoke to afterwards emphasized how the presentation, and in particular the insights I offered into the Brazilian state, helped them to think about different forms of MST–state engagement. Of course, the limit of this research was that many of these political and economic openings were conjunctural, depending on the particular alignment of internal actors and external social forces at a particular moment in time. In my forthcoming book (Tarlau 2019), I try to draw out some broader lessons that emerged from these conjunctural possibilities, for example: activists are most effective when combining disruption, persuasion, negotiation, and co-governance into their tactical repertoires. Through expansive leadership development, social movements can implement alternative educational programs in local schools, even under conservative governments. Schools are important sites for activists to prefigure, enact, and develop the social and economic practices they hope to use in the future. My hope is that these broad lessons, based on a comparative ethnographic approach of diverse regions, will tread the difficult line between respecting local specificity and the need for drawing out some more general lessons. In the end, my guess is that these lessons will be more novel and useful for US social movements than the MST itself.

Here, I also want to offer a bit of caution. My research was a comparative ethnography, whereby I lived with and embedded myself in the daily lives of MST educational activists for over 20 months. I believed that this type of long-term and in-depth research on the daily lives of MST activists would be the only way to fully understand both the possibilities and contradictions of the movement, and the strategies activists employ to implement their educational program in the formal school system. Nonetheless, it is important to note that this is *not* the movement's preferred approach to research, especially with international researchers. In a recent communication with the CRI, the coordinators acknowledged that in the great majority of cases, the MST has no influence on academic research projects, as these proposals arrive at their doorstep already finalized, simply requesting permission to conduct a study. The movement's position is that this is not a problem. Even if the research is purely academic, as long as it is aligned politically with the MST then the movement will organize interviews and visits for the researcher to different MST communities and programs. However, the movement no longer authorizes longer periods of stay in these movement spaces. This is partially due to the movement's own internal capacity. However, just as important is the caution the movement must take about researchers entering internal decision-making spaces, where conflicts and contradictions are abundant. The movement does not pretend that these internal tensions do not exist, but the leadership wants to avoid these tensions being taken out of context and perhaps even used to undermine the movement.

In the case of researchers that are more connected to the movement and want to design a research study in dialogue with the movement, the leadership encourages studies about their enemies: for example, the advance of agribusiness in a specific region, the actions of a particular multinational company, etc. This research is directly valuable to the movement, as it helps the leadership develop internal strategy. In terms of applied research, the movement sees these projects as more complicated because they often involve an intervention in a local reality. As already mentioned, the movement encourages its own activists to engage in this form of research-action, or praxis, under the supervision of allied professors or local movement leadership. Although it is possible for foreign researchers to engage in this type of research, the CRI has emphasized that applied research in camps and settlements should only be conducted by people that the movement already knows and confides in.

Research-political engagement in the United States

When my data collection came to an end in December 2011, one of the movement's major "asks" was that I join the Friends of the MST – the movement's official solidarity organization in the United States. The MST discourages individualism and prefers collective decision-making processes. For the previous year I had conducted research as an individual; now I was asked to join a *collective* that supported the MST. Since 2012, I have been an active member of the national coordination of the Friends of the MST, while continuing to publish academic articles about the movement. Perhaps unexpectedly, this has contributed to the quality of my academic publications, as being part of this group means that I am always abreast of the movement's actions and shifting political positions. The Friends of the MST does not attempt to direct my research, but they indirectly act as a form of accountability, as I am in constant dialogue about my work with a group of people committed to supporting the movement. Importantly, the Friends of the MST has also helped bridge my scholar and activist identities. Previously, I saw myself as a researcher of the Brazilian MST and an activist in the United States. Through the Friends of the MST, I now identify as an activist-scholar engaged in transnational solidarity and organizing efforts informed by my long-term research commitments.

Interestingly, through these research and political engagements with the MST, I have also become one of the gatekeepers for others' research. Given the MST's limited capacity, the CRI coordinators now request that the Friends of the MST vets any proposals from US academics or social movement leaders to study or spend time with the movement. We have a survey with a dozen questions that we send anyone who makes such requests. These include questions about the purpose of the research or exchange, how the person will contribute to the movement, the source of funding, other activist engagements, etc. Often, after we send this initial survey we never hear back from the person, illustrating that even minor forms of gatekeeping can help clarify who is dedicated to establishing a long-term and collaborative research relationship with the movement. If a person does respond, we assess their answers and make a recommendation to the CRI, whose coordinators make any final decisions.

Since I first began researching the MST in 2009, I have presented on the movement dozens of times in diverse spaces. Of course, as an academic I often present in conferences, and those presentations are usually in dialogue with other educational theorists and social movement scholarship. When possible, I try to invite MST leaders into those spaces; for example, when the World Comparative Education Society met in Argentina in 2013 I collaborated with another colleague to bring two MST leaders from southern Brazil. During an exchange of three MST leaders in the United States, I made sure to invite these activists to present with me at multiple conferences and classroom presentations. Presenting about the MST in these academic contexts, whether with or on behalf of the movement, is an important form of political engagement, as it legitimizes grassroots knowledge production within the academy. I also prioritize presentations in community-based contexts, whether the Marxist Library in Berkeley, or within a labor union, or to a local Teachers4Social Justice chapter. Again, I do these presentations as a member of the Friends of the MST, but also as an academic researcher of the MST's educational programs. The enthusiastic responses I have had from grassroots organizations after these presentations illustrates the real necessity for hope in the US context – the desire to see and learn from positive examples of expansive social change.

Finally, a big part of my research-political engagement has been developing educational programs with community groups in the United States. My understanding of the importance of political education – of internal study, reflection, and analysis within movements – is a direct result of my research with the MST. Beyond simply presenting about the MST, I have tried to introduce the MST's ideas about education to US movements in concrete ways. For example, after the occupation of a piece of land owned by the University of California in 2012,[2] I helped to organize the educational programming within the occupation. More recently, I organized a six-week political education program for a group of students in the Student Organic Gardening Association at UC Berkeley. During our weekly meetings we talked about Marxism, intersectional analyses of capitalism, the global food system, and how to develop a conjunctural analysis. However, just as importantly we learned and practiced the MST's central educational principles: work, culture, collective organizing, social struggle, and history (Mariano, Hilário, and Tarlau 2016). I have also participated in other grassroots educational spaces, always attempting to share my research with the MST in ways that help US organizations think beyond the box of what they already know and dream of new possibilities of social organization and struggle. I see these local commitments and projects as part and parcel of my long-term political and research engagement with the MST itself.

Conclusions: current challenges and future research paths

What conclusions can we draw from these experiences and the movement's own internal determinations about research engagement? First, if a researcher engages in a long-term study of a movement, whether through critical ethnography or participatory action research or another methodology, it is important to focus not only on the movement but also on the environment in which the movement is embedded. Whether this means researching the state, or land grabbing, or new agricultural technologies, this *state–society relational* approach to social movement research is critical for providing strategic insights for the movement. Second, anyone who plans to do research with a social movement needs to always *respect their collective processes* and determinations. This might mean letting go of some individual autonomy and submitting one's own research and political engagement to a broader collective. This does not mean that research cannot be rigorous and critical, but it should be developed in dialogue with a collective of people that have clear insights about the needs, necessities, and requests of the movement. Third, the *political engagement* of the political-research engagement approach is central. In the long term, academic publications will contribute much less to social movements than other forms of disseminating research, or employing research findings to contribute to building stronger social movements. This might mean learning from a movement in one location, and then using those lessons to contribute to movements in other global contexts. Or, as in the case of the MST in Brazil, it might involve being an active mentor and supporter of activist-researchers within movements, who are trying to study and intervene in their own local reality.

In conclusion, we want to emphasize that the MST, over its three decades of struggle, has always prioritized research. The movement believes that research is central, to both understand the essence of reality and intervene in that reality. The movement prioritizes research in all of its educational programs, forming activist-researchers who will take more strategic actions because they understand the world around them and the possibilities for social transformation. Furthermore, activists acknowledge the role of external research for and with the movement. As one MST leader once said, "The problem is not all of the researchers arriving at our doorstep. The problem will be when the researchers stop arriving".[3] The fact that there is a demand to research, study, and learn from the MST is a testament to its success transforming society over the past three decades. Now this recognition is more important than ever before. Brazil, like other countries globally, is passing through a moment of polarization that has led to the rise of neo-fascism. The current president in Brazil, Jair Bolsonaro, has declared open war on the movement. At one campaign stop he said, "Here I want to say to the MST scumbags that we're going to give guns to agribusiness, we're going to give guns to the rural producer, because the welcome mat for a land invader is a bullet, 247 caliber".[4] This atrocious statement already comes in the wake of a series of assassinations of MST leaders.[5] This violence is likely to get much worse. The MST needs domestic and international supporters to condemn these actions. Research with and for the MST is critical in garnering this support. Indeed, politically engaged research may never have been so important in Brazil as in the current political movement.

Notes

1 Education of the Countryside is a new approach to rural education inspired by the MST's educational program in the late-1990s (Tarlau 2015).

2 www.dailycal.org/2012/04/23/protesters-continue-occupation-of-uc-owned-land/ [Accessed October 22, 2018].

3 Informal conversation with an MST activist in Rio Grand do Sul, January 2011.

4 www.nybooks.com/daily/2018/03/05/blood-on-the-land-in-brazil/ [Accessed October 22, 2018].

5 https://news.mongabay.com/2018/10/landless-movement-leader-assassinated-in-brazilian-amazon/ [Accessed October 22, 2018].

References

Fernandes, B.M. (2008). Educação do campo e território camponês no Brasil. In Por uma educação do campo: campo – políticas públicas – educação. Brasília: INCRA.

Mariano, A., Hilário, E., and Tarlau, R. (2016). Pedagogies of struggle and collective organization: the educational practices of the Brazilian Landless Workers Movement. Interface: A Journal for and about Social Movements, 8(2): 211–242.

Marx, K. and Engels, F. (1986). A ideologia alema. São Paulo: Hucitec.

Morissawa, M. (2001). A história da luta pela terra e o MST. São Paulo: Expressão Popular.

MST. (2001). O MST e a pesquisa. Veranópolis: ITERRA.

MST. (2014). II Encontro Nacional de Educadoras e Educadores da Reforma Agrária II ENERA (Boletim da Educação no. 12, Edição Especial). São Paulo.

Ribeiro, D. (1995). O povo Brasileiro: a formação e o sentido do Brasil. São Paulo: Companhia das Letras.

Stédile, J.P. (2012). A questão agrária no Brasil: o debate na esquerda – 1960–1980. São Paulo: Expressão Popular.

Tarlau, R. (2015). Education of the countryside at a crossroads: rural social movements and national policy reform in Brazil. Journal of Peasant Studies, 42(6): 1157–1177.

Tarlau, R. (2019). Occupying Schools, Occupying Land: How the Landless Workers Movement Transformed Brazilian Education. Oxford: Oxford University Press.

Wolford, W. (2010). This Land Is Ours Now: Social Mobilization and the Meanings of Land in Brazil. Durham, NC: Duke University Press.

3 | CRITICAL ORAL HISTORIES AND THE PEDAGOGIES OF DISPOSSESSION AND RESISTANCE IN BRAZIL'S LANDLESS WORKERS' MOVEMENT

David Meek

Introduction

Research has incredible potential to be a political tool for social mobilization. Grassroots movements throughout the world are increasingly training their own members to be activist-scholars. These emerging researchers gather data on the contradictions within their own communities, and develop methodologies for advancing social transformation. Movements' own researchers often engage in collaborations with allied academics. In this chapter, I focus on the potential for critical oral history research to create transformative spaces of dialogue between these disparate researchers. Critical oral history work can serve a dialectical function. Movement researchers uncover histories of dispossession and struggle through their own oral history work with other movement members. Through participating as subjects in oral history projects with allied academics, these emerging movement scholars are able to more deeply contextualize and valorize their own histories, and their placement within them as organic intellectuals.

In this chapter, I disentangle histories of dispossession and resistance within an agrarian reform settlement of Brazil's Landless Workers' Movement (O Movimento dos Trabalhadores Rurais Sem Terras) (MST) in the southeastern Amazon. I present and analyze the oral history of one young MST activist, whom I call María, whose life has been characterized by movement, and shaped by migrations in search of education. This quest for education has helped form her political identity. When I first met her, María was 18 years old and peripheral to the movement. Over seven years of repeated field visits, I had the opportunity to watch María's political participation ebb and flow as she became more involved with the movement, and its educational program. Drawing upon María's oral history, I seek to show how our own relations intersected: how her educational history, own process of research, and history of political activism intersected in complex ways, and in turn with that of my own work. For both María and myself, critical oral history work was crucial to understanding processes of dispossession and resistance.

Regional context: agents of dispossession and alternative development

Processes of dispossession have long characterized southeastern Pará. Since the 19th century, small-scale farmers and extractivists harvested Brazil nuts in the region. During the 20th century, large landed oligarchs began to appropriate this land, converting the extractivists into indentured workers. Governmental efforts to colonize the region have oscillated between a large-scale colonization program that settled thousands of migrants along the Transamazon highway, and the financial support of large-scale actors of dispossession. Owing to the prevalence of government subsidies, climatic conditions, and international markets, cattle ranching has become solidified as a hegemonic form of production, and its agents have become central in the struggle over land.

Mineral extraction is another major driver of dispossession and environmental degradation in the region. In 1979, gold was discovered at Serra Pelada in southeastern Pará. A gold rush rapidly ensued: within weeks more than 25,000 miners were sifting through ore by hand, and over the next few years approximately 100,000 miners migrated to the southeastern Amazon from throughout Brazil. When Serra Pelada was closed by the government, the marginalized laborers dispersed to work in various small illegal mines. These were incredibly difficult times as violent conflicts frequently ensued between the miners, hired gunmen, and landowners. Large corporations have become pivotal actors in the struggle over the region's natural resources. The mining giant Vale do Rio Doce opened the Serra das Carajás mine in the early 1980s. It has since grown to be the largest iron ore mine in the world. In recent years, social movements have mobilized against the mining giant, as it is extracting resources from the region and transporting them via rail line through social movement territories.

This description of capitalist dispossession is more than contextual. It is a point of origin for this chapter, because these histories of dispossession are intertwined with histories of social mobilization in the region. Prior to the 1990s, agrarian social movements were not active in southeastern Pará. Rather, unorganized groups of squatters, known as *posseiros*, would occupy land, seeking to gain title to it through active cultivation. Brazil's Landless Workers' Movement, which began in the early 1980s in southern Brazil, had up until this point avoided engaging in direct action land reform in the Amazon, arguing that the government should engage in land reform throughout the country. However, given the large numbers of marginalized workers living in shanty towns surrounding the mines, and the waves of migrants searching for a better life and a piece of land, the MST brought the organized struggle for land to southeastern Pará.

During the early 1990s, the MST began to organize these *garimperos* (miners) and other marginalized workers. Many interviewees recounted a nearly identical story of entering the movement: they remember MST activists driving a car with giant speakers around these frontier cities, broadcasting announcements that the poor should occupy unused land, saying that doing so was their right. In 1995, after signing a ledger and entering the movement, thousands of landless workers set up an encampment on the outskirts of Curionópolis.

In early April 1996, the MST made a petition to the National Institute of Colonization and Agrarian Reform (INCRA) that the Fazenda Maxaceira in the municipality of Eldorado dos Carajás was an unproductive farm that should be expropriated, and created as a settlement for those encamped in Curionópolis. INCRA, however, disagreed that Fazenda Maxaceira was unproductive, and offered to settle the MST members in a settlement project in Tucuruí. MST members were discontent with this offer, and on April 10, 2000 MST members began to march to the state capital of Belém in protest (685 kilometers). On April 16, the group reached Eldorado dos Carajás and blockaded highway BR-154 in protest at a location known locally as the "S-curve". A spokesperson from INCRA reached a deal that day with these MST members where they would re-open the highway in exchange for transportation to Marabá, where they could discuss their demands with INCRA's superintendent. However, on the next day (April 17) the MST learned that

INCRA had no intention of providing transportation or engaging in dialogue, and so the MST re-occupied the highway. Several hours later, two battalions of military police arrived, surrounding the roadblock from the directions of both Paraupebas and Marabá. Although the exact events that transpired remain disputed, it is clear that the military police opened fire and killed 19 MST members.

The massacre of Eldorado do Carajás can be understood as part of a larger pattern of land violence that has come to characterize Amazônia. In Brazil, between 1980 and 2003, a total of 1,671 rural landless activists were murdered during land conflicts. More than half of these murders occurred in Amazônia, and the overwhelming majority of these in southeastern Pará (Simmons 2005: 308). This Amazonian "land war" is not just a late 20th-century phenomenon, but can be understood as a regional place-based process with historical antecedents in the War of Canudos (1821), Ronco de Abelha rebellion (1851), Quebra-Quilos rebellion (1874), Contestado rebellion (1912), and various other land-based conflicts (Simmons 2005).

Seen through the lens of dispossession, agrarian conflicts characterize the region because of a persistent tension between resource abundance and scarcity. The abundance of natural resources, such as rubber and Brazil nuts, fomented rapid settlement. Additionally, the perceived abundance of land in the Amazon in comparison with the concentration of land in other parts of Brazil provided the incentive for a largely landless population to migrate to Amazônia. However, land is not abundant, but actually scarce, because it is concentrated in the hands of powerful groups that frequently rely upon fraudulent titles. This Amazonian land war is a place-specific process that is at once grounded in conflicting local histories of resource use, but also tied to larger-scale processes of land concentration and material transformation that are mediated by political and economic power.

The politics, potential, and pitfalls of research with the MST

For more than two decades, extensive academic research has been conducted on, alongside, and with Brazil's MST. International and Brazilian scholars external to the movement have engaged in much of this research, shedding light on everything from the spatialized histories of social mobilization, to the role of dance and theater in pedagogy, to the constraints facing agroecological production. However, the MST has long been concerned with questions surrounding the political and ethical implications of the research process. As Moraes and Witcel (2014) – two activist-scholars from within the MST – note, the question of research brings up the issue of:

> Who is doing research and what is the objective of these researchers? There is no neutrality in research. We believe that research is either done with the intention of contributing to the process that is being studied, or it is done from the position of a different social class. Depending on the ideological point of view of the researcher, the research itself takes a certain tone. It can contribute to the process of struggle, of practice and reflection; it can also provoke concern, indignation, provocation – depending on the intention of the researcher. (2014: 53)

The MST's concern with the politics of research tracks a broader critical scholarship on the epistemologies, ethics, and methodologies of activist research (Maxey 1999; Bevington and Dixon 2005).

The MST has developed a Secretariat for International Relations (SRI) to help vet external research proposals, and ensure that research being done with the MST contributes directly to its struggle. At present, if an international researcher contacts the MST directly, their proposals will be sent on to the US Friends of the MST Scholars' Collective, which works with the SRI to evaluate the proposed ethical protocols and potential for the research to directly support the movement's goals. Rather than encouraging allies to research the movement itself, the MST's SRI is pushing scholars to draw upon their institutional legitimacy to analyze agribusiness. Rather than researching the movement directly, scholars are encouraged to advance the movement, and its struggles directly, by identifying the forces of dispossession. Yet, it is not only external scholars who have been engaged in research on the MST. Like many social movements throughout the world (Choudry 2013), the MST has prioritized research within its organization by training its members as activist-scholars.

Research within the MST is closely intertwined with its alternative vision of education, known as *Educação do Campo*. More than a set of pedagogies, *Educação do Campo* is a national education reform movement comprised of a various rural social movements including the

MST, National Confederation of Agricultural Workers, Movement of those Affected by Dams, among others. As a movement, *Educação do Campo* is

> defined by its demands for quality and free education from infancy through university, and the construction of a distinctly rural school that is guided by a vision of rural development, which is based in social justice, agricultural cooperation, environmental respect, and the valuing of rural culture. (Munarim 2008: 61)

As a pedagogy, *educação do campo* consists of a series of teaching practices that explicitly value the knowledge systems of rural agricultural communities. One of the key formats that such learning takes place is through an alternating pedagogy (*pedagogia de alternância*), where students rotate between periods of time in both their home and school communities. A key part of the alternating pedagogy is that during these periods, students are conducting critical research in their home communities.

The MST's vision of research is strongly influenced by Brazilian critical pedagogue Paulo Freire's concepts of conscientization and praxis. Conscientization – or developing critical consciousness – refers to learning to perceive social, economic, and political contradictions, and to take action against that oppression. Praxis is the action and reflection on the world in order to change it. MST activists engage in research to deconstruct taken-for-granted assumptions about social forces, and develop methodologies for social transformation. Moraes and Witcel (2014: 51) emphasize that within the MST, "research is a process of raising critical consciousness, of peeling back the layers of reality". They expand on this sentiment, noting:

> Research becomes a mirror that we are reflected in, and through which we can listen and learn about the history that we have lived. We have to be vulnerable and open to the reflections that come out of this reading of our reality. This forces us to think about our practices. The richness of the experiences that we have lived – once problematized and studied – will help us understand our reality so we can again transform it. (2014: 52)

Critical self-reflection is an important practice that is cultivated within the MST. Activists will meet in small groups to engage in a process whereby they critique their own part in problematic social relations, and how the way those behaviors represent broader contradictions within society. Returning to Moraes and Witcel (2014: 53), "it is always necessary to question the contradictions, difficulties, and divergences of our social movement, because it is only through these new understandings that we can learn to answer, intervene, educate, and develop new practices".

In navigating the relationship between activism and research, I found it helpful to engage in similar processes of self-critique and group discussion with the young activists with which I worked. My intention in helping to foster this dialogic space was grounded in the recognition that my role was not one of intervention. Moraes and Witcel (2014) once again help to clarify this distinction:

> The role of a researcher is not to impose her ideas, to lecture, or to "bring" consciousness to the movement, or to dictate actions based on what she thinks is most appropriate. (2014: 53)

As a scholar interested in agroecology's capacity to help achieve food sovereignty through advancing cooperative systems of production, I was very conscious about not allowing my political and ideological leanings lead to proposing particular actions. Within our dialogic spaces, this was a source of confusion, and debate. For some activists, my ultimate purpose was to help advance community development through bringing "projects", literally agricultural credit, into the community. These discussions were challenging, in that they called me to question my role within the community, and the ways in which I was either engaged or not, in advancing its struggles. As Moraes and Witcel indicate on this dynamic:

> Researchers must interact with the reality they are researching, and their insertion into this reality must be connected to practice. Consciousness and knowledge must be constructed through a process of action and reflection, which must have a connection to real social processes. Capturing the conflicts and contradictions of reality opens the way to ruptures and changes. This is the job of the researcher; to allow herself to be educated

by the experience she is living. In truth, what a researcher brings us is a dimension of the everyday life of one particular community, from the perspective of that community's dreams, aspirations, and hopes. (2014: 54)

Informed by the MST's vision, my objective was not to "bring development", but rather to help shine light on the "conflicts and contradictions of reality". I sought to give a voice to the settlement's hopes, its challenges, and ultimately potential methods of transformative social and ecological change by negotiating these educational spaces and research processes alongside emerging MST youth leaders.

My research questions and methodologies emerged through participating in the Evolução da Juventude Camponsea (EJC) group, which was an emerging space of youth political formation within the 17 de Abril settlement. When I first began attending EJC meetings, the youth were interested in knowing about how my own activism and research aligned; how was it, they asked, that my work was contributing to the MST's broader struggle? Motivated by these research relationships, I have become increasingly involved in thinking about how to advance the movement's objectives. I now serve on the National Coordinating Collective of the Friends of the MST – a solidarity organization that supports the MST – and am a founding member of the Scholars' Collective, which is seeking to develop a protocol for activist-scholars interested in working with the MST. All of these moments for increased engagement began with the discussions I had with these youth activists, who pushed me to think about the politics of engagement in new ways.

Through oral history work with these young activists, I learned that perpetual movement has long defined their lives. I now present the oral history of María, a young MST activist whose life has been characterized by movement, and shaped by migrations in search of education. Over seven years of repeated fieldwork in the 17 de Abril, I found that María's educational history, own process of research, and history of political activism intersected in unexpected ways, with that of my own work and political development.

A life of movement

María's life, like many in the 17 de Abril settlement, is characterized by movement. Most inhabitants of this community are not native *Paraense*, and either migrated to Pará from the neighboring state of Maranhão in the 1980s, or from Brazil's south within the last decade. Aside from this initial experience of migrating to the state, processes of movement are part and parcel of individuals', and families', lives. Household heads routinely travel in search of work, family members leave the settlement to join other land occupations, activists travel to lend support to new occupations, and students often commute to nearby cities for specialized or higher education. These linkages between movement, education, and political participation are central themes in María's narrative.

In April 1997, María moved with her family to the recently founded 17 de Abril settlement from Paraupebas, an urban center approximately two hours away. The family of 11 moved to the settlement because María's eldest brother had joined the movement, and was able to secure land following the massacre of Eldorado dos Carajás. In 1997, houses had not been constructed in the settlement's village, and so María's family immediately moved to the rural land parcel they had received from the government, which was quite distant – nearly 15 kilometers away on very rough roads. That first year was very difficult. They lived in a rudimentary shelter made from thatched palm fronds, which leaked whenever it would rain. María's memory of this era is characterized by duress, and epitomized by an argument between her father and mother, which culminated in him abandoning the family on the farm.

María, and many others, have moved in and out of the settlement over the years in a search for educational opportunities. During the late 1990s, the settlement's school was very poorly developed, providing basic education through the 4th series (approximately 3rd grade in the US system). This school was physically precarious: the wooden walls were flimsy, and there was concern they might simply collapse. When it rained, the water came in through the gaps between the boards. Like many families, María's mother wanted her daughter to have a quality education, and so in 2000 sent her to the neighboring state of Maranhão to live with her grandparents and start school. She entered the age-appropriate grade, but the teacher soon realized that María couldn't read. After spending three years with her grandparents, María returned briefly in 2003 to be with her family in the settlement. However, María's mother found the settlement's school to be still inadequate, and so sent María to the city of Redenção, approximately four hours away, to live with her brother, and attend school there. María lived with her brother for three years, and then in 2007 returned to Maranhão to live with her grandmother, returning in 2008 to live once again with her mother in the 17 de Abril. Laughing, she tells me, I really traveled a lot during that period.

When she moved back to the settlement, María became pregnant at 13 years old with her first son. The father of the child wanted María to have an abortion, demanding that she choose between him, and her son. María chose her son. Although she had her mother's support, as a new teenage mother it was very difficult for María to continue school. María spent a year out of school before moving to the nearby city of Paraupebas, where she lived with her sister, and finished basic education. In 2011, María returned to the 17 de Abril settlement, and started her secondary education, but it was at this point that she became pregnant at the age of 15 with her second child. With her mother providing childcare assistance, María completed her secondary education. Upon graduation, María wanted to attend university, but didn't have the financial resources.

One of the most commonly mentioned benefits of the MST is that it provides scholarships to young activists to attend diverse university programs, ranging from agronomy to teacher education. These university scholarships are financially supported through the National Program of Education in Agrarian Reform (PRONERA), which funds partnerships between state and federal universities and social movements. In January 2015, María received a call from the MST's state leaders that a spot had become available in a teacher-training program in *Educação do Campo* offered at the Federal University of South and Southeastern Pará (UNIFESSPA). As María describes it, the course is grounded in the realities of rural subjects. Up until this point, María's education had been largely in the traditional education system, where rural livelihoods and spaces are often seen as backwards, and urban life differentially valorized. In addition to the pedagogical content, María's access to this education had been through a process of displacement, which involved traveling to distant urban areas. The course in *Educação do Campo* challenged this spatial and cultural displacement. "It's a course that seeks to train educators to work in the campo, where they will bring methodologies that are relevant to the life of those in the campo, whether they are landless, or indigenous".

Learning to counter hegemony

María's *Educação do Campo* program was organized around two pedagogical strategies that created connections between local and broader regional processes of dispossession, and emerging counter-hegemonies. The first is the alternating pedagogy, which is grounded in the dual recognition that agricultural labor has a pedagogical value, and that rural youth play a crucial agricultural role in their families during harvesting, sowing, and other parts of the local agricultural calendar (Ribeiro 2008). In courses, such as María's, which are grounded in an alternating pedagogy, students conduct critical research in their communities, enabling them to identify processes that have led to uneven development and dispossession. During periods of time in 17 de Abril, María, and the three other students from the 17 de Abril settlement, collected approximately 20 oral histories, through which they learned new details about the massacre at Eldorado dos Carajás, and the process of development by dispossession that transpired in the community. One of the biggest lessons that María took from these narratives surrounds the political economy of dispossession.

María's research participants discussed the time period immediately following the massacre as the era of *cala boca* (shut your mouth). They remembered this as a time when the government rushed to create various development projects in the settlement. These facilities, which included a manioc-processing factory, industrial swine and chicken production areas, all failed nearly immediately. In the late 1990s, there was neither electricity to power these facilities, nor individuals trained to operate them, or roads capable of getting the products to market. These development projects were financed through state loans to the community, which given the projects' failures, it was never able to repay. The settlement's elders saw this rush of projects as the government's attempt to silence the survivors through a quick payoff, but to do so in a way that would keep them in perpetual poverty, and ultimately cripple the community. These facilities have long been defunct, and sit in shambles on the perimeter of the village, festering relics of a potential future.

María and her cohort synthesized the lessons surrounding the massacre and ensuing politics of development and dispossession into two small books entitled, "What is it that the 17th has?" and "Portraits of a History". They presented these oral histories in public fora in the school's auditorium, during which they discussed the history of the community, the various struggles that it has waged over the years, and the process through which its inhabitants have been able to move forward with their objectives. Students read sections from the various oral histories, and then collectively reflected on their broader linkages to regional patterns of development and displacement.

The second pedagogical strategy draws upon the educational importance of movement to teach students about the linkages between local and regional processes of dispossession. This is what Godlewska (2013) might refer to as a *dislocation* pedagogy, whereby students are "removed from what has become familiar to them, disrupting their geography (where they and others belong in the community that is home to the university (*school*)) and their assumptions about life course and the authority of academic knowledge" (2013: 384–385). Throughout the two years of the program, María's cohort took a variety of research trips, ranging from two days to two weeks, to aluminum smelters, cattle ranches, and mines, as well as farmers' markets, agricultural cooperatives, and land occupation encampments. The cohort traveled to the mines of Serra dos Carajás – the largest iron ore mine in the world – where they collected the oral histories of miners. María learned about the linkages between the miner's marginalization in the early 1980s, when tens of thousands of miners worked in perilous conditions. Dispossessed of a livelihood, and without access to land, many miners would come to join the MST, and for those who survived the massacre of Eldorado dos Carajás, found the 17 de Abril settlement. From there, the cohort traveled to the MST's Frei Henri encampment. This encampment, like many others in the region, is a perpetual zone of violent conflict. Hired gunmen hide behind earthen walls, opening fire on the MST activists at irregular intervals. Walking into houses whose mud walls were pocked with bullet holes, the cohort interviewed many of the encampment's inhabitants, gaining a textured understanding of what dispossession looks like at present, and how it is connected to broader historical, political, and economic processes of agrarian conflict dating back to the 19th century. Then the cohort traveled further south to the MST's Palmares II settlement, located just outside the city of Paraupebas. While in Palmares II they stayed at the Agroecological Institute of Latin America-Amazonia (IALA-Amazonia). This is an agroecological training school that is part of the transnational social movement La Via Campesina's network of more than 40 agroecological schools spread throughout Latin America, Africa, and Asia. The cohort spent three days at IALA-Amazonia, visiting small farmers' agroecological plots. Through these field visits, María and her cohort learned about how agroecology can function as a form of resistance to dispossession. Her course visited the land of farmers who were creating diverse agroforests with papaya, açaí, and passion fruit. Against a broader landscape of cattle ranching and land consolidation, these farmers were creating diversified agroecosystems, developing the conditions whereby their children could earn viable livelihoods, and remain living on the land.

Education and the agrarian question

María moves in her narrative from talking about the course, to the future. She begins by explaining the pressing question of *ficar ou sair* (to stay or leave), which defines the lives of youth in the community. "Many youth leave the 17 de Abril at the end of high school, because they don't have the money to enter the university, or they need to work, and so they move to Paraupebas or Marabá". What María describes is in no way unique to the 17 de Abril settlement. Rather, throughout the world a broader phenomenon of depeasantization is taking place, as rural youth migrate to urban areas. Throughout my time in the 17 de Abril, I recognized that various youth were telling similar stories; education plays a complex role in the question of whether or not the peasantry remains on the land.

María explains that there are various educational opportunities within the community aside from traditional schools. For example, an agricultural extension agency offers short courses through a partnership with the government. Yet, these courses don't provide employment for people.

> Take me, for example, I did a course in producing milk derivatives (such as yoghurt and cheese), but where am I going to work? The dairy didn't hire anyone who had done the course. I think there were 20 of us from the 17 de Abril that did the course. Or, to give another example, I did a course on agroextractivism; many of us did that course, but no one is working in that area, because … it was a basic course lasting just

three months ... So all of these people are just sitting around with their certificates and training. This includes me. I have certificates from good courses, but don't end up working in them.

María's perspective is best understood in the context of a persistent debate surrounding the function of education. Scholars argue that education plays a major role in the social reproduction of society and, from an intersectional perspective, its racialized, gendered, and classed hierarchy of power. Within the neoliberal model, education functions to produce laborers who will work within the existing model of society. However, as María indicates, there are no existing job opportunities. Certificates from courses hold little value. Yet, one of the key insights that both María and I came to, is that education can serve an alternative function. From a Gramscian perspective, education can be a tool to bring an embryonic vision of society into existence (Schugurensky 2000). And individuals, like María, can become organic intellectuals within this process.

For María, the purpose of her course isn't simply employment. It's about stemming the processes of depeasantization, and contributing to repeasantization by decolonizing knowledge, and promulgating an alternative vision of the relation between nature and society. Following the completion of the program, María will have the necessary training to work as a teacher in any community. But, she has no intention of leaving. The intention of this program was for "us that are from these areas, who live along the rivers, the indigenous, those encamped, and those in the settlements, for us to stay in the areas where we are, so that we can begin giving classes at any level within our school". María reflects on the model of education that will ground her engagement, as a teacher, with students and the landscape. She changes the tempo of her voice, speaking extremely slowly to emphasize the words "It's as if it was a pedagogy ... but a pedagogy of the land. Or, perhaps, a pedagogy of agrarian reform". "What does a 'pedagogy of the land' mean?" I ask her

It's how you conserve the knowledge of a community; it's just like with an indigenous group; you wouldn't go to an indigenous community and have it be like "this is how everyone in Brazil studies", because everything that we study in school, it's what happens in the capitals, in São Paulo, or maybe in the

United States. We don't study what happens within our territory. So, it's about studying what is happening within our community, preserving customs, introducing pedagogical materials about the importance of agriculture, and emphasizing the practical aspect as well. But also, not forgetting about the origins of the MST. Because, today, we're here because of the movement, which we entered at the beginning. It's about not forgetting this root of us all.

For María, the pedagogy she has come to embody is one about creating linkages between peasants and the land. It's a pedagogy of repeasantization. By helping students learn about agroecology, María will be decolonizing education, resisting its traditional negation of rural livelihoods and ecologies. She will be working as an organic intellectual, inculcating the memory and value of struggle in her students. I found that this is one of the critical aspects of education within the MST; its capacity for political formation. The Portuguese word *formação* can be translated as training or development, but both translations miss the broader significance. I think of *formação* as a process of literally forming, or molding, the individual. María reflects on the importance of education in her own life in this process of political formation.

I think this aspect of education is very important, because just speaking about myself [she laughs a lot], I never knew many of the chants of the MST, because I never participated extensively in the youth group, I never participated in the meetings of the *Sem Terrinha*, so not participating in these things enabled me to forget my origins; even though I've lived in this settlement, I've never had that degree of intimacy with the movement.

The movement just never mattered to me so much, I always acted like "I'm not Landless"; I didn't place much value on it. But after I entered the university, it woke up a desire in me to recover this root of struggle.

Like many youth, María's relation to the MST has been complex. Although she has lived in one of its settlements since she was a child, the movement was never particularly important to her. Having not participated in the MST's youth programs for *Sem Terrinha* (little landless ones), María never learned about the movement's, or her own, origins. However, this changed when she entered the university; participating in the course lit a spark within her.

Since entering this program, I've found María increasingly involved in movement activities. This was a marked change: in the seven years I had been working in the settlement, I had never known María to be active within the movement. She was never present at rallies, occupations, or movement debates. This all changed in 2015. Just the week before, she participated in a three-day conference of MST educators at the MST's Palmares II settlement. In addition to her course at the university, the conference was an incredibly important event, because it helped her think critically about the linkages between education, depeasantization, and repeasantization. At the conference, María and other MST educators discussed the differences between rural schools, urban schools, and *escolas do campo*. Both rural and urban schools differentially valorize urban lifestyles and livelihoods while debasing rural culture as archaic and in need of modernization. *Escolas do campo*, by contrast, are grounded in the ideology of *Educação do Campo* – a system of education that explicitly values peasant cultural traditions and forms of production. María learned through participating in the conference that the traditional school system is imbricated in the process of depeasantization, but that *escolas do campo* have the capacity to connect individuals back to the land.

> *Escolas do campo* need to engage with all of these aspects that are related to the campo; for example, children will learn know what a hoe is, because today, no one wants to go to the fields, but this is something learned; it's culture. Everything needs to be passed on.

María describes learning all of this, about what it means to be *Sem Terra*, about the differential role that education can play in forming agrarian subjectivities, as a process of literally awakening. "Now that I've awoken, I'm going to participate in everything (movement activities) that I am able". What is being awoken is her political identity.

I ask María how the movement mediates the relationship between identity and education. She tells me:

[T]he question of identity is about the value of what has happened; for example, I didn't know the entire history of the 17 de Abril. I never tried to write it down; it was never important to me. I didn't know who it was that died in order for us to get access to this land. I didn't know their names. And Professor Rivagne (who is one of the teachers in the university program as well as an MST state leader), talked about this at the conference: the importance of preserving identity. And so I've been paying more attention, and I'm interested in joining this youth group, the Evolução do Juventude Camponesa, which I've entered now, to help get the group going.

The identity of *Sem Terra*, of being landless, is one forged through prolonged histories of colonization and dispossession. Even though María was not present at the massacre of Eldorado dos Carajás, her life was forever shaped by it, as well as the structural oppression that her parents and other pioneers endured in the mines. Yet, like too many youth, the details of these periods are perceived as something that happened exclusively in the past. They are seen as irrelevant. Education functions as a means of recovering and reinforcing cultural memory, and in the process solidifying political identity. María not only uncovered the names of those who were massacred, she discovered herself in the process. Formed by her participation in this *Educação do Campo* course, María is now becoming engaged as a leader within the political youth group. Education is certainly not a one-time experience of political formation. Pedagogical moments are omnipresent within social movements, and build upon each other. As María relates,

> These events are where one begins to become passionate about
> the movement; it's through learning the history, through the
> debates – where you get to put forth your ideas – it's there
> that you become passionate, and you then begin to follow
> the path, participating in the youth meetings, the pedagogical
> encampment, and so on.

María starts laughing as she tells me, "Look, I hadn't been to any, and now I want to go to them all!"

What María helped me understand is a complex feedback loop exists between education, political participation, dispossession, and resistance. Through education, emerging MST leaders gain the critical tools necessary to uncover histories of dispossession and resistance. Through this learning process, their political identity is forged by the collective memory of social struggle. Galvanized as organic intellectuals, their political participation increases, and they in turn become more enmeshed in a process of movement that brings them more into the moments of everyday political education. María's journey – from seeing the movement as irrelevant to wanting to be consumed by it – is inextricable from political processes of education.

I conclude my conversation with María by asking her to reflect on our relationship and the impact that this type of research-political engagement might, or might not, have on processes of social mobilization. María pauses for a prolonged moment, and then responds, telling me:

> When we come into contact with people who have the same type of ideological thought as us, we realize that what we believe in isn't some sort of fairy tale, it's real. It's something that is hard to attain, and many times we don't attain it, but when we begin to study, to debate with people who understand, and who are able to explain to us, we're able to see better, and arrive at the point where we can better understand what is all around us, and those might be good things, or they might be bad [she laughs], but it changes us, as it forms us.

Dialogue can contribute to a process of social transformation. The oral history work that María and I have each engaged with has, as is said within the movement, given value to the struggle (*dar valor a luta*). It's made the process of social transformation not something imaginary, but real. Crucial to that recognition is a critical visualization of social context. Understanding that context, and one's role in it, not only adds value to the struggle, but it itself forms us. This is the reciprocal and dialectical process of dialogic learning through critical oral history.

Conclusion

Research can be a form of political engagement. For the MST, there is no neutrality; research is a political endeavor. If allies conduct with objectives of social transformation, it can contribute to the broader process being studied. In this chapter, I've described the multiple, and intersecting ways, through which oral history can intervene in contexts of dispossessions and resistance. In conducting her own oral histories as part of a university course, María actively uncovers how intertwined processes of explicit and structural violence have functioned as techniques of state dispossession, leaving her community in perpetual poverty. María also explored the flipside, investigating how emerging agroecological practices, such as agroforestry, function as strategies of resistance that solidify connections between the peasantry and the land. For María, education at a broad scale, and research in particular, are means of political engagement. Through her course and the conference, María's relation to the movement transformed from one of apathy to commitment. Research, for both María and I, have been intersecting processes of reflexive self-awareness. Through these experiences we have completed what Moraes and Witcel (2014) put forth as our job: learning from our experiences of collaboration, and helping to foster critical reflections on the everyday struggles of a particular community.

References

Bevington, D. and Dixon, C. (2005). Movement-relevant theory: rethinking social movement scholarship and activism. *Social Movement Studies*, 4(3): 185–208.

Choudry, A. (2013). Activist research practice: exploring research and knowledge production for social action. *Socialist Studies*, 9(1): 128–151.

Godlewska, A. (2013). Dislocation pedagogy. *The Professional Geographer*, 65(3): 384–389.

Maxey, I. (1999). Beyond boundaries? Activism, academia, reflexivity and research. *Area*, 31: 199–208.

Moraes, M.Z. and Witcel, E. (2014). The "responsibility" of being educators in a social movement school. *Postcolonial Directions in Education*, 3(1): 42–56.

Munarim, A. (2008). Trajetória do movimento nacional de educação do campo no Brasil. *Educação*, Jan/Apr: 57–72.

Ribeiro, M. (2008). Pedagogia da alternância na educação rural/do campo: projetos em disputa. *Educação e Pesquisa*, 34(1): 27–45.

Schugurensky, D. (2000). Adult education and social transformation: on Gramsci, Freire, and the challenge of comparing comparisons. *Comparative Education Review*, 44(4): 515–522.

Simmons, C. (2005). Territorializing land conflict: space, place, and contentious politics in the Brazilian Amazon. *GeoJournal*, 64(4): 307–317.

4 | PARTICIPATORY RESEARCH FOR SOCIAL CHANGE IN MINING AND AGRIBUSINESS SETTINGS IN COLOMBIA

Irene Vélez-Torres

This chapter addresses the question of how to endorse participatory research in mining and agribusiness encounters in such a way that the research practice can encourage community action for social change. It is described how gold mining and sugarcane agribusiness are connected to dispossession of local communities, particularly indigenous and Afrodescendant communities that are traditional inhabitants of the Alto Cauca region. Further, significant strategies and motivations to enhance social participation in research and community actions for social change are explained, with two cases being elaborated in more detail. Finally, some conclusions are drawn to shed light on the epistemology and practice of research by (i) reflecting on the importance of defining the *telos* of research and (ii) detailing important practical decisions that in contexts of dispossession may have the potential to lead to community action.

Settings of dispossession in the Alto Cauca, Colombia

Economic relations in Latin America have shaped geographies of dispossession. Dependency theorists have shown that a tendency of re-primarization of the national economies in the region have expanded the frontiers of agrarian and mining extractivism to new territories in the last three decades (Escobar 2000; Cardoso and Faletto 1979; Veltmeyer and Bowles 2014; Acosta 2013).

In Colombia, dispossession has been researched in the last decade from different perspectives, including the institutionalized arrangements that have led to violence and accumulation (Gutiérrez-Sanín 2014; Peña, Parada, and Zuleta 2014); the connections between the internal armed conflict and the dispossession generated by cattle, mining, and other extractive industries (Cotte-Poveda and Duarte-Rojas 2014; Vélez-Torres 2014); and the connections between forced displacement, land abandonment, and accumulation (Ganzález-Galindo 2009; Vélez-Torres 2013).

Three main milestones reveal the recent history of institutional arrangements for economic accumulation in Colombia. The first is the promotion of the development rhetoric since the 1950s. It leads to the construction of several governmental plans that promoted an agrarian economy based on international trade and infrastructural development for the agro-industrial sector (Escobar 2011). The second refers to the structural shift of the national economy towards privatization and re-primarization of the national economy, commonly known as the neoliberal turn in 1990 (Pérez-Rincón, Vargas-Morales, and Crespo-Marín 2017). And the third consists of the institutional arrangements carried out during the last two decades to welcome international investment and enhance the articulation of the national economy with global trends of extractivism (Vélez-Torres 2014); such institutional arrangement has resulted in softening regulatory frameworks in all extractive processes. The promotion of mining and flex crops – such as palm oil and sugarcane – have been two major fields of institutional fixing to attempt entering the global economy from the strengthening of the primary sector/a strengthened primary sector.

Economic processes of accumulation in Colombia have intertwined with actors, mechanisms, and expressions of armed and quotidian violence. Furthermore, paramilitary violence in Colombia has taken part in the intrinsic formation of the nation (Grajales 2011). In other words, violence has shaped the state in such a way that the spheres of government and civil society have essentially been embedded in all kinds of extra-economic violent actors, actions, and dynamics. As a result, accumulation, violence, and dispossession can be argued to be interconnected components of the post-colonial state-building process in Colombia.

The unequal distribution of wealth, the violent means of accumulation in the extractive industries, and the differentiated access to development are connected processes that have increasingly worsened the quality of life and environmental sustainability of territories inhabited by peasants and ethnic communities. Though heavily impacted in their territorial and communal rights, communities have responded with a diverse repertoire of social and legal acts of resistance (Göbel and Ulloa 2014).

TABLE 4.1 Ethnic population in the region of study according to the 2005 Census

Department	Afrodescendants (%)	Indigenous (%)
Cauca (North)	21.5	21.8
Valle del Cauca (South)	27.0	0.5
Total average in Colombia	10.4	3.3

Source: Based on Urrea Giraldo (2010)

The Alto Cauca is located at the southwest of Colombia, in the upper basin of the Cauca River Valley, between the central and western Andean mountain chains. The region is populated by a large proportion of indigenous and Afrodescendant communities (see Table 4.1). While indigenous people inhabited the national territory before the colonization by the Spanish, the first Black communities were forcedly brought from Africa as slaves to work in the colonial gold mines and haciendas. Both Afrodescendants and indigenous communities since then remained subordinated to the hegemonic political and economic powers, led by creole elites who have engaged in private capital accumulation in the agribusiness and mining sectors. In this constellation of actors and power relations, ethnic communities have been historically marginalized from access to wealth and well-being, and particularly access to land and quality environmental goods. The result has been the permanent dispute over access to, property of, and control over environmental goods and services.

While the Alto Cauca region hosts an outstanding ethnic diversity, it has been reported that 64.3 percent of the land in the Valle del Cauca Department is owned by 5 percent of the population and 61.5 percent of the land in the Cauca Department is owned by 5 percent of the population (Rodríguez and Cepeda 2011). The land property concentration could also be analyzed in relation to its geographical distribution, to discover that the flat and fertile Cauca River Valley is occupied with sugarcane while the less accessible piedmont is distributed between a great number of peasants and ethnic communities. Inequality in use and property of, and control over land has entangled with other forms of discrimination, deeply rooted in post-colonial contexts. In particular, ethnic differences have crosscut class inequities, bringing together a context of marginalization and impoverishment to indigenous and Afrodescendant communities from the Alto Cauca. In contrast, two models of production have prominently strengthened in the region and ensured accumulation of profit and political power in a few hands: the sugarcane agro-industry, located in the flat area of the valley; and the mechanized medium and large-scale gold mining, located higher up in the mountains.

The historical landmarks of dispossession as described in the introduction continue to be visible in these models of production that have shaped the economic geography of the Alto Cauca. Firstly, the progressive expansion of the sugarcane monoculture was promoted by the national government and the private industry as an exemplary model of development since the 1950s. Various government stimuli and the commitment of the sugar industrials allowed an exponential advance in the area of sugarcane cultivation (see Table 4.2).

Expansion of the agro-industry was done at the expense of the peasants' economies and traditional ways of life, in particular of the Afrodescendant communities that had inhabited the flat area of the Cauca River Valley since its colonization in the 16th century. The wetlands that had been primary spaces of production for the Afrodescendant peasants had disappeared while the traditional ways of life, that were adapted to the hydrological cycle of the Cauca River, had almost extinguished. The radical change of the local landscape over the course of three decades can be observed in Figure 4.1.

Secondly, the neoliberal turn in the economy had an important effect in the promotion of agro fuels in the country. With regard to sugarcane, the promotion of ethanol aimed primarily at satisfying

TABLE 4.2 Expansion of the area of sugarcane cultivated in the Cauca River Valley plains (Valle del Cauca, Cauca, Risaralda, and Caldas Departments)

Year	Sugarcane cultivation (ha.)
1962	32,211
1974	96,939
1984	138,567
1994	181,063
2004	197,130
2015	232,070

Source: Rojas (1983: 142) and ASOCAÑA (2016: 79)

El Hormiguero District, aerial photograph taken before 1984.
Photographic archive from Biblioteca Departamental
del Valle del Cauca.

El Hormiguero District, aerial photograph taken in 2014.
By Adriana López.

FIGURE 4.1 Visual comparison of landscape change in three decades

Source: Composition of photographs by Adriana López and the archive from Biblioteca Departamental del Valle del Cauca

the internal consumption for a newly targeted 10 percent obligatory mix in gasoline. This policy gave a new air to the sugarcane agroindustry by welcoming a diversification of its products. While this may had given economic advantages to the sector, it also implied an expansion of the monoculture at the expense of the confinement and displacement of rural inhabitants and their traditional peasant ways of life.

As mentioned above, the second production model that is central to the economy of the region is gold mining, which is going to be described in relation to the third landmark referred to in the introduction as the institutional adjustments in the laws and regulations to welcome foreign investment. Since the establishment of the Mining Code in 2001, the governmental entitlement to private mining projects rose exponentially (see Table 4.3). As a result, private actors protected by law had been more successful in securing formal control over the local natural resources. Seen as illegitimate by the

TABLE 4.3 Mining entitlement in the Cauca River piedmont (Cauca Department)

Year	2005	2006	2007	2008	2009	2010
Allocated mining titles – Cauca	44	56	84	117	168	225
Allocated mining hectares – Cauca	65,128	75,732	109,960	242,972	149,414	428,241

Source: Based on the Anuario Estadístico Minero Colombiano (2010)

communities, legal entitlements have been resisted by local inhabitants from the piedmont of the Cauca River. Afrodescendants and
indigenous peoples have defended their right to traditional mining in
the territory as practices deeply rooted in their history and culture.

While the mining landscape in the region could be seen as the
result of a process of privatization through entitlement, illegal
mining parallels the extractivist landscapes, as observable in some
statistics: according to the latest mining census in 2011, 72 percent
of the mining at the national level corresponds to small-scale mining, while in the Cauca Department 90 percent of the small-scale
mining does not hold a mining title and can therefore be considered
illegal (Güiza 2013).

Illegal mining can be understood as a result of the legislation
shift that opened the extractivist frontier to foreign investment
and large-scale mining in 2001, while at the same time made it
difficult for small-scale miners to achieve the new requirements of
formalization. As a consequence of this particular legal adjustment,
informal small-scale mining became illegal. Formalization meant
illegalization to those who could not achieve or demonstrate the
required standards.

Formalization did not increase the state's capacity to ensure control over land-based resources, nor to improve the environmental
and social standards of extractive activities. Instead, the state's interest in formalization added to the unregulated exploitation of mining
resources at the local level. First, because the state does not have
enough mechanisms for local control, while in other situations has
demonstrated a lack of political will to exercise such control. And
second, because the formal mechanisms to control mining, such as
norms, plans, projects, institutions, and information systems, do not
always dialogue and are not necessarily compatible and complementary. This uneven institutional constellation is reflected in the messy
local settings of mining control.

In addition to having to confront governmental mining entitlement, local Afrodescendant communities who are traditional miners
have to confront the violence, contamination, and environmental
damage of small-scale mining done by foreign actors to the territories, and who frequently make use of contaminating substances. In
this context, Afrodescendants' traditional livelihoods and territories
are under threat from large-scale mining, supported by the national
government as the "engine of national development", as well as from

non-traditional illegal mining, aggressively expanding their activities secured by illegal armies, big machinery, and deadly chemicals along traditional habitats of impoverished rural communities.

Research for social action and environmental justice in the sugarcane monoculture and the gold mining landscapes

I have developed most of my research between the sugarcane plantations and the polluting artisanal gold mines. In these landscapes of research, I have positioned myself as an activist researcher (Chatterton 2008; Hale 2006) and a politically engaged academic (Borras 2016). The integration of these concepts means something very simple and at the same time very profound in my research practice: (i) that I stand for a critical understanding of the contexts under research; (ii) that I opt for a participatory and interdisciplinary approach to understand problems in order to create feasible solutions; (iii) that in my research I explicitly and continuously commit to social change. We can look at these pillars in more detail.

First, a *critical account of reality* requires academics to analyze social problems and solutions considering the distribution of power and wealth in a constellation of social actors. It implies an accounting for the way in which socio-environmental problems are structured, formed, or induced by relations of power where a sector of society accumulates to the detriment of the environment and the impoverishment of another social group. By understanding context from the perspective of power, the researcher is impelled to take a position from her academic knowledge or professional practice in a boarder constellation of actors and power relations.

Second, *interdisciplinarity and participation* are complementary tools to acknowledge complexity and to contribute to problem understanding and problem solving. By integrating different disciplinary knowledge, a broader and more complex comprehension of problems emerges. Also, by bridging the community with academia, the academic knowledge is nourished by the communities' actions, feelings, and understandings of their surrounding; the strong connection that is created between the academic work and the community life makes academic knowledge socially rooted and potentially meaningful to the local people involved in the research. Academic knowledge becomes relevant in the scientific sphere at the same time as knowledge tools are collectively created for community use and empowerment.

Third, commitment to *action for social change* implies that the research engages with the communitarian interests, priorities, and perceived problems in such a way that people feel their problems and worldview are acknowledged and recognized in the research. Insofar as the problems in which the research is centered feel their own, a motivation could arise within the communities to transform those problems.

Beyond participation as a legitimating practice in academic research (Kindon 2005), a revaluation and re-centering of the action for social change (Fals-Borda 1979; 2001) has the potential to transform academic research into a complex of educational and knowledge tools to empower and strengthen communities' social and political practices of resistance of dispossession.

Figure 4.2 develops a Participatory Action Research (PAR) model that details the aforementioned pillars and suggests different steps in the participatory research, from problem-identification to actions for social change.

FIGURE 4.2 PAR cycle

Source: The author

The model departs from the people's perception of a particular problem. Communities may feel discomfort in relation to a great diversity of situations: massive numbers of fish dead, suspicion of worsening water quality, privatization of land, restricted access to land, restricted access to water, possible eviction of traditional miners, air pollution by pesticides, human health problems possibly connected with pollution, etc. Often, when the research team comes onto the scene, the communities will have already tried to get assistance from governmental institutions without having received clear responses that indicate the willingness or capacity to protect their rights. Having limited options available to transform their current realities has proven to be a milestone in the emergence of socio-environmental conflicts. The entrance of the researcher or academic intervention has the potential to represent a new opportunity to try to understand, solve, and lobby the state to address their concerns.

In the fields of research and academia we mobilize different resources in order to contribute to understanding and create suitable solutions for the problems perceived by the communities. We build institutional alliances and look for national and international collaborations to tackle the complexities of the communities' problems; technical and interdisciplinary collaboration is therefore a key feature of the model. Above all, it is crucial to collaborate with the communities at as many stages of the research process as possible. Particularly, we believe in the relevance and importance of the knowledge that the communities may already hold in the creation of different educational, technical, and knowledge tools that can be useful to change the issues at stake. The model, therefore, closes its first cycle by enhancing social actions; participatory and academic research thereby acquires its double function by contributing to the academic body of knowledge as well as being integrated into the communities' social organization processes and agendas for change.

The model has been used in various cases in which dispossession is the structuring context of the local landscape. The first case I would like to discuss is the Afrodescendant community from La Toma, who are traditional gold miners – who mine without the use of mercury or cyanide in the extraction of gold – and whose activity has been threatened by large-scale gold mining as much as by artisanal, polluting gold mining developed by people who are foreign to the territory. In La Toma, collaboration was activated when

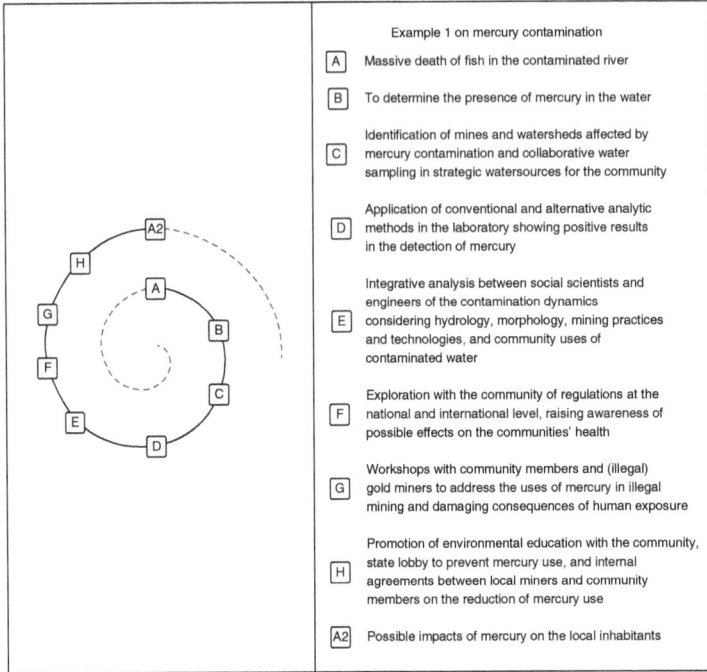

FIGURE 4.3 PAR applied in the context of mercury contamination in illegal mining

Source: The author

the fishermen reported the death of massive numbers of fish in the Ovejas River (as shown in Figure 4.3).

Eight years earlier, I started to work with the community council from La Toma on the processes of forced displacement originated in the dispossession of local communities. Our collaboration in research and political activism has taken us to different topics of research and strategies of social organization. In this case, the concern was directed to the possible causes of an environmental disaster originated in the water contamination and generating direct impact of the community's traditional livelihoods.

After having studied the mining situation in La Toma for almost a decade, I knew that the appearance of dead fish could well be the result of some type of contamination coming from the recently installed gold mines by miners who are foreign to the territory. In order to respond to the call for help by social leaders, I decided to team up with a biological engineer from Universidad del Valle, specialized in creating easy and cheap technology for communitarian access, and a biological engineer from University of Florida, specialized in designing technology for planetary health (Vélez-Torres et al. 2018).

To understand what kind of contamination was affecting aquatic life in the river, we decided to characterize and visit the different mining sites that could possibly be releasing waste to the river. Soon we realized that, besides the concerns of the social leaders, there was little knowledge about what chemicals the miners may have been using and how those chemicals could affect the local people and environment. Between the academics and the social leaders, we decided to develop strategies to characterize mining contamination and strengthening local education on mining and environmental monitoring.

After two years of collaboration on mercury contamination, several actions have been carried out by the community, such as lobbying the governmental institution in charge of environmental protection; making agreements with the foreign miners on a plan to reduce the use of mercury in mining; and enacting educational projects for environmental monitoring of the contamination. Out of these community-based processes, new questions are emerging, for example on the impact of exposure to mercury on the community's health.

The second case in which I used the described model was a research project developed between the ethnic communities of El Tiple and Lopez Adentro. Both territories have been affected by the expansion of the sugarcane monoculture, and ended up confined and surrounded by sugarcane. The common worry among these communities was related to the effects of glyphosate (a broad-spectrum systemic herbicide used by the agro-industry and evaluated by the World Health Organization (WHO) as "probably carcinogenic in humans") on their traditional farms.

Together with the community, we formulated a five-year research project that aimed to analyze conflicts over natural resources in the Cauca River Basin. An important result of this study was the need to more clearly establish the connections between land-use change and the use of pesticides as part of agrarian development in the region. Figure 4.4 illustrates the different stages of this PAR process, enhanced by the Afrodescendants' community council from El Tiple and the indigenous Cabildo from Lopez Adentro.

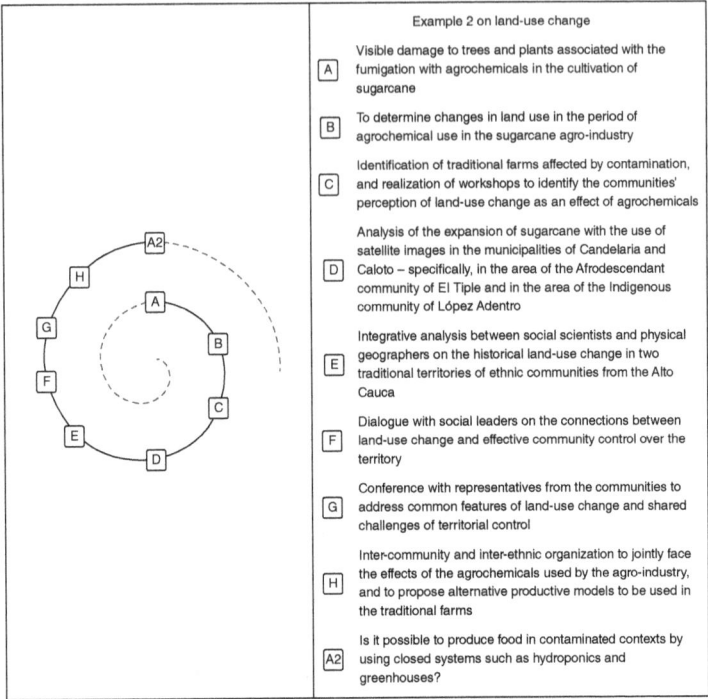

Example 2 on land-use change

A — Visible damage to trees and plants associated with the fumigation with agrochemicals in the cultivation of sugarcane

B — To determine changes in land use in the period of agrochemical use in the sugarcane agro-industry

C — Identification of traditional farms affected by contamination, and realization of workshops to identify the communities' perception of land-use change as an effect of agrochemicals

D — Analysis of the expansion of sugarcane with the use of satellite images in the municipalities of Candelaria and Caloto – specifically, in the area of the Afrodescendant community of El Tiple and in the area of the Indigenous community of López Adentro

E — Integrative analysis between social scientists and physical geographers on the historical land-use change in two traditional territories of ethnic communities from the Alto Cauca

F — Dialogue with social leaders on the connections between land-use change and effective community control over the territory

G — Conference with representatives from the communities to address common features of land-use change and shared challenges of territorial control

H — Inter-community and inter-ethnic organization to jointly face the effects of the agrochemicals used by the agro-industry, and to propose alternative productive models to be used in the traditional farms

A2 — Is it possible to produce food in contaminated contexts by using closed systems such as hydroponics and greenhouses?

FIGURE 4.4 PAR applied in the context of land-used change resulting from the expansion of the sugarcane agro-industry

Source: The author

An interdisciplinary research process was initiated to simultaneously study the change in land cover, as shown by satellite images by LandSat and RapidEye (Correa-García et al. 2018), and the communities' perceptions on the effects of the sugarcane expansion through using agrochemicals as a key component of the agricultural engineering model. A salient and unexpected result of this integrative analysis was the loss of control over land and land-based resources by the local communities while at the same time the agro-industry was strengthening its position in the region. The most important result of the project in terms of the communities' actions for social change was the decision to, together, confront the effects of the agrochemical contamination and generate a collective process of social organization and juridical response to the sugarcane mills responsible for the fumigation.

This decision was taken in mid-2017, and up to now there have been no clear results of the inter-ethnic mobilization. We have not found this to be surprising as the political and economic power of the agro-industry makes it difficult for the local communities to effectively respond to the impacts of the monoculture. Yet, an important new question has arisen among the communities in relation to how to adjust the traditional food production model in ways that can mitigate or solve environmental agrochemical contamination. One possible solution has emerged from the participatory and action research in the form of hydroponic systems that, being controlled encounters, can be integrated into the traditional production of food and medicinal plants.

Conclusions

Defining the aim of the research is crucial in contexts of dispossession. Iniquity, at the basis of accumulation by dispossession, does not only refer to the material distribution of nature, labor, and power; it also brings forth an ethical consideration on how such distribution affects marginal, impoverished, and minority groups. From the perspective of distributive conflicts, environmental justice is a useful concept as it denotes the unequal exposure to hazard, risk, and damage, which can ultimately reinforce exclusion and marginalization of certain societal groups (Bowen 2002; Bullard and Johnson 2000; Martínez-Alier 1997).

Inquiring about iniquity in context of dispossession implies the conviction that there are different power structures that are possible and desirable, and that it is the role (and responsibility) of scientists and academics to contribute to such a distinct constellation of social relations. In a way, it implies recognition that the researcher is a social actor that plays a role not only in responding to science-based questions but also in its connection to the social world that is of concern to her research. "Why", "for what reason", and "with whom" are three connected questions that an engaged researcher has to answer in order to coherently deal with an activist approach in contexts of exploitation, usurpation, and grabbing.

Beyond characterizing the interests, features, and structures of communities' limited access to social and environmental goods, Participatory Action Research is a suitable method for bringing together two elements that are crucial in research on contexts of dispossession: scholar-activism and community actions for social change. Three main pillars support the epistemology of such an approach: (i) a critical understanding of reality that emphasized power relations; (ii) interdisciplinarity and participation in the process of producing knowledge; and (iii) the enhancement of social actions for change.

A model was drawn to systematize a series of steps that, in different settings of dispossession, have been articulated to ensure that the research stands on grassroots participation and community actions for social change. The modeled strategy has placed the *action* back in the center of Participatory Action Research, to overcome the instrumental use of social participation and to return the transformative strength of the PAR approach. Two cases were developed in order to illustrate the application of the model, and four core features can be highlighted:

1. To formulate the research as a response to the communities' concerns helps in appropriating the research project, process, and products.
2. What scientific and technical capacity should be incorporated into the project will depend on the different questions raised by the communities in different time and spaces. While knowledge, alliances and strategies are therefore dynamic, institutional arrangements and projects should also couple to change and remain as plastic as possible.
3. To dedicate time and space to the communities' participation and the interdisciplinary integration of scientists can strengthen the research outcomes in terms of comprehensive understanding of the problems, as well as organic responses by local communities.
4. Though communities' actions may not be a guarantee of success or complete problem solving, the emergence of new questions, needs, and problems demonstrate social change; it is crucial to acknowledge that such concerns emerged from an experience and an understanding of the problem that was not there in the first place.

The suggested account of PAR commits to produce knowledge that could contribute to counter social and environmental inequalities, and to support actions for social transformation. In other words, it encourages a research practice that takes position as part of a process of social change. On the one hand, this understanding of PAR invites the creation of scientific knowledge that is relevant to academia as much as it can be used by the local communities in their social organization agendas. On the other hand, it promotes community actions for claiming and making socio-environmental justice.

The PAR model created implies a deep engagement of the researchers with the contexts and the people with whom they develop their research. Such engagement has the potential to enhance social engagement from the side of the academic or scientist, and can positively impact community actions to transform the social realities as lived by the communities and that are in drastic need of alteration. This coupled strategy has been revealed to be useful in contexts of dispossession, such as the mining landscape in the piedmont of the Alto Cauca and the sugarcane monoculture in the flat lands of the Cauca River Valley. The analysis presented on the different settings of dispossession demonstrates how the local constellations of actors are highly relevant in defining geographies of extraction and dispossessed communities.

References

Acosta, A. (2013). Extractivism and neoextractivism: two sides of the same curse. In Miriam Lang and Dunia Mokrani (Eds.) *Beyond Development: Alternative Visions from Latin America*. Quito: Rosa Luxemburg Foundation and Amsterdam: Transnational Institute.

Anuario Estadístico Minero Colombiano. (2010). *Ministerio de Minas y Energía*. Available at: www.simco.gov.co/LinkClick.aspx?fileticket=rDDN5zSCgE0%3D&tabid=96 [Accessed February 20, 2017].

ASOCAÑA. (2016). *Informe anual de Asocaña 2015–2016*. Available at: www.asocana.com.co/modules/documentos/11992.aspx [Accessed February 20, 2017].

Borras, S. (2016). *Land Politics, Agrarian Movements and Scholar-Activism*. The Hague: International Institute of Social Studies.

Bowen, W. (2002). *Environmental Justice through Research-based Decision-making*. New York: Routledge.

Bullard, R. and Johnson, G. (2000). Environmental justice: grassroots activism and its impact on public policy decision making. *Journal of Social Issues*, 56(3): 555–578.

Cardoso, F. and Faletto, C. (1979). *Dependency and Development in Latin America*. Los Angeles, CA: University of California Press.

Chatterton P. 2008. Demand the possible: journeys in changing our world as a public activist-scholar. *Antipode*, 40(3): 421–427.

Correa-García, E., Vélez-Correa, J., Zapata-Caldas, E., Vélez-Torres, I., and Figueroa-Casas, A. (2018). Territorial transformations produced by the sugarcane agroindustry in the ethnic communities of López Adentro and El Tiple, Colombia. *Land Use Policy*, 76: 847–860. DOI: https://doi.org/10.1016/j.landusepol.2018.03.026.

Cotte-Poveda, A. and Duarte-Rojas, A.M. (2014). Conflicto armado, despojo de tierras y actividad ganadera: indagando entre el testimonio no oficial y las cifras estatales en el Departamento del Meta-Colombia. *Revista iberoamericana de estudios de desarrollo*, 3(1): 32–57.

Escobar, A. (2000). El lugar de la naturaleza y la naturaleza del lugar: ¿globalización o postdesarrollo? In E. Lander (Ed.), *La colonialidad del saber: eurocentrismo y ciencias sociales. Perspectivas latinoamericanas.* Caracas: Ediciones FACES/UCU.

Escobar, A. (2011). *Encountering Development: The Making and Unmaking of the Third World.* Princeton, NJ: Princeton University Press.

Fals-Borda, O. (1979). Investigating reality in order to transform it: the Colombian experience. *Dialectical Anthropology*, 4: 33–55.

Fals-Borda, O. (2001). Participatory (action) research in social theory: origins and challenges. In P. Reason and H. Bradbury (Eds.), *Handbook of Action Research: Participative Inquiry and Practice.* Sage: London.

Ganzález-Galindo, W. (2009). El desplazamiento forzado y el despojo de la tierra: efectos de un modelo capitalista de producción en Boyacá. Periodo 1997–2007. *Revista Apuntes del CENES*, 28(47): 133–154.

Göbel, B. and Ulloa, A. (Eds.). (2014). *Extractivismo minero en Colombia y América Latina.* Bogotá: Universidad Nacional de Colombia.

Grajales, J. (2011). The rifle and the title: paramilitary violence, land grab and land control in Colombia. *Journal of Peasant Studies*, 38(4): 771–792.

Güiza, L. (2013). La pequeña minería en Colombia: una actividad no tan pequeña. *Dyna*, 80(181): 109–117.

Gutiérrez-Sanín, F. (2014). Propiedad, seguridad y despojo: el caso paramilitar. *Revista Estudios Socio-Jurídicos*, 16(1): 43–74.

Hale, C. (2006). Activist research v. cultural critique: indigenous land rights and the contradictions of politically engaged anthropology. *Cultural Anthropology*, 21(1): 96–120.

Kindon, S. (2005). Participatory action research. In I. Hay (Ed.), *Qualitative Research Methods in Human Geography.* Oxford: Oxford University Press.

Martínez-Alier, J. (1997). Environmental justice (local and global). *Capitalism Nature Socialism*, 8(1): 91–107.

Peña, R.D.P., Parada, M.M., and Zuleta, S. (2014). La regulación agraria en Colombia o el eterno déjà vu hacia la concentración y el despojo: un análisis de las normas jurídicas colombianas sobre el agro (1991–2010). *Revista Estudios Socio-Jurídicos*, 16(1): 121–164.

Pérez-Rincón, M., Vargas-Morales, J., and Crespo-Marín, Z. (2017). Trends in social metabolism and environmental conflicts in four Andean countries from 1970 to 2013. *Sustainability Science*, 13(3): 635–648.

Rodríguez, D. and Cepeda, E. (2011). Concentración de la tierra en Colombia. *Comunicaciones en estadística*, 4(1): 29–42.

Rojas, J.M. (1983). *Empresarios y tecnología en la formación del sector azucarero en Colombia, 1860–1980.* Bogotá: Fondo de promoción de la cultura del Banco Popular y Departamento de Publicaciones de la Universidad del Valle.

Urrea Giraldo, F. (2010). Patrones sociodemográficos de la región del sur del Valle y norte del Cauca a través de la dimensión étnica-racial. In L. Castillo (Ed.), *Etnicidad, acción colectiva y resistencia: el norte del Cauca y el sur del Valle a comienzos del siglo XXI.* Cali: Universidad del Valle.

Vélez-Torres, I. (2013). Desplazamiento y etnicidad: fracasos del multiculturalismo en Colombia. *Desacatos*, 41: 155–173.

Vélez-Torres, I. (2014). Governmental extractivism in Colombia: legislation, securitization and the local settings of mining control. *Political Geography*, 38: 68–78.

Vélez-Torres, I., Vanegas, D., McLamore, E., and Hurtado, D. (2018). Mercury pollution and artisanal gold mining in Alto Cauca, Colombia: woman's perception of health and environmental impacts. *Journal of Environment and Development* (in print).

Veltmeyer, H. and Bowles, P. (2014). Dynamics of extractivist resistance: linking Latin America and northern British Columbia, Canada. FLACSO-ISA Conference. Buenos Aires. Available at: http://web.isanet.org/Web/Conferences/FLACSO-ISA%20BuenosAires%202014/Archive/c646a4bb-d64a-4958-8a32-08ceb4386f2e.pdf [Accessed September 12, 2018].

5 | ANTICOLONIAL PARTICIPATORY ACTION RESEARCH (APAR) IN ADIVASI-DALIT FOREST DWELLER AND SMALL PEASANT CONTEXTS OF DISPOSSESSION AND STRUGGLE IN INDIA

Dip Kapoor[1]

> We fought the British thinking that we will be equal in the independent India. There will be a land settlement, for instance ... but the *savarnas* (upper castes) and the rich people have controlled (*akthiar*) the land, including Adivasi land. (Kondh Adivasi male, EA leader, Kapoor 2009a: 36)

> The Forest Department comes and asks us to create a Forest Protection Committee (*jungle surakhshya manch*). Protection from whom should I ask? We do not cooperate because they really do not care about the forest. We need to protect the forest from them. (Kondh Adivasi woman, EA, Kapoor 2010: 29)

> We all know that our problems today are because of colonialism (*samrajyobad*) and capitalism (*punjibad*) and these MNCs, NGOs, DfID [Department for International Development, UK] and the government are its forces. (Niyamgiri Surakhya Samiti, NSS anti-bauxite mining Dalit activist, Kapoor 2017b: 71–72)

Introduction

The pertinence of engaged academic research in contexts of colonial capitalist dispossession in India includes and encompasses more than knowledge production for and with anticolonial struggles against forest-land dispossession by Adivasi (original dwellers/Scheduled Tribes or ST) and Dalit (untouchable outcastes/Scheduled Castes or SC) forest dwellers and small and landless (indentured labor) peasants.[2] An anticolonial participatory action research (APAR) informed by an oppositional politics addressing colonial continuities pertaining to place/land/territory, labor/bodies, culture/knowledge/racialized identities, and production/social relations, actively works towards extending the potential for flattening hierarchical social relations of knowledge/cultural and material production. This includes democratizing engagements between academic researchers enmeshed in colonial capitalist relations and attendant non/academic institutional arrangements and ST-SC movement intellectuals working in communal-collective modes (e.g. *entra* or collective labor arrangements on small plots) of production/ distribution and meaning making in forested-rural contexts. APAR also means directing knowledge engagements towards enhancing the material and cultural prospects of projects for communal-collective economic relations given the increasing colonial (violent) penetration and expansion of iniquitous capitalist social relations of production usurping spaces where ST-SCs are unequivocally oppositional (saying no to the mine).

APAR research relations augment socio-political efforts towards the increased commoning and collectivization of research knowledge production and its utilizations, emphasizing collective usage for the immediate socio-political productivity of the struggle at hand. This approach would also adhere to democratizing knowledge production processes, if not rely on multiple, often contradictory and messy epistemological engagements (e.g. from the ST-SC historical-sacral to colonial state land classification schemes in relation to land-based conceptualizations/knowledges). APAR assumes a place for continuous reflexivity on the part of all actors engaged in the work thereby remaining open to addressing the regressive and anti-democratic prospects of reproducing elitisms to popular political basism (Freire 1970) potentially characterizing, to varying degrees, hierarchical relations in any social formation (emergent capitalist, feudalist, and/ or historical communal-collective).

Other possibilities for APAR relations might include: collective approaches to research resource determinations and sharing (including institutional academic funding), re-distribution and re-purposing for an anticolonial collectivist politics in contexts of dispossession; popular education and organizing work; popular (movement) organization building, including the establishment of in/formal sub-altern research organizations; networking/scaling-up anticolonial formations; the selective leveraging of academic researcher (including university) resource opportunities, institutional networks, and political capital for a ST-SC rural politics and more.

This chapter seeks to sketch some of the possibilities of a cross-locational if not contradictory (in social structural terms) engagement between participatory action researchers in academia (the author) (Kapoor 2009a) and movements/struggles of social groups and/or emergent subaltern classes in contexts of rural dispossession, pau-perization, and exploitation (Kapoor 2017a) by selectively drawing on two decades of work with ST-SC organizations including the Center for Research and Development Solidarity (CRDS) and the Ektha Abhijan (EA) Adivasi-Dalit social movement organization, in the east coast state of Odisha, India. Processes of dispossession and resistance have long characterized the situation for ST-SC/other marginal forest dwellers in this state (Kapoor 2013; 2015; 2017b). While STs for instance constitute 8 percent of the population of India, they account for 40–50 percent of development-displaced persons (DDPs) and in the state of Odisha, they make up 22 per-cent while constituting 42 percent of DDPs (Fernandes 2006: 113; Munshi 2012: 9). Given its lucrative mineral reserves in bauxite, coal, and iron-ore, including timber/forest resources, state-corporate land grabs (e.g. Kashipur and Niyamgiri) handing over Scheduled Area lands and forests to private industry (e.g. Norsk Hydro, Vedanta, or POSCO) are being opposed by ST-SC and allied social movement formations (see discussion of Lok Adhikar Manch or LAM later in this chapter or Kapoor 2015).

After providing a brief overview of what is being referenced here as an anticolonial (Fanon 1963; Mariategui 1996; Zibechi and Ryan 2012) PAR methodological approach (APAR) with Third-Worldist political-contextual origins (Fals-Borda 1979; 1988; Freire 1970), the chapter considers some deployments of APAR with respect to a ST-SC land-forest oppositional politics addressing colonial capitalist social relations in contexts of racialized state-capitalist dispossession (Robinson 1983). In so doing, we try to demonstrate both, the process (including some methods) and political developments from an APAR initiative over two decades between subaltern movement intellectuals (ST-SC members/leaders of CRDS and the EA) and academic (university) researchers (the author) across political-economic and cultural modes, inter/national, caste, class, gender, and rural–urban divides and locations.

APAR and ST-SC land-forest struggles: building popular organizations, movements, and networks and producing movement-relevant knowledge for claims against land-forest dispossession

Research and eventual and lasting friendship have defined the author's working relations with CRDS and the EA, if not ST-SCs in south Odisha since the first doctoral experience in the early 1990s whereafter a group of 10 ST-SCs (also research participants for the doctoral study) from villages in south Odisha, working for development NGOs and popular social movements in the area, approached the author to consider getting involved with Adivasi-Dalit movement assertions. Working for NGOs for wages, these individuals were also active with local social movements in the region as animators/cultural workers, adult educators and organizers on land-forest and cultural-social issues and were largely critical of NGO development interventions and politics driven by donor priorities and charitable (paternalistic) purposes which tended to eschew an oppositional politics in contexts of development dispossession and neo/colonial land grabbing (Kapoor 2005; 2013; 2017b). As was subsequently shared, the group was intrigued and encouraged by the author's line of questioning, scrutinizing NGO work for the doctoral research, and were thereby encouraged to broach the subject of working together.

With little clarity or confidence on the author's part around what was to transpire next, we remained in touch and kept up discussions pertaining to a research-based approach given the potential political productivity (as interpreted by the group in Odisha) of my then precarious academic location as a sessional lecturer as I saw it. This approach would, as determined by the group of 10 ST-SC women and men and the villages engaged in organizing work with them, include adult education and organizing for socio-political action on land-forest issues and concerns, including addressing exploitation of peasant labor (feudal and displaced state-capitalist forms) and related socio-cultural issues such as ST-SC politics. The process would be rooted in already nascent ST-SC social organization and movement building work by the group of organizers being nurtured in a 30-village area – villages that the organizers were from. The rudimentary political approach then discussed (mid-1990s) was to work with and against the state as dictated by circumstance, issue, and available legal space. Initial locally determined assertions over land-forests were to be taken up when and where such claims were more likely to be secured through existing Constitutional rights (Scheduled Areas Act), safeguards, and state policy directives to the extent possible, while exploring if not stretching the porosity of these boundaries via organized direct action when necessary and warranted.

It thereby followed that the guiding and primary purpose for this emergent APAR across several episodic and dis/continuous longitudinal engagements over two decades has been to stimulate, inform, and augment popular Adivasi-Dalit assertive politics to secure land-forest territory in the Scheduled Areas, i.e. territories that are Constitutionally protected but nonetheless continually colonized and usurped by non-Adivasi caste-class-urban and state-corporate interests, often enacted by the state via "eminent domain" and "for the public good" claims. These are contemporary examples of racialized *terra nullius* justifications as is often alluded to by ST-SCs in this region (Kapoor 2007; 2009b), especially around cases of development dispossession by dams (e.g. Upper Kolab and Harbhangi projects) and in bauxite mining zones like Kashipur and Niyamgiri (Kapoor 2017b) involving multi/national corporations and the state.

APAR questions (pre-determined, emergent, and in retrospective recollection) over the years for CRDS, the EA movement, and the author, whether as a part-time non-tenure-track academic for the first eight years or as a tenured academic since 2003 for another 15 years (including two grant-funded projects in the region between 2006–2009 and 2014–2019) have generally focused on or remained in the vicinity of the following:

1. How has land-forest been colonized (usurped)? Who are the primary agents and actors, and what are their strategies today? What was/is the state of land-forest control for ST-SC and other backward caste forest dwellers? How would (should) this ground analysis of the *politics of dispossession* inform appropriate organized *response (resistance)*?

2. How to stimulate and *build strong ST-SC organizations* to spearhead such responses (resistance)?

3. What kinds of *education*, knowledge, and learning need to be and become a part of this process of organizing and assertion? Whose knowledge, why, when, and what for?

4. What needs to be done to enhance prospects for *unity (ektha)* across subaltern social groups and emergent classes? What needs to be done in this regard towards addressing casteism and untouchability and related horizontal conflict and tensions among subaltern social groups, including gender politics, which threaten subaltern ST-SC solidarity?

5. How to expand *networking and coalition building* among anti-dispossession movements in the region (*trans-local activism*)? How should/can we go about *magnifying these assertions in a geographically contiguous Scheduled Area* (initially in three districts) in order to ensure a critical mass engagement in an anticolonial politics against forced displacement, dispossession, pauperization, and migration to urban slums in search of income/wages and the ongoing colonization of the social and cultural fabric of ST-SC communities?

APAR in this context, as it gradually became apparent to the author, is anticolonial in terms of PAR contributions towards an ST-SC praxis in such struggles over place, land, forests, and exploitation of indentured labor with its British colonial and Hindu feudal and landed-caste antecedents. Today in the post-independence period this oppositional politics was being directed at Hindu feudal and landed caste, caste-class, and state-corporate inter/national colonial capitalist dispossession (Kapoor 2007; 2015). The importance of the historical continuity of these struggles is compelled by the reality that "all the colonized (ST-SC) has ever seen on his land is that he can be arrested, beaten and starved with impunity" while knowing full well that "the land is the most meaningful ... and it is land that must provide bread and natural dignity" (Fanon 1963: 9). Hence, APAR in south Odisha recognizes the social mobilizing importance (bred by conditions of colonial capitalist development violence) of a contested politics of land-forest/place, including the significance of working towards ensuring that the economic activity (production) on a given territory is supporting its inhabitants as determined by those facing the prospects of development dispossession, pauperization, and labor exploitation.

APAR praxis is also anticolonial in terms of its contributions towards ST-SC struggles to address the continued colonial dehumanization and racial erasure (neo/colonial relegations to the sub-ontological zone of non-beings or "jungle inhabitants/*vanvasi*") of Adivasis (often equated with animals in the way of development) and Dalits (untouchable polluted outcastes), thereby seeking to instate the possibility of an open-ended dialectic which is only conceivable between "beings" (however un/equal) predicated on mutual recognition as such (Fanon 1963; Guha 1997). APAR in this context then would seek to contribute towards the historical movement of ST-SC land-forest and indentured/forced migrant ST-SC labor struggles against social structures and conditions of feudal/caste and caste-class neo/colonial inter/national capitalist dispossession, pauperization, and exploitation.

APAR and the period of germination: popular education,
organizing and movement building in ST-SC villages and the
emergence of EA (1996–2006)
The research relationship could be conceived in terms of two linked temporal periods. First in relation to early germination and when the author was a part-time non-tenure-track academic (1995–2002) and the second in relation to becoming a tenure-track academic with better access to grant possibilities (2003–now), eventually including two grant-funded episodes between 2006–2009 (Learning in Adivasi Social Movements) and 2014–2019 (caste politics and resistance in schools/social contexts). The latter period (discussed in the next section) is when political momentum pertaining to the guiding research/political questions developed significantly in and around the grant-funded period. The early years of germination involved consistent/deliberate adult education-organizing and *ektha* (unity) building focused APAR exercises moving towards an eventual consolidation of collective aims around land/forest assertions for a potential ST-SC movement formation called the Adivasi-Dalit Ektha Abhijan or EA.

Several individuals of the 10-member team (referenced hereafter as the "research team") were familiar with Freirian and ST-SC approaches (*our ways knowledge*) to popular education and organizing work, which provided an initial knowledge link of sorts with the author given academic familiarity with Freirian pedagogy. Cycles of action–reflection–action and political awareness and consciousness raising (praxis) were key aspects of the work among ourselves as a social action research team and then with the 30-village ST-SC constituency that this effort focused on originally. The author's growing familiarity with Gramscian Marxism and the initial contributions of subaltern studies (Ranajit Guha), including anticolonial conversations from the work of Frantz Fanon (1963), were also brought in to these engagements with the research team who decided what and when to work with around these concepts/analytics. Caste-class "hegemony" (Gramsci 1971: 506), for example, if not "dominance without hegemony" (Guha 1997), provided conceptual analytics for political reflection concerning colonial capitalist and feudal dispossession and exploitation of ST-SCs, often proving to be generative in dialogical actions with the ST-SC base being engaged in APAR as praxis vis-à-vis the guiding and emergent research questions.

Initial themes (largely pertaining to or guided by research questions 1–4) that emerged from the team's own experiences and through work with the villages and that provided some direction for praxis included a combination of historical, material, and cultural foci and were as follows: (1) historical memory, place, identity in relation to land and ancestors and the foregrounding of cultural knowledge; (2) hunger and landlessness (feudal and state-capitalist incursions around usurpation of forests, land, and bonded/exploited labor); (3) alleged forest encroachment and state-market responses; (4) Adivasi-Dalit conflicts/unity, historical and symbiotic relations, and the divisive role of caste politics; (5) gender relations and alcoholism/other; (6) usury and money-lending-related debt-bondage/land alienation; and (7) ST-SC relations with the petty bureaucracy and its extensions in to Adivasi-Dalit Scheduled Areas (e.g. forest guards, revenue agents, police, and para militaries).

Generating historical memory and cultural knowledge were central to early village gatherings. As noted by Fanon (1963: 210),

Colonialism is not satisfied with holding people in a grip and emptying the native's brain of all form and content. By a kind of perverted logic, it turns to the past of the oppressed people, and distorts, disfigures and destroys it.

Bakhanis (narratives imbued with historical and mythical significance establishing Adivasi cosmological and epistemic claims to place, including symbiotic relations with Dalits/Panos or Dombs in this context) (see Kapoor 2007), for instance, were and remain central to the popular education and organizing work of the research team. Such narratives enabled *ektha* while simultaneously providing the impetus for formalizing organized socio-political action grounded in struggles against land-forest and cultural dispossession. The period of germination focused on extending and deepening EA movement understanding/purpose that were eventually channeled towards organized ST-SC contestations and assertions around a land-forest anticolonial politics of place, autonomy, and self-governance (Kapoor 2009b).

The aforementioned themes guiding APAR as praxis were broached (depending on what was most germane to a given village/area) via multiple culturally significant mediums including: skits/plays (street theatre); puppetry; poetry; songs/ballads; elder narratives/soliloquy; musical events; interactive dialogues and debates on social issues (e.g. gender relations and alcoholism) etc. An APAR approach, deliberately schemed by the research team and the author but always open to emergent possibilities in dialogue, began regularizing this otherwise haphazard process to date on weekly, monthly, and bi-monthly rotations across villages depending on distance and local/political situations. When it was determined by the group that certain villages were beginning to welcome the team and the analysis of issues being addressed (relationship and collective ST-SC understanding were maturing), the idea of establishing village-based organizations was broached with the concerned village(s). All members of the village were deemed participants; a whole village approach in the name of the emergent EA organization and ST-SC movement prospect focused on land-forest assertions, revival of ST-SC forms of organizing/collective leadership, and a cooperate–agitate approach towards the "encroaching state" and in relation to addressing public services/programs that villages deemed useful and necessary after close political and cultural scrutiny.

Reflection–action–reflection then began to involve establishing tasks and responsibilities and setting schedules to address material issues initially pertaining to the immediate resource base/productive activities at the village level. These included: strengthening collective grain and seed banks; collective labor practices (*entra*) on small plots (the entire area was officially landless or holdings were under 2 acres per family); charting a course of systematic "encroachment" on vacant land (*anawadi* state land classification zones) to extend land control prospects at collective (was prioritized in the form of fruit orchard claims/development) and individual/family levels (vegetable gardens) based on existing state directives (discussed in more detail later in this chapter – see IF/CFR discussion); and several organized initiatives to agitate and demand state services/programs that were either defunct or never initiated in the first instance (paved roads, small irrigation, tube wells, drinking water, electrification, public health centers, BPL/Below the Poverty Line cards for access to state-subsidized rations, etc.).

Organizing and EA building work gathered momentum and strength as material assertions became viable/visible and more land began to be brought under cultivation (paddy/millet/pulses/ragi). Village-based EA organizations for women grew in strength as organized agitations over time systematically destroyed local liquor distilling establishments along with money-lending networks (usually linked to the liquor trade). The petty business-caste appropriation of Public Distribution Centers (PDC outlets providing essential state-subsidized food/daily rations) that exploited ST-SCs and prevented them from availing of this public facility was gradually challenged and taken over by EA women's organizations in the region; some 32 in all to date.

Claims on hutment land (all villages were deemed as "encroachments/squatters" or dwellings without title) also galvanized the organizing process for the emergent EA as some 5,200 households eventually secured non-transferable *pattas*/deeds of a tenth of an acre each ensuring that summary eviction of villages is no longer possible as had been the case to date. The research team accompanied villages that engaged in these processes and shared knowledge on when, where, how, and with whom to initiate these various actions until such time as inter-village EA organizing gradually began to become a reality and village-based EA organizations assisted and taught each other with facilitation/initial oversight by the research team.

The gradual development of sustained organized pressure (an emergent reality as the EA grew in strength in terms of width and depth) when demanded in relation to any of these initiatives included: *gheraos* (encirclement of state offices/officers); *dharnas* (sit-ins); blockades; memorandums/demands and petitions; staging of large-scale cultural events by the EA projecting political strength, etc. Direct action has been enabling ST-SCs to work together in reclaiming land/forests, establishing culturally centered organizational technologies/practices, and all while moving to take control of state services and programs (at the *panchayat*/local village governance level enabled by legal developments such as the Panchayats (Extension to Scheduled Areas) Act, 1996) when and where this has been deemed useful if not politically necessary perhaps in terms of enhancing ST-SC autonomy on a land/forest base which remains continually enmeshed in a process of claims and counter-claims (more on this aspect below).

The APAR team has been central in this development as described and has gradually vacated the political center of the process as EA organizing and leadership depth and width have matured. Initiated in the mid-1990s, the APAR process as briefly described has facilitated the development of an EA movement/organization which today includes a core area of strength in 150 ST-SC villages or 26,000 people organized in to 150 village-based EA organizations; 20 *panchayat*-level organizations with a gender-balanced leadership participation of 300 leaders from these villages; two block-level organizations which draw from the *panchayat* level including 16–24 leaders each in the Mohana and Daringbadi blocks; and a central EA committee of 15 leaders (gender-balanced). The central organization can only make decisions on any subject once initially suggested and ratified by all village-level EA organizations in a consensus-compromise-all-village approach. A wider peripheral and secondary concentric layer of EA organizations (varied strength and levels of engagement and still emergent) encompasses some 350,000 Dalits and Adivasis in a 500-village contiguous region.

APAR roles for the author/researcher (university academic) have gradually shifted from frontline/village-level popular pedagogical work with the team (3–6-month visits/year were regularized given part-time employment as a sessional instructor), where after five years or so of being introduced as the "friend/brother from Delhi" proved inadequate in terms of addressing the limitations of caste, gender, class, urban/rural, linguistic/cultural, and inter/national difference. A watershed event of sorts wherein the author/researcher was received/greeted with a welcome fit for an upper-caste politician (banners, drums, and marigold garlands included, not to mention that the word was out on a Canadian/foreign connection) much to our political dismay if not a naïve consternation at the time, led the research team to conclude that the author's involvement in this capacity was mostly becoming (or already had been but was now a post-realization/learning) counter-productive for the organizing effort. With the growing political maturity and regional presence of the EA and the increasing tensions in the area rife with a Hindu fundamentalist to a Maoist guerrilla politics, the author's village-level participation was eventually deemed a liability for all concerned.

Subsequent APAR roles for the author shifted further in to the background (in relation to village-level interaction) over the years including: helping with documentation (e.g. strategy, pedagogical/ organizing methods, internal reporting, institutional development, accounts, knowledge collation and dissemination for internal consumption as part of APAR public dissemination within EA constituencies, which included a newsletter or quarterly issues of *Amakatha*, Our Word/story shared in village-based reading circles); intellectual/pedagogical support (pertinent outside knowledge/ research and information gatherer) and research team motivation; and securing meager funds which were organized from abroad through regularized personal giving from a small group of friends as university/grant funds were not a prospect for sessional instructors. This was largely used to support the research team and village-level organizing efforts around collective land/forest expansion efforts; seed funds which were eventually not necessary as tree-saplings for fruit orchard expansion was procured by the EA from state nurseries once village-based EA organizations matured. In due course, formal academic grant writing (from about 2003), including translating the meaning of this process/content for the research team while translating the collective understanding back into grant language also became a key task for the author/researcher.

Knowledge produced through APAR praxis is multifarious but the general pattern of contribution has been in keeping with and in relation to research questions 1–4 (guiding praxis) and the key themes identifying the popular education work of the research team when APAR was initiated and then gradually refined along the way. For instance, our ways/historical knowledge and memory was produced and activated in the moment and sometimes audio-taped for reuse and circulation in other EA villages (Kapoor 2007). Specific knowledge generated via the politics of land reclamation and "encroachment" (e.g. policies and politics of classifications) was shared in *Amakatha* and orally in village-level meetings or with groups asserting claims while in the process (Kapoor 2009b; 2010). Video recordings and films around cultural knowledge production came into the picture later, once research funding became available via grant funds, along with website-based public dissemination in the vernacular and in English.

Six years in to the work, the author brought up the question of academic publication/knowledge dissemination (in relation to the APAR research questions) and its potential significance vis-à-vis formal research grant prospects in the event that a tenure-track position was indeed achievable in the near future. Publication in academic venues (journals and dissemination in conferences) then became a prospect as the research team, largely through the author's interjections on this front, began to see some sense in formalizing/academizing different aspects of knowledge generation from this multifarious APAR, as publications for international academic journals. These publications to date are shared and reviewed prior to dissemination and have become an opportunity for reflexive learning for the research team, including the author. They have also played an institutional part in securing regular grant funding, now for some eight years in total.

When a tenure-track position materialized in 2003, we began to develop a research grant proposal together (Learning in Adivasi Social Movements) which came to fruition in 2006 for a three-year period, one of the objectives being the formal establishment of a popular Adivasi-Dalit small peasant/forest dweller research center, namely CRDS. Work done to date and new work related to the grant proposal informed this participatory research endeavor which not only provided the research team (now formally referred to as Research Assistants or RAs) with a semi-regular modest stipend for their familial needs/obligations but also helped resource a CRDS office, secure mobile phones, motorbikes, bicycles, grain for new grain banks (initial seeding to expand these village-based efforts) justified (in formal research budgets) as a culturally appropriate form of payment for village-based "research participants", audio-visual equipment, etc. This not only formalized the research in the shape of a popular research organization (a brain/dissemination center with satellite centers in the expanding EA zone) but also amplified EA movement organizing work as transportation and communication networks for one, were now on a new and enhanced footing altogether. A new training mandate (linked to grant-based public dissemination and community engagement) enabled sharing these experiences and strategies with other popular organizations in the region, seeding other similar (to the EA approach) parallel initiatives; some 14 in all spanning eight districts.

APAR had now developed in scope and was poised to experiment with more expansive aspirations expressed by CRDS and the EA which is what we turn to next, briefly, in terms of research question/area #5 pertaining to expanding the scale of land-forest social action and developing trans-local forms of networked solidarity and activism with other ST-SC anti-dispossession movements and struggles in south Odisha.

APAR and the period of maturation: funded research, CRDS, and knowledge production for anti-dispossession land-forest EA social action (2006 onwards)

Formally funded research from 2006 defined by academic priorities (e.g. *understanding* learning in Adivasi social movements to develop emancipatory knowledge for academic consumption) and its peculiar ethical-professional boundaries, enabled both engagement and disengagement from EA political interests to continue to utilize research (as APAR or described otherwise in grant applications) more explicitly if not completely towards applied prospects addressing ongoing land/forest anti-dispossession initiatives at work. Always seeking to merge priorities to the extent possible, formal "data collection" events/opportunities (e.g. focus groups) were deliberately structured as per demands of academic research institutional protocols and research questions, while seeking to enable EA politics to the extent possible/permitted (e.g. research-funded activities could not be used to support an extra-institutional oppositional politics of direct action challenging land/forest control). That said, as independent bodies and extra-institutional movement formations (from grant funding agencies supporting the academic/author and his institution), CRDS and EA were able, if they deemed necessary, to deploy knowledge produced from formally funded time-bounded research activities (where they were also research agents/participants) towards EA movement ends and actions.

For example, focus group or knowledge dissemination events (popular conferences with movement actors) often produced knowledge and enabled prospects for solidarity which participants could then utilize and build upon in relation to their own organizing work thereof and well beyond a particular research/data collection moment. That is, knowledge production for academic purposes (conceptual and theoretical if not empirical interests, emancipatory or otherwise, replete with unavoidable objectifications no matter the democratic intention) and for movement purposes sometimes cohered, and at other times the former was used as an opportunity for CRDS and the EA to move beyond what the funded events had generated and on their own terms as independent organizations active around an ongoing APAR processes. The latter drew from but went far beyond the boundaries established by a formally funded participatory (interpretive) research process with little pretention towards PAR let alone APAR.

Land/forests activisms, for instance, in relation to Individual Forest Rights or IFR (from the mid-1990s) and subsequently collective or Community Forest Rights (CFR) enabled by the new Forest Rights Act (2006) (FRA) which have been central to an APAR process from the mid-1990s, prompted the development of grant-funded foci (a program of funded research) which, among other possibilities, produced knowledge for and with ST-SCs and the EA, which in turn were taken up by them to realize land/forest-related objectives. Funded research from 2006 was timely in this regard and then again from 2014 to now (where the focus is on caste politics in schools including wider caste contexts and different expressions of resistance by EA/Dalit organizations). Timely in terms of both operationalizing and growing CRDS and in terms of creating numerous and regular opportunities for the RA team and EA villages/regions to come together and discuss land-forest politics (dispossession/resistance), law/policy (FRA), and bureaucratic information (Rules as per the Act for making claims, e.g. 11(3) as per amendment Rule of 2012) including procedural technicalities and the order for enacting same (e.g. the 17 steps towards completing a voluminous claim). These "formal funded research" sessions were necessary for initiating an organized process of pre-meditated claiming on a larger scale in the Scheduled Areas backed by an organized EA political presence, as land claims are always more than info-technical legal exercises and foremost always about politics (control), despite the available openings created by the FRA in 2006, now some six decades after independence.

Prior to 2006, Scheduled Areas where ST-SC and non-tribal forest dwellers have resided over several generations in some cases (the current Act requires proof of domicile for 75 years prior to the Act), were simply regarded as "government forests" in the state's exercise of eminent domain and by implication, *terra nullius* in connotation and practice as Adivasi and other forest dwellers were relegated to the pariah non-status of encroachers on their own land. ST-SCs are subsequently fair game for petty corruption and regular harassment by the lower reaches of the state bureaucracy including forestry officers, revenue agents, and the police, subjected to eviction and compelled to pay bribes (often in chickens, liquor, or cash) as "encroachers" when they carried out regular hunter-gathering, collection of minor non-timber forest products, and swidden/other forms of cultivation on the hill slopes of the ghats. State land classification schemes, mining, state plantations (cashew), conservation reserves/zones (elephant corridors), bamboo (mafia) plantations/processing, petty business caste/class (illegal) incursions in to Scheduled Areas for agriculture, and access to supply lines for retail purposes in towns and cities (e.g. turmeric production from Kandhamal is a lucrative trade) are some of the sources of pressure on land/forest where ST-SC and non-tribal forest dwellers are deemed to be in the way with little juridical status/recourse to date.

The FRA (2006), and the CFR provision in particular, now grants legal recognition/sanction for tribal and non-tribal forest dwellers to control, protect, and manage their customary forests. Land/forest claims are non-saleable/commodifiable (under IFR or CFR) and activation of Gram Sabhas (village-level government) and Forest Rights Committees (FRC) is central for making these provisions a reality for forest dwellers. It is estimated that at least 32,711 villages in Odisha will be eligible for CFR rights recognition for 23,000 sq. kms of forested area and in tribal majority districts (which is the EA zone) like Gajapati, Kandhamal, and Rayagada, forest land eligible for such recognition/claims could be in the vicinity of 73 to 84 percent of forest cover. Scheduled/forest districts account for 16/30 districts in the state populated mainly by ST-SC and other backward castes. The Act recognizes the rights of forest dwellers over forests, valleys, streams/rivers, grazing land, burial grounds, traditional places of worship (sacred land), as well as forest resources and gives them the rights to protect, conserve, and manage these resources (irrespective of ethnicity, caste, or creed) for their betterment.

A few examples (foci) of formal funded research-generated thematic discussions and research-enabled data collection processes/methods pertaining to the FRA and ST-SC learning in social action (including caste politics) regarding land/forest claims (e.g. "data episodes" via focus groups; key informant interviews; dialogical sessions/village level; collective critical incident analysis; photo-research/territory; elder/expert narratives on forest histories/claims; mapping exercises, etc.) in Gajapati, Kandhamal, and Jharsuguda districts (EA zone) included:

1. culture and the politics of a state-defined land/forest claims process (FRA and IFR/CFR);
2. FRA and CFR information and process;
3. land/forest mapping exercises/claims learning; and
4. identifying and preparing for EA responses to address an anti-ST/SC claims politics.

In relation to (1), ST-SC participants discussed land/forest/water and the FRA approach to territorial claims and its political potential as a (contradictory?) means for asserting ST-SC ontological-epistemic conceptions and convictions (e.g. the whole question of land as property in the sense intended by the state) predicated on their historical relations with land/forest as place, ancestral home, and spiritual abode (Kapoor 2010) while providing a commons for all traditional forest dwellers (Adivasi-Dalit alike as understood in the EA areas) addressing material/production needs in keeping with cultural traditions and ways. While IFR claims were restricted to STs (divisive politics of claims), CFR was available to all non/tribal forest dwellers, making this a strong reason for potential adoption, not to mention some acknowledgment of commons although competing CFR claims would mitigate this. Both claims were non-commodifiable/saleable but both were discussed in terms of the possibility of subsequent changes to the law enabling eventual commodification making land saleable and its divisive/colonizing potential by market forces (e.g. World Bank encouragement of small-holder claims and Joint Forest Management/JFM in Madhya Pradesh/elsewhere experience was introduced by the RA team in relation to the discussions regarding this future possibility), if not caste-divisive politics already inherent in IFR rules. CFR also enabled spatial claims that were greater in scale and with potentially more in keeping with traditional ways/knowledge of land/forest cultural signification.

In relation to (2), for example, techno-informational learning pertaining to the Act's provisions for different claims including three types of rights including: (1) *land rights* for individuals and families of under 4 acres each (with proof of occupation); (2) *user rights* to collect and use minor forest produce (fruits, roots, tubers, and leaves of plants gathered as per tradition) excluding timber but also including access/use of water/bodies, shifting cultivation, and pastures/grazing land; and (3) the right to protect, manage, and conserve forests as communities (CFR) recognizing *rights over forests*, valleys, streams, grazing land, burial grounds, sacred spaces, etc. The 17 steps in filing claims are points of further deliberation in this regard.

In relation to (3) mapping is learned through walking around and drawing the region as per categories prescribed under the Act and is reliant on the villager's knowledge of use patterns and meaning. For example, Rule, Article 3(1)(G) points out traditional rights pertaining to: (a) wood use, (b) burial grounds, (c) sacred trees, (d) sacred caves, (e) divine places, (f) forest paths, (g) cattle paths, (h) sacred ponds, (i) use of stones, (j) swidden cultivation areas, (k) places to preserve fire wood, (l) forest harvesting grounds, etc. GPS verification by the government and counter-verification by EA/RA team (carried out as a check on the state) is also undertaken after these hand-drawn sketches are included.

In relation to (4), analytical discussions pertaining to past and current experiences working with claims are the focus of conversations. Key anti-claim actors/agents and their strategies for subverting claims processes are considered including past/potential EA role/responses in relation to addressing these political constraints and obstructions. Actors/tactics have tended to include the *state bureaucracy*. For example, issues exposed dwell on the tendency of the lower

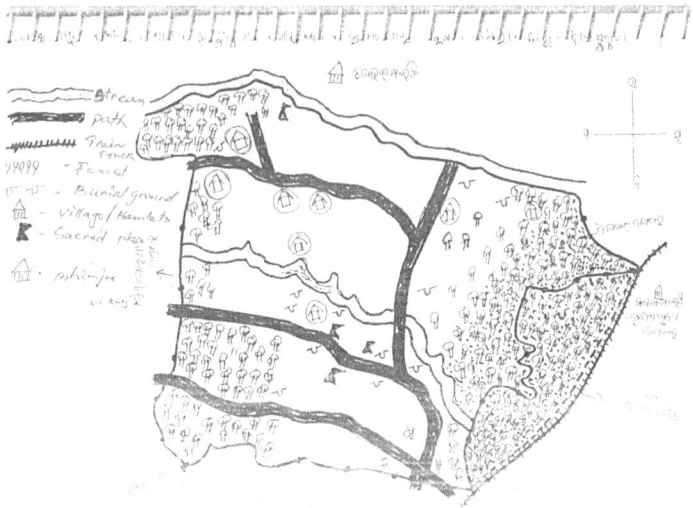

FIGURE 5.1 Hand-drawn map for CFR claims

Source: The author

reaches of the bureaucracy to ignore or be slow to respond to bigger CFR claims as opposed to IFR claims which are less time consuming and exclude SCs (casteism among officials). Furthermore, the government's approaching to CFR/IFR is seen to be one of bestowing favors as a prince would a subject, when this is a matter of popular/ legal rights assertion, not to mention non-systematic *suo-motto* or ad hoc/at will granting of claims by District Collectors (senior levels) on a preferential basis, while recognizing that village claims could be much bigger as would be the case when done by the EA. Cases are discussed where Collectors have either offered bribes to stop Gram Sabha meetings to initiate CFR or have outright insisted that EA restrict themselves to other matters at these meetings (e.g. health/ schooling) and not CFR.

Mining/logging mafias are other anti-claims agents frequently using intimidation and violence in relation to CFR given the extent of these claims, while *Hindu fundamentalist* saffron groups (casteist) obstruct the process since SCs are included in CFR claims and work, in order to drive a wedge between STs and SCs, including propagandizing the EA as either Christian missionaries or Maoist (guerrilla) cadres, as do petty trading castes in towns who often

TABLE 5.1 Ektha Abhijan movement land and forest claims

DISTRICTS	IFR (acres)		CFR (acres)	
	Claimed (# of villages)	Settled	Claimed (# of villages)	Settled
Gajapati (since 1997)	13,500 (#104)	8,435	21,410 (#104)	0
Kandhamal (since 2007)	36,980 (#132)	33,000	13,428 (#132)	8,989
Jharsuguda (since 2014)	6,486 (#46)	2,005	14,575 (#52)	14,575
TOTALS	56,966 (#282)	43,440	49,413 (#288)	23,564

Source: CRDS and author

collude with mining/logging mafias to affect the same. Maintaining unity/*ektha* and conflict mitigation between STs and SCs and non-tribal forest dwellers is also a continuous challenge discussed in this context, not to mention conversations regarding moribund Forest Rights Committees ignored and/or discouraged by state neglect. To date (over a decade now since the Act), given that 60 percent of villages are forest villages in Odisha, the EA zone claims are path-breaking as the first CFR claims in the state.

Initiating trans-local networking and solidarity among ST-SC anti-dispossession movements and the Lok Adhikar Manch (LAM) (2014 onwards)

The EA FRA process has encouraged the movement to consider tentative engagements with other ST-SC and related subaltern anti-dispossession struggles in the state in a bid to explore the potential for networked solidarity and learn from respective experiences, if not begin to develop joint platforms for scaling up this politics in a locally meaningful manner. Funded research engagements with CRDS exploring learning in Adivasi social movements and caste politics have created, via data collection episodes and popular dissemination exercises expected by granting agencies, several opportunities over the years for multiple movement/struggles to come together in popular conferences and meetings to share perspectives and politics (some of which was documented as part of the research endeavor) and begin to initiate trans-local networking in the form of the LAM, a name, and a joint LAM People's Manifesto that emerged in the second such meeting of ST-SC movements (Kapoor 2015: 26–27). Whether such engagements develop in strength still remains to be seen but early research supported and focused gatherings for data collection purposes have included up to 15 seasoned (some past movements) to new organizations opposing dispossession due to land alienation (affected by money lending/petty business classes), forest plantations, mining, industrial development, dams, military installations, conservation, and tourist zones. Even fisher groups from the coast addressing shrimp cultivation to mechanized fishing (depletion of stocks) and the Coastal Regulation Zones have participated in these fora. Funded research and the CRDS have been instrumental in making this research process possible, and knowledge shared at these events in relation to the five guiding research areas/question and beyond has been shared among ST-SC constituencies and in academic fora (international conferences/publications) where empirical, theoretical, and conceptual understandings have also received due consideration when warranted.

Concluding reflections: academic research, APAR, and ST-SC small and landless peasant land-forest struggles

Over time, sustained (non/funded) academic research engagements built in to previous (non-academic) movement engagements can become a politically productive avenue through which to work with and augment dispossession and exploitation related social struggles and movement formations if there is a defining and conscious move towards democratizing the social relations of knowledge production between academics and movements/intellectuals. This includes actively moving these relations towards producing movement-relevant knowledge/education for enhancing and deepening the prospects for an anticolonial material and cultural process of democratization in an oppositional politics addressing colonial capital today. While the examples considered in this chapter are brief and several in order to provide a sense of what is possible, elaboration of any one of these interactions would suggest a dialectical appreciation for a process that has moved towards new forms of thesis-antithesis-synthesis that are progressively enhancing the prospects for an anticolonial, anti-dispossession, anti-proletarian informal labor politics, if not a related forced migrant emergent foot-loose labor politics (not discussed in this chapter but another area of work for CRDS-EA over the past five years in relation to the National Rural Employment Guarantee Scheme and matters of compensation and ST-SC labor exploitation and organizing) wherever colonial capital creates contradictions and crises.

The role of a popular research process (including academic research/ers) whereby systematic interrogation of the quotidian use and abuse of political, economic, and cultural/religious power by castes/classes, urban-dwellers (*shahariyas*/city dwellers) and variously by the agents of the state, market, and civil society, has been integral to CRDS-EA-organized ST-SC political learning and anti-colonial anti-dispossession social action efforts to date. Needless to state, these processes are uneven in development, sporadic in their accomplishments, and require continuous engagement, especially in times when the spectacle of heightened challenges (e.g. when villages are being demolished by bulldozers to make way for a refinery) by the state–capital nexus are seemingly not there to provide the necessary level of confrontation to compel greater prospects for unification across social groups and classes (magnification of plausible resistance) at any given point in time. With this in mind, academic research/er engagement too needs to be sustained, continuous, cognizant of movement cycles and rhythms, adjusting itself to the need of the day/hour while extending academic boundaries (contrary to tendencies towards reproducing hegemonically inspired academic researcher self-disciplining exercises for/in ruling relations) in the gray zones (for example ethical and/or grant-funded perimeters of the im/possible) to the extent possible and when movement-related demands continually challenge such political-ideological limitations of academic-movement relations seeking to limit the scope and possibility of the politics at hand.

Hence the importance of popular institutions of research (building same) closer to/within movements (see the first chapter on the MST in Brazil for instance in this regard) that can independently carry out what an institutionally bounded (funded) academic project cannot or will not address. Here too, formal academics could be asked to play "voluntary consultancy roles" (as do academics for the state, market, and civil society) in a movement-defined APAR project.

Once engaged and trust and reciprocity if not critical political alignment become plausible (a continual process of critical learning and
political-cultural reflexivity), the possibilities for making productive
contributions as a researcher-educator then remain open.

Notes

1 Authorship of this chapter
includes, in different capacities, several
members of CRDS and EA organic
intellectuals from ST-SC communities,
too many to name here, including
and especially Mr. Kumar Prasant
who has been an instrumental if not
irreplaceable SC/Panos-ST-small
peasant leader and animator in all the
efforts discussed here. His continuous
commitment and contribution over
the decades towards the germination

of EA, CRDS, and this APAR cannot be
exaggerated.

2 Adivasi or "original dwellers" are
referred to by the state, for ameliorative
purposes, as Scheduled Tribes (STs)
(denied state recognition as indigenous
peoples in India) while Dalits or "the
downtrodden" are similarly referred
to as Scheduled Castes (SCs) and are
pejoratively relegated to being "polluted
peoples/outcastes" in relation to the
Hindu caste hierarchical structure.

References

Fals-Borda, O. (1979). Investigating reality in order to transform it. *Dialectical Anthropology*, 4(1): 33–56.

Fals-Borda, O. (1988). *Knowledge and People's Power: Lessons with Peasants in Nicaragua, Mexico and Columbia*. New Delhi: Indian Social Institute.

Fanon, F. (1963). *The Wretched of the Earth*. New York: Grove Press.

Fernandes, W. (2006). Development related displacement and tribal women. In G. Rath (Ed.), *Tribal Development in India: The Contemporary Debate*. New Delhi: Sage.

Freire, P. (1970). *Pedagogy of the Oppressed*. New York: Continuum.

Gramsci, A. (1971). *Selections from the Prison Notebooks*, edited and translated by Q. Hoare and G. Smith. London: Lawrence & Wishart.

Guha, R. (1997). *Dominance without Hegemony: History and Power in Colonial India*. New Delhi: Oxford University Press.

Kapoor, D. (2005). NGO partnerships and the taming of the grassroots in rural India. *Development in Practice*, 15(2): 210–215.

Kapoor, D. (2007). Subaltern social movement learning and the decolonization of space in India. *International Education*, 37(1): 10–41.

Kapoor, D. (2009a). Participatory academic research (par) and people's participatory action research (PAR): research, politicization and subaltern social movements in India. In D. Kapoor and S. Jordan (Eds.), *Education, PAR and Social Change: International Perspectives*. New York and London: Palgrave Macmillan.

Kapoor, D. (2009b). Adivasis (original dwellers) "in the way" of state-corporate development: development dispossession and learning in social action for land and forests in India. *McGill Journal of Education*, 44(1): 55–78.

Kapoor, D. (2010). Learning from Adivasi (original dweller) political-ecological expositions of development: claims on forests, land and place in India. In D. Kapoor and E. Shizha (Eds.), *Indigenous Knowledge and Learning in Asia/Pacific and Africa: Perspective on Development, Education and Culture*. London and New York: Palgrave Macmillan.

Kapoor, D. (2013). Social action and NGOization in contexts of development dispossession in rural India: explorations in to the un-civility of civil society. In A. Choudry and D. Kapoor (Eds.), *NGOization: Complicity, Contradictions and Prospects*. London and New York: Zed Books.

Kapoor, D. (2015). Subaltern social movements and development in India: rural dispossession, trans-local activism and subaltern revisitations. In D. Caouette and D. Kapoor (Eds.), *Beyond Colonialism, Development and Globalization: Social Movements and Critical Perspectives*. London and New York: Zed Books.

Kapoor, D. (Ed.). (2017a). *Against Colonization and Rural Dispossession: Local Resistance in South and East Asia, the Pacific and Africa*. London and New York: Zed Books.

Kapoor, D. (Ed.). (2017b). Adivasi-Dalit and non-tribal forest dweller (ADNTFD) resistance to bauxite mining in Niyamgiri: displacing capital and state-corporate mining activism in India. In D. Kapoor (Ed.), *Against Colonization and Rural Dispossession: Local Resistance in South and East Asia, the Pacific and Africa*. London and New York: Zed Books.

Mariategui, J. (1996). *The Heroic and Creative Meaning of Socialism: Selected Essays of Jose Carlos Mariategui*. Amherst, NY: Humanities Press.

Munshi, I. (Ed.). (2012). *The Adivasi Question: Issues of Land, Forest and Dispossession*. New Delhi: Orient Blackswan.

Robinson, C. (1983). *Black Marxism: The Making of the Black Radical Tradition*. London: Zed Books.

Zibechi, R. and Ryan, R. (2012). *Territories in Resistance: Cartography of Latin American Social Movements*. Minneapolis, MN: University of Minnesota Press.

6 | CONSERVATION AND PALM OIL DISPOSSESSION IN SUMATRA AND SULAWESI: THIRD-WORLDIST PARTICIPATORY ACTION RESEARCH, INDIGENOUS AND SMALL PEASANT RESISTANCE, AND ORGANIZED ACTIVISMS

Hasriadi Masalam

Introduction

The historical emergence of Third-Worldist Participatory Action Research (PAR) (Fals-Borda and Rahman 1991; Freire 1979/2000; Hall, Gillette, and Tandon 1982) triggered by attempts to acknowledge and even promote different epistemologies which stand for the interests of oppressed groups, continues to derive a contemporary significance from small peasant and indigenous people's struggles addressing colonial accumulation by dispossession (ABD) in the "post colony" (Harvey 2005; Kane 2001; Kapoor 2017). As Fals-Borda (1988: 5) suggested PAR is "an endogenous intellectual and practical creation of the peoples of the Third World". driven by the fundamental motive as a "critique of colonial scholarship, imperialistic history, and continuing neo-colonialist presence" (Swantz 2008: 36), i.e. "Third-Worldist-PAR" is committed to decolonization and popular democratization with marginal rural and urban social groups and classes (Kapoor and Jordan 2009; Kapoor 2017; Masalam 2017) in contexts of ABD.

The common threads in the research leading to this chapter are not just instigated by intellectual curiosity but also by an inspiration to contribute towards a praxis that is more transformative and democratic. Such an impetus as an engaged researcher-cum-organizer have, to a large extent, shaped my approach to popular education work with rural social groups in different parts of Indonesia for almost two decades now, especially through my affiliation with ININNAWA and Indonesian Society for Social Transformation (INSIST), a network of social movement-oriented NGOs. It also defined my methodological orientation towards doing action-oriented participatory research for and with peasant and indigenous people affected by development dispossession (DD). As someone who was born and grew up in the rural frontier of Sulawesi Peninsula in the eastern part of Indonesia and with extensive popular education work with rural social groups, my search for methodological strategies in social inquiry, which embrace critical theoretical approaches while encouraging trans- formative practices, led me to participatory action-oriented inquiry for knowledge creation and collective agency.

This chapter demonstrates the educational and popular knowl- edge production role of Third-Worldist-PAR praxis and learning in social action (Foley 1999; Kapoor 2009; Masalam 2018) in two locations in Indonesia and in two temporal periods. The first instance shared here pertains to the struggle to address conserva- tion dispossession by indigenous peoples in the Serampas Highlands of Sumatra between September 2011 and June 2012, where we deployed PAR as activists with ININNAWA and INSIST. The sec- ond instance concerns PAR with small peasants in Baras in West Sulawesi addressing palm oil agro-industrial dispossession and where I worked as a doctoral researcher doing PAR in conjunc- tion with activists from the Karsa – a land rights social action NGO based in Palu (capital of Central Sulawesi) – between May 2015 and February 2016. Both cases demonstrate how PAR can be used to assist with collective analysis and knowledge production to enhance and undertake learning and organized responses in these struggles.

Context of conservation dispossession and PAR engagements in Sumatra

The history of the upland communities in Southeast Asia is the history of resistance, including the Serampas people, a *marga* (clan) inhabiting the remote rugged terrain of Bukit Barisan, strands of mountains stretching along the west coast of Sumatra, Indonesia, which according to archeological studies inhabited the region at least since the 11th century. Based on the historical records and archeological remains, some scholars argue that the highlands were the demographic and political center of Sumatran civilization during the pre-colonial period. Despite the pressure of the nation state to modernize the rural frontiers, the customary systems that the Serampas had established to manage their internal and external social dynamics and lands remain an important reference in communal decision-making. However, the presence of Village Government Law No. 5/1979, which homogenized all forms of settlement into the village administration, had limited the space for Serampas institutions.

Today, Serampas is the name of both the place and the *marga* (clan) that inhabits five villages, namely Renah Alai, Rantau Kermas, Lubuk Mentilin, Tanjung Kasri, and Renah Kemumu, administratively located in Merangin District, Jambi Province, Indonesia. The first three villages encountered when entering Serampas region by vehicle will be Renah Alai, Lubuk Mentilin, and Rantau Kermas as they are located in the buffer zone of the Kerinci Seblat National Park (KSNP), one of the most important protected areas in Indonesia due to its endangered biodiversity, while the other two villages, Tanjung Kasri and Renah Kemumu, are inside the national park zone.

Since the declaration of the highlands as part of the KSNP in 1982, the Marga Serampas have continued to resist the metaphorical erasure of the long history of their ancestral presence on the land. Therefore, through resorting to a dual system, Serampas strive to pursue what is perceived as a preferable socio-cultural way and as one villager summed it up, "If the stamp of our *depati* (local chiefs) is valid outside Serampas, we actually don't need the government" (Interview notes, December 2011).

Third-Worldist-PAR addressing conservation dispossession in Serampas Highland

The PAR praxis with members of two Serampas villages, Renah Kemumu and Rantau Kermas (September 2011–June 2012) was intended as a process of knowledge construction by facilitating joint analysis of the socio-politic, economic, and cultural contexts of these changes. My engagement with this PAR work was facilitated through my affiliation with ININNAWA and undertaken in collaboration with a team of activist researchers from Mitra Aksi, a member of INSIST in Jambi Province. The PAR processes utilized a Freirean pedagogy of problem-posing methods, primarily through interviews and focus group discussions to identify the generative themes (Freire 1979/2000),

emerging from the analysis of the socio-economic and political constructions at play in the immediate surroundings of Serampas, while
connecting this with wider political-economic contexts (e.g. inter/
national market dynamics and agents of dispossession). The PAR
processes have been mainly focusing on facilitating the processes of
communal learning/shared analysis of socio-political, economic, and
cultural dimensions of the current circumstances faced by inhabitants
in this area. At the same time, questions were also raised throughout
the study to identify common interests that could nurture resistance
against the process of state conservation imposed incarceration and
marketization and commodification of land/forests and exploitation
or estrangement of labor (free labor). The process of knowledge
production started from identifying concrete daily issues as well as
the cause/s, actors, and impacts, before broaching the conversation
around interventions to address the same.

Collective analysis on political-economic contour of
conservation-DD politics

Through the PAR processes, we jointly-identified three main generative themes: conservation agendas, privatization of agriculture,
and problematic development programs. As far as the Serampas
were concerned, the conservation agenda was seen as one of the
main state–capital agendas contributing towards dispossession in the
area. In addition, the dependence on export-oriented and import-
dependent agricultural initiatives, especially for coffee and cinnamon,
exacerbated this situation because "we depend on chemical agricultural inputs, which means our life and death is for the *toke* (money
lender)" (Interview notes, November 2011).

The two commodities are indeed very vulnerable to fluctuation of
prices in the global commodity markets, which adds to uncertainty
around livelihoods. Moreover, the government campaign to modernize the rural communities, especially the forest-dependent ones,
as the prerequisite for national economic growth imperatives, was
seen to jeopardize the social fabric of Serampas people. The com-
pulsory modernization of forest/rural social groups has "changed
everything, as they abolished our rules, and now we lose our deep
affection for our land, and eventually our love for each other" (Focus
group notes, December 2011).

TABLE 6.1 Serampas joint analysis on political-economic contours of conservation-DD politics

Policy/Programs	Agents of DD	Processes of DD	Impacts of DD
Conservation	World Bank, WWF, local NGOs, Ministry of Forestry, park patrols, KSNP authority, ICDP, District government	Restrictions of access, imposition of park zones on ancestral lands, gradual self-evictions, lack of transparency in the zoning/mapping processes, Village Conservation Agreement	Change of land and forest use (from shifting cultivation to agroforestry), individualized land ownership/no recognition of communal/customary land use system, constant threat of evictions, criminalization of "forest encroachers"/ambiguous legal status
Privatization	District agricultural office, *tauke* (money lenders), external inputs providers, commodities exporters	Promotion of export-oriented and import-dependent agricultural initiatives	Environmental degradation, food insecurity, loss of biodiversity (e.g. local seeds) and local practices, dependence on external agricultural inputs, impoverishment cycles due to debts
Development	Ministry of Internal Affairs, *Bupati* (head of district), Agricultural Office, NGOs	Change of local leadership and value systems	Erosion of social cohesion and affinities, dependence on external supports

After the declaration of the area as a national park, the Serampas, as customary holders, were immediately re-defined as "forest encroachers". Furthermore, in 1992 the Head of Sarolangun District imposed a "Transmigration Program for Forest Encroachers" for the villagers of Tanjung Kasri and Renah Kemumu, who continue to reside inside the park zone, as opposed to the other three villages in Serampas who are located in the buffer zone. The villagers rejected the transmigration scheme. In the Serampas estimation, it was the state through the KSNP authorities that had encroached on their ancestral lands. The conservation scheme is considered a heavy burden, as one elder from Renah Kemumu remarks, "Why us? Why are we being chosen to pay the price? They now even call us 'the guardians of earth lungs', while before this we were forest encroachers!" (Group discussion notes, February 2011). The sharp remark references the shift of the conservation approach from fortress conservation towards the new Integrated Conservation and Development Project (ICDP), funded through World Bank loans and implemented by the World Wildlife Fund (WWF) and local NGOs between 1996 and 2002 to improve the economic standard of the villages bordering the national park and to enable them to develop alternatives to hunting, collecting non-timber forest products (NTFPs), and opening up agricultural land. Through the Village Conservation Agreement, the ICDP offered the forest-edge communities aid packages including, for instance, micro hydroelectric generators and a few other small-income-generating projects.

Yet in Renah Kemumu, similar agreement was not achieved as they insisted that what the KSNP authorities considered as forest is indeed part of their *rapohen*, the reserve land that they periodically cultivated following the shifting cultivation cycle. In fact, the concepts of biosphere park/co-management, Community Based Natural Resource Management (CBNRM), Integrated Conservation and Development Project (ICDP) popularized by the World Bank and international development organizations have been criticized for the lack of genuine participation of the local communities. It is also testimony to state/outsider ignorance of the traditional and communal land and forest use system, if not an active attempt through inventing and delineating the park zoning scheme, to compel villagers to pursue allegedly pragmatic strategies of opening up new farming lands to the extent possible, which could then become the basis for individual claims of ownership (private as opposed to communal), whenever the national park authorities decided to exercise a more exclusionary approach.

The Serampas also learned that even when they are not physically evicted from their ancestral land, the conservation policy and development programs imposed on them have, nonetheless, actually generated the process of ongoing dispossession. Thus, although the establishment of a national park does not automatically mean physical eviction, often the communities living inside the natural conservation zones are neglected in terms of public service provisions as a way to "encourage" them to leave their ancestral land; facilitating a process of "gradual self-eviction". This is particularly the case after extensive embedding of Serampas in market export-oriented agriculture, especially for coffee and cinnamon, which became the main drivers for converting the forests into farm lands. The focus on export-oriented products made the region and the people more vulnerable to fluctuating world market prices that proved to become an additional pressure to convert more land every time the market was booming. Therefore, market dynamics have played a very substantial role in encouraging farmers to engage harmful farming practices against their immediate environment. The Serampas are now sandwiched between the dual pressures of following the dictate of market prices and the pressure to maintain sustainability under the terms of the conservation agenda. The sustainable development discourse frequently places the blame for environmental destruction not on capitalist development but on its victims, those often marginalized by these "development schemes". Thus, they become double losers as they are sacrificed to the demands of both commercial agriculture and the conservation movement.

Ongoing roles of PAR in addressing conservation dispossession in Serampas

Based on the identification and exploration around the three generative themes and since the inception of this PAR work in 2011, the following initiatives are now ongoing: (1) reclaiming of customary forest in response to the recently changed law on forest management (legal activisms), (2) building of a learning center to revitalize the local farming systems/knowledge (local knowledge and organization building), and (3) an ongoing attempt to revive and strengthen the politics of unity as Marga Serampas, which has been strained by the imposition of a uniform village government model by the modern nation state of Indonesia, along with market-induced competitive individualism (property rights) and commodification previously alien to these areas.

Reclaiming of the customary forest

As a result of the legal struggle by the indigenous movement in Indonesia led by the Indigenous Peoples Alliance of the Archipelago (AMAN), on May 16, 2013, by the decision of case Number 35/PUU-X/2012, the Constitutional Court determined that the indigenous forests are no longer classified as state forest, but part of the forest right (*hutan hak*) of a customary community (Rachman and Masalam 2017). Indigenous forest (*hutan adat*) is determined in accordance with the fact that the relevant customary law community still exists and is acknowledged. Utilizing this political and legal opportunity, with the support of a national network demanding the immediate implementation of the court decision, the Serampas people are mobilizing pressure on the local government machinery, as the new law requires recognition by the Head of District of the indigenous status in order to file the reclaiming of the customary forest, which is under the national park zone. Historical documents of *Piagam Serampas* have also been used to organize counter-mapping in challenging the zoning system as stipulated by the national park authorities. The participatory mapping processes also provide the opportunities to learn and incorporate the spatial knowledge of Serampas, particularly women, often ignored in modern (colonial) Western cartography.

Revitalization of food sovereignty

The damaging impacts of the green revolution campaign as well as the promotion of export-oriented commodities and imported chemical agricultural inputs are also identified as key issues of the development dispossession that the Serampas feel the need to address. Challenging the narrative of "official seeds" – the phrase used by one Merangin District Agricultural Office staff member to describe hybrid rice seeds – through the PAR work, Serampas have collected at least 16 types of seeds which are proven to be more tolerant to the specific weather and soil conditions in upland areas.

While the district official continues to narrate the green revolution myth by arguing that "If farmers still plant rice in the dry paddy fields, there will be many who are starving" (Group discussion notes, February 2012), the villagers observed that the hybrid rice seeds distributed by the Agriculture Office are only suitable for paddy fields on flat land with adequate irrigation, and not for rugged terrain such as in Serampas. And this is barring the fact that the seed supply from the government rarely reaches Serampas on time when the planting season is getting more uncertain due to climatic variations. Therefore, an ongoing initiative for local rice seed breeding has been started by some villages who see the sense in Serampas knowledge and practices.

Some participants have also reconsidered their focus on cash crops, particularly coffee and potato, at the expense of subsistence food production as they prefer to "plant their rice in Vietnam" (Interview notes, December 2011), a satirical remark for farmers whose rice supply depends on imported rice. Based on a survey of rice production and consumption in the two villages, the PAR participants are also concerned about the threat of hidden food insecurity due to the abandoning of the *bilik nagari* (communal rice barn) system, which had proven to be helpful during harvest failures, natural disasters, or even as social insurance for individual calamities.

This is also an identified area of potential action to counter the government version of food security after the designation of the region as "the rice barn of Merangin District", which aimed to boost rice production for markets/export as opposed to local consumption. In fact, the traditional custom in Serampas considered it a taboo to sell newly harvested rice to ensure the needs of all households in the village are fulfilled first and prioritized.

Politics of unity as Marga Serampas

In responding to the erosion of social cohesion and historical affinities as Marga Serampas, due to the change of local leadership system as well as market and state-led development interventions that exacerbate dependence on external supports, the PAR work also recognizes the importance of reviving historical resilience/ memory as a cultural and political strategy to address corporatized state-led development dispossessions. According to one PAR participant, echoing the sentiment of many, "Our ancestors were probably 'poorer' in material terms but they definitely had more freedom and dignity than we have today" (Group discussion notes, December 2011). The reason for such a situation as shared, was, because "we have fallen in to the trap of 'divide and conquer'" as part of the development dispossession strategy being imposed.

The different treatments, resulting from the various development schemes with predetermined rules/controls by external actors (government, NGOs, or corporate entities), created a sense of disunity among the five villages that historically come from one ancestral clan. For instance, Tanjung Kasri and Renah Kemumu are more geographically isolated as the national park authorities did not allow for the construction of a permanent road. Hence, they are often looked down upon as being left behind when compared to the more developed neighboring villages.

On a contrary note, during the big earthquake in the region in 2010, these "relatively more developed villages" learned that it was their kin from the neighboring villages that provided emergency aid until the external aid providers from the government and NGOs managed to reach the area. Therefore, an initiative is now underway which addresses going beyond state-defined village administrative borders by revitalizing the traditional communal decision-making structures to deal with externally driven development schemes (e.g. *kawa* tradition) where the *depati* (traditional leaders) and elders of Marga Serampas meet together. The initiative commenced in 2007 and has now grown in to the Forum Marga Serampas (Forum of Serampas Clan) whose main aim is to maintain the practice of traditional laws and customs, as well as to strengthen local claims and emotional and historic bonds to ancestral lands. The Serampas pursue a politics of unity through the use of cultural modes of knowledge production, including songs and elders' wisdom (role of historical memory), which nurture the emergence and eventual maturation of development dispossession-related struggles by engaging and activating "our ways" (including sacred knowledge) (Kapoor 2009; Masalam 2018).

Context of palm oil dispossession and PAR engagements in West Sulawesi

The PAR praxis on addressing palm oil dispossession involved the affected social groups in Baras, administratively located in North Mamuju District of West Sulawesi Province. The main protagonists are members of social groups located in four villages, including: Sipakainga, Tamarunang (Duripoku Subdistrict), Bulu Parigi, and Towoni (Baras Subdistrict) with a total population of approximately 4,000 households, involved in the land contestation against PT Unggul Widya Teknologi Lestari, one of the largest palm oil companies in the area. Sipakainga and Tamarunang are relatively new villages, where the majority of the people are the migrants from the neighboring province, particularly South Sulawesi. Bulu Parigi and Towoni have a much longer history of presence in the region dating back to the pre-colonial era as Baras villages, with ethnolinguistic origin from Kaili Uma of Kulawi, now part of Central Sulawesi Province.

West Sulawesi is a relatively newer and isolated province established in 2004 as part of the decentralization euphoria after the fall of the centralistic and authoritarian Suharto regime. The isolation can be traced back to the 1950s to mid-1960s when the Darul Islam Movement, a secessionist group fighting for the establishment of an Islamic state, led by Kahar Muzakkar, occupied the area. Throughout the rebellion period, the area was scarcely populated and the main means of transportation was primarily through the sea. Massive capital expansion began to open up the region in the 1970s in the search for timber, particularly ebony wood, either from legal and illegal logging. The region became the site of plunder for Suharto's cronies through forest concessions that the villagers described as the highly valuable forest commodity *"mainan Cendana"* (Cendana's toys), symbolizing Suharto's presidential palace in the capital city of Jakarta. Some villagers in Baras recalled that at the beginning of logging concession expansion in the 1970s they were intimidated by the forest concession companies who told them that the hardtop vehicles and helicopters transporting the timbers, as the symbols of the company's presence on their land, belong to Ibu Tien, Suharto's first lady (Kapohu elder, interview notes, August 2016). The opening of the palm oil plantation by the Astra Group in the 1990s, through its subsidiaries, i.e. PT Letawa, PT Pasangkayu, PT Suryaraya Lestari, and PT Mamuang, further exacerbated the land alienation of the local population. These plantation companies are joint ventures of the Soeryadjaya conglomerate, original owner of Astra Group; with Sulawesi Wanabakti Lestari, owned by a timber businessman from Toraja, South Sulawesi, Salahudin Sampetoding; Salim Group, owned by Liem Sioe Liong and Soeharto; Lumbung Sumber Rejeki group, owned by Radius Prawiro, a former minister in the Suharto era; and Adi Upaya Foundation, owned by Indonesian Air Force officers.

Third-Worldist-PAR addressing palm oil dispossession in Baras

The PAR praxis with small peasants in Baras in West Sulawesi addressing palm oil agro-industrial dispossession was part of my PAR doctoral engagements in close collaboration with activists from Karsa, a land rights social action NGO based in Palu (capital of Central Sulawesi), between May 2015 and February 2016. After initial discussions with the Palu activists, who have been supporting the palm oil DD-affected social groups in Baras since 2014, we agreed to introduce the PAR work as an attempt to strengthen the land reclaiming action, through joint analysis of the strategic and tactical actions they have been taking, as well as to jointly identify further interventions coming out of the collective agreements between the activists and the peasant groups.

Collective analysis on the political-economic contour of palm oil DD politics

The PAR engagement with the directly affected palm oil DD rural social groups in Baras is primarily aimed at helping to map the politics of DD and the responses that they have been taking to date in order to disentangle the *bannang siroca* (Bugis, means knotted thread) and identify possible interventions to strengthen their positioning in this land contestation. The joint analysis has been particularly useful in explicating the imposed politics of DD, i.e. main actors, tactics deployed, and its multi-faceted impacts in living the life that they have reason to value.

This section shares the localized analysis on the capital expansion into the rural frontiers through the framing of the capital invasion as a prerequisite for modernizing imperatives of developmentalism pursued by the state–capital nexus and the complicit role of the supposedly sympathetic civil society actors in obscuring if not distracting the land struggles. Figure 6.1 outlines the joint analysis coming out of the PAR praxis on micro-macro power construction at play leading to DD, as well as the tactics deployed and the subsequent impacts, generated from the joint analysis with the land struggle constituents and the Karsa land activists.

Collective analysis on contours of palm oil DD in Baras

At the beginning of the PAR engagement, the villagers' analysis on the actors affecting DD generally focused around two key antagonists, PT Unggul Widya Teknologi Lestari (UWTL), the palm oil

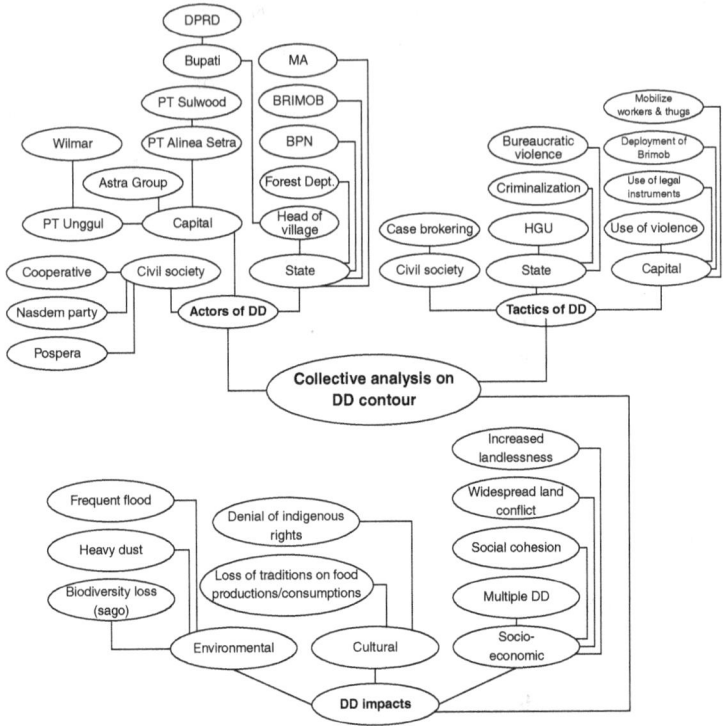

FIGURE 6.1 Collective analysis of development dispossession

company with whom they are in conflict, and Brimob, the special force police. This analysis was understandable considering the fact that these were the most tangible and immediate actors with whom they have had direct contact in their day to day experience as victims of ongoing dispossession. As we developed a structural and historical investigation on the micro and macro context of DD, a more complex picture of the institutional and geographical background of the actors involved continues to emerge, yet still focusing on state and capital-based actors. The complexity of the analysis was also influenced by their socio-historical background, for instance, the historical identification by the *pakkampong* groups, which obviously involved a longer time span, was richer than the peasant migrants.

In addition, the informational learning delivered by the activists and I, particularly in terms of the macro context of DD actors, was deployed through a historical perspective in problematization exercises of the key actors affecting their land dispossession. It was through this typical learning that the *pakkampong* groups started to see their DD experiences as gradual dispossession. They were not focusing any longer on the current experience, which began in the 1970s and early 1980s when massive capital expansion began to open the region for timber,[1] particularly ebony wood, through legal and illegal logging. One of the companies that the villagers recalled was PT Sulwood, the logging company owned by Salahudin Sampetoding, one of the timber barons who was granted by the Ministry of Forestry a large forest concession in Sulawesi.[2] It began to operate in the area and brought workers mostly from outside the region. A subsequent series of massive capital expansions took place in the 1990s through the opening of palm oil plantations by the Astra Group, through its subsidiaries, i.e. PT Letawa, PT Pasangkayu, PT Suryaraya Lestari, and PT Mamuang. In addition to opening up land for their own plantation, these companies were also clearing up the forest for the transmigration scheme, mostly from Lombok Island, as part of the company's obligation mandated by the government to involve smallholders under contract farming. Although the early dweller groups did not clearly categorize the transmigrants as actors of DD, they generally saw the transmigration program as part of the palm oil expansion scheme.

After the peasants had cleared and cultivated the land since late 1990s, in 2003 PT Unggul Widya Teknologi Lestari, the key perpetrator of land dispossession according to local peasants' analysis, came onto the scene. PT Unggul Widya Teknologi Lestari (UWTL),[3] one of the top 50 high-performance palm oil corporations in Indonesia,[4] is a subsidiary of Widya Group, a national private corporation focusing on palm oil commodities with plantation sites located in West Sulawesi, South Sulawesi, Bengkulu, and East Kalimantan. Since 1985, Widya Group has been running a palm oil plantation and processing plant with a total area of 41,680 ha. To support the company's operation in producing crude palm oil (CPO) and palm kernel, Widya Group built five processing mills with a production capacity of 45–60 tons/hour in each operation site. PT Unggul is a supplier for Indofood Agri Resources Ltd., a subsidiary of Salim Group, and Wilmar, the leading agribusiness multinational corporations in Asia. Another subsidiary of Widya Group operating in West Sulawesi is PT Manakarra Unggul Lestari, with a plantation (9,350 ha) and processing mill in Tommo Subdistrict, Mamuju District.

In the collective analysis of the DD-affected social groups in Baras, the actual presence of this new actor could take place only under the protection of the state through the special force police personnel (*Brimob*) deployment to guard the PT Unggul workers demolishing and bulldozing the crops planted on the contested land, destroying houses and huts, and replacing the crops with palm oil trees. Yet the role of the state apparatus was not only as guardian of the capital; as the villagers later found out there were cases, for instance, of local police officers (*Babinsa*) being involved in the land transactions over the contested site. This convinced the villagers that the concession claim was indeed unfounded. The skeptical questions increased as personnel of *Brimob* served as an intermediaries by buying palm oil fruits from the contested land and selling them to the company's mill.

Other actors that the villagers identified as indirectly complicit to the land dispossession are some individuals from local NGOs and political parties trying to take advantage from their pursuit of reclaiming the land. Although they recognized and even appreciated the constructive support of Karsa activists in helping them confront the police criminalization and demanding the withdraw of *Brimob* troops stationed during their successful land reclaiming campaign in 2014, the villagers noticed the vested interests of other civil society actors, even "hidden" competition to represent their case before the state institutions or mass media. Both the *pakkampong* and peasant migrant groups mentioned that some individuals from local NGOs and political parties have approached them offering help in securing legal recognition from the state over the reclaimed land.

In terms of the tactics deployed by the state–capital nexus in effecting DD, similar to their collective analysis on key DD actors, the two most common tactics identified across the groups were the use of legal instruments to deploy the forest (HPH) and land (HGU) concessions by the logging and plantation companies as well as the constant use of violence and intimidation, both directly by the companies or via the hands of the state apparatus. Both the early dweller and peasant migrant groups throughout the collective analysis repeatedly characterized the use of legal instruments to dispossess them of their lands as the manifestation of the colonial territorialization policy, where "*negara sudah merdeka, kami masih dijajah*" (the state is independent already, but we are still colonized) (Sipakainga villager, interview notes, June 2016).

As for the deployment of violence and intimidation to effect land dispossession, as mentioned above the villagers recalled the early days of logging concession expansion in 1970s when they were intimidated by the logging companies who constantly reminded them that the vehicles and helicopters transporting the timber belonged to Ibu Tien (Kapohu elder, interview notes, August 2016). During the heyday of the Suharto authoritarian regime, the logging companies owned by Suharto cronies were compelled to indirectly deploy the corrupt state centralistic power to intensify the intimidation. Ironically, under the post-Suharto regime, which was supposed to be more democratic, PT Unggul was even more obvious in demonstrating their power to request the deployment of *Brimob* to guard their workers in demolishing and bulldozing the crops cultivated on the contested land, destroying houses and huts constructed by the villagers, and replacing their crops with palm oil trees. Physical abuses by the police became the daily experiences of those who dared to return to the land now planted with palm oil trees, as one Sipakainga villager described: "they acted like a scarecrow for the company, they shot their guns into the air every day just to scare us away" (Interview notes, August 2016). In addition to using the state apparatus to perpetrate the violent modes of the DD tactic, PT Unggul also mobilized their workers and hired thugs (*preman bayaran*) to intimidate the land struggle constituents, especially after they managed to occupy the land in 2014. Since then, violent conflicts between the peasant groups and the company's workers have recurred every time the company has tried to enter the reclaimed land.

Collective analysis on the resistance to address DD

Figure 6.2, on the resistance addressing DD, was generated primarily with the assistance of the Karsa land activists in facilitating separate group discussions with the five social-historical groupings of the land struggle constituents, i.e. the Bantayan and Kapohu villagers, primarily where the early dwellers reside, Sipakainga and Tamarunang, mostly migrant peasants, and the camp inside the reclamation area that consists of villagers of both origins. Although there were some members from different groups involved in the discussion in the village outside their own – for instance, the villagers of Sipakainga attended the discussion in Bantayan and Kapohu – the PAR engagement has not been successful in organizing wider cross-villages meetings. Despite the constant attempts to triangulate between different groups, this figure was the result of bringing different pieces into this joint analysis.

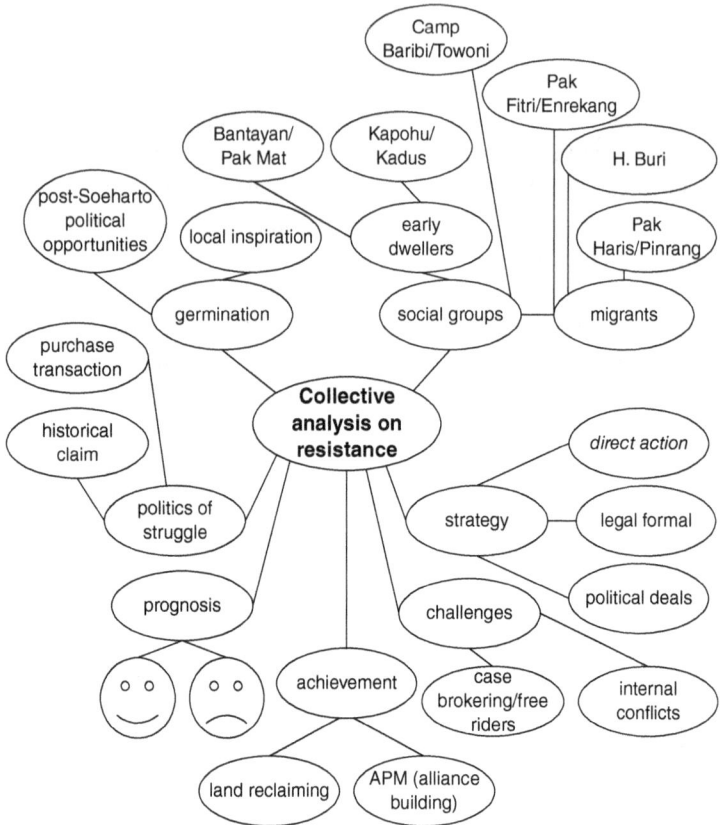

FIGURE 6.2 Collective analysis of resistance to development dispossession

Collective analysis on resistance in Baras

In July 2014, the social groups from these five villages started land reclamation on their own terms by building huts and planting banana trees as markers or symbols of reclamation. The police have destroyed the huts several times since, but these are promptly re-constructed by the Baras. After the occupation, the next stage was building a *bantaya* (traditional building for communal meetings), both a symbolic and functional means of determination in tackling the challenges of the collective decision they had made to occupy the land. After the agreement was reached to take the path outside the court, the next collective strategic decision they made was that the contested land must be physically occupied and turned into settlements and farming sites. At the same time, the establishment of the new settlement also attracted many small and landless peasants from neighboring villages who were in conflict with other plantation companies and interested to learn about the reclaiming process.

To further strengthen their claim and normalize the daily life in the newly established settlement surrounded by palm oil trees planted by the company, the constituents also built a *mushalla* (small prayer space). The *mushalla* is also a symbol of unity in their resistance as they learned after their temporary huts were destroyed by the *Brimob*: "a thousand huts we built and were destroyed by *Brimob* will have no meaning compared to destroying this one small *mushalla*, which will make many people angry" (Group discussion notes, June 2016).

For the early dweller groups, historical messaging was also an important strategic and tactical mode of resistance. Some elders are rekindling the history of fighting the colonial Dutch plantations. A symbol of resistance against the Dutch is, for example, an old canon that is venerated to this day as a tombstone for honoring their elders and martyrs. To nurture a spirit of unity, elders often repeat the story when their ancestors collected the coconut harvest, one of the most lucrative commodities at the time, and bartered them for guns used in the armed struggle against the Dutch colonialists. They recount how their ancestors managed to halt the expansion of Dutch coconut plantations along the Lariang River in defense of their villages which were subsequently never colonized.

> I am not a fearless old man, but I am determined to fight for the rights of my people. What will happen to my grandchildren if no more land is left? They will probably curse me as an irresponsible grandpa!
>
> ...
>
> You can see some remnants of our old villages inside the plantation, the bodies of our elders were buried there. If I quit this struggle, wouldn't that be a big betrayal (*pengkhianatan besar*)? (Bantayan elder interview note, June 2016)

To some extent the historical learning was also intended to respond to the need for a sense of unity between the *pakkampong* (early dwellers) and *pendatang* (peasant migrants) as they recognize "we need to know the history of the arrival of people to this land. Hopefully by listening to these stories we can meet again more often" (Group discussion notes, June 2016). Similarly, for the peasant migrant it can convey the message of appreciating their "*bekas tangan*" (results of hard work), because "[a]fter leaving my village, then migrating to Malaysia for so many years, until I managed to secure this piece of land in Baras, would I just let the company take it from me?" (Interview notes, Tamarunang villager, August 2016).

During the collective group reflection on the repertoires of strategies and tactics that they have pursued throughout their struggle since PT Unggul confiscated their land in 2003, they generally agreed on the importance of direct action, compared to the costly and timely legal standing and making political deals during the election. Moreover, the struggle constituents across generational and gender groupings developed their analysis pertaining to the collusion-of-power structure, i.e. the state apparatus, and capital, i.e. the palm oil company, in effecting the PT Unggul-led DD by confronting the continuous violent intimidation by the state apparatus and the company.

Road blocking is another direct-action tactic that they have continued to deploy and which has been proven to be an effective one because they are aware of the company's urgent need to get the recently harvested palm oil fruits to the mills as soon as possible, before they go bad, as they have to be processed in a fresh condition. Thus, road blocking is an effective way to slow down the company's operation. They also developed *jalur tikus* (literally means "mice road" or short cut) to counter the company's control of the road system passing the plantation area that allowed them to navigate the road connecting the villages inside the plantation.

One important lesson from confronting the police and company's ongoing intimidation throughout the deployment of direct-action tactics was the importance of documenting such repressions. As Ipul, a young member of the land struggle, mentioned, "we now record, secretly, any encounter we have with the police. Other than as evidence of police violent actions, it's also a useful tool to educate my fellow young people here in Baras about the land struggle and why it is important to play more active roles" (Interview notes, August 2015). The villagers also learned to involve media, printed or electronic, as a shield to avoid harsher repression from the state apparatus. On one occasion they managed to cancel *Brimob* deployment, under the company's request, in Baras.

For the constituents of the struggle, they are not only fighting for land (means of production), it is also about building a new structure of equal relations among the different social groups (means of meaning making) involved. This is particularly the case after some signs of division started to emerge after they managed to occupy the disputed land and started to plan for the redistribution. At this point, the PAR praxis can be a potential means of re-consolidating the struggle as one group leader substantiates the need to strengthen the ideology of unity and solidarity across social groups

The PAR engagement has been focusing on internal reconsolidation to disentangle this *bannang siroca* (knotted thread) from the problem-posing exercises of analyzing the contour of multiple dispossessions that both the *pakkampong* and *pendatang* groups have experienced as well as reflecting on their own tactics and strategies in addressing DD. One possible solution identified in the group discussions with the land struggle constituents was organizing series of reconsolidation meetings with the key representatives from each group. Afterwards, the next step is having larger group meetings with the entire land struggle constituents from the four villages to ensure all possibilities for solutions are agreed to by all members. The meeting will also be an opportunity to affirm the agreements over the direction of the land struggle, particularly with the current circumstance of being deeply incorporated into the terrain commodification.

There were several main agendas proposed for this large meeting, i.e. strengthening the claim over the contested land, solving the issue of conflicting claims, and re-consolidating the collective identity of the struggle. In addition, the collective analysis of their current circumstance demonstrated the need to learn from other struggles facing similar challenges, particularly in dealing with the politics of unity and other more technical issues they are grappling with related to market violence, such as the fluctuating price and soaring costs of maintaining the palm oil production cycles (agricultural inputs, like fertilizer, etc.), and even the palm oil DD-affected rural social groups who have started the post-palm oil route as their response to the unfair and unprofitable export-oriented commodity production system.

Concluding reflections on Third-Worldist-PAR and indigenous and small peasant struggles

The entire process of data collection and analysis in the Third-Worldist-PAR praxis in Serampas and Baras were geared towards collective learning and participation directed at mobilization. Thus, the methods adopted were designed as a praxis of resistance, where the strategies of joint data generation and data analysis contributed towards a development of spaces for solidarity building through learning, organizing, and acting generated in a PAR process. The reflections and knowledge dissemination in this PAR work are continuous attempts to politicize the issues transpiring throughout the process of learning in social action. The analytical frameworks were specifically deployed to track the key areas of convergence in histories and current analysis, as well as areas of divergence if not difference that will need work down the road among the villagers and among activists engaged in the land struggle organizing efforts. It was also utilized to sketch out tentative directions for PAR interjections that may be useful for all concerned. The collective PAR reflections on the achievements and challenges of their land struggles have also demonstrated the political significance of taking extra-legal (direct) actions, from road blockades to riots, and these have been found to be the most rewarding in terms of forcing the corporation and the government to meet some of their claims for land, even partially.

The PAR praxis, both as political education and as a practical material intervention has brought the indigenous and the marginalized small peasant to the center of the contentious struggle of who gets to determine if not develop notions (knowledge) pertaining to whose power is being reproduced and whose power is being curtailed, if not what an appropriate politics of resistance does and should be about. Looking at concrete practices and idealized aspirations and excavating contradictions between these two realms will continue to be an important exercise in building relevant knowledge leading to collective action and the constant problematization of emerging contradictions learned through resistance addressing DD. Both cases have demonstrated how historicizing their collective analysis on the imposition of DD politics at the micro-macro levels has led to the emergence of a localized mode of organized political mobilization.

The complexities of maintaining the primary commitment of a Third-Worldist-PAR towards organizing, networking, and learning in social action in anti-dispossession struggles, while engaging in and seeking to understand the multiple modes of small peasant and indigenous learning and knowledge production processes embedded in resistance to address DD has had its challenges. Some complexities include (and for those considering such research as graduate students): (1) the tensions of engaging with the practical terms of facilitating movement interventions that require a longer time commitment from a PAR praxis than is usually afforded by a doctoral project; (2) the challenges of crisscrossing between the boundaries of being a PAR researcher committed to a relevant political praxis in the immediate context of engagement on the one hand and the academic imperatives of knowledge generation for academic (thesis) purposes often limited to if not challenged by, for instance, the parameters of research ethics as defined in a university setting in a country and culture (Canada) far removed from the political-ethical commitments and contexts of a small peasant in Sulawesi; and finally, (3) the challenges associated with addressing the imperatives of conducting Third-Worldist-PAR in the "post colony" while addressing predominantly Eurocentric knowledge and theoretical imperatives that set certain limits around what constitutes and what is considered to be legitimate knowledge generation for academic purposes in the West (Masalam, Kapoor, and Jordan 2016). The road ahead suggests a need for greater attention towards how we may work towards decolonizing hegemonic approaches to PAR in non-Western contexts.

Notes

1 There were at least 21 large logging companies operating in the region, Central and West Sulawesi, especially for the multi-million commodities of "black gold"/ebony wood, mostly connected to Bob Hasan, former Minister of Forestry and long-time crony of the Suharto family (Aditjondro 2001).

2 As an illustration, today the Sulwood Corporation is operating 500,000 ha of forest concession in Central Sulawesi for carbon trading in collaboration with Keep the Habitat, an Australian environmental organization. http://nayu2.blogspot.co.id/2009/06/dana-karbon-dukung-pelestarian-hutan.html.

3 PT WUTL was established on February 3, 1997 by Dr. Ir. Muin Pabinru (Director General of Food Crops Agriculture), Ir. Hasjrul Harahap (former Minister of Forestry during the Suharto era), Tjiungwanara Njoman, Johanis Izaak Andi Lolo, and Tjokro Putro

Wibowo Tjoa, leading members of the
Indonesian Palm Oil Association.

4 www.cdmione.com/
source/50TopKelapaSawit2015.pdf.

References

Aditjondro, G.A. (2001). Suharto's fires. *Inside Indonesia*, 65 (Jan.–Mar.).

Fals-Borda, O. (1988). *Knowledge and People's Power: Lessons with Peasants in Nicaragua, Mexico and Columbia.* New Delhi: Indian Social Institute.

Fals-Borda, O. and Rahman, M.A. (1991). *Action and Knowledge: Breaking the Monopoly with Participatory Action-Research.* New York: Apex Press.

Foley, G. (1999). *Learning in Social Action: A Contribution to Understanding Informal Education.* Leicester: NIACE.

Freire, P. (1979/2000). *Pedagogy of the Oppressed.* New York: Continuum.

Hall, B.L., Gillette, A., and Tandon, R. (1982). *Creating Knowledge: A Monopoly?* New Delhi: Society for Participatory Research in Asia.

Harvey, D. (2005). *A Brief History of Neoliberalism.* New York: Oxford University Press.

Kane, L. (2001). *Popular Education and Social Change in Latin America.* London: Latin America Bureau.

Kapoor, D. (2009). Adivasis (original dwellers) "in the way of" state-corporate development: development dispossession and learning in social action for land and forests in India. *McGill Journal of Education*, 44(1): 55–78.

Kapoor, D. (Ed.). (2017). *Against Colonization and Rural Dispossession: Local Resistance in South an East Asia, the Pacific and Africa.* London and New York: Zed Books.

Kapoor, D. and Jordan, S. (2009). *Education, Participatory Action Research, and Social Change: International Perspectives.* New York: Palgrave Macmillan.

Masalam, H. (2017). Our crops speak: small and landless peasant resistance to agro-extractive dispossession in Central Sulawesi, Indonesia. In D. Kapoor (Ed.), *Against Colonization and Rural Dispossession: Local Resistance in South and East Asia, the Pacific and Africa.* London: Zed Books.

Masalam, H. (2018). *Participatory Action Research, Learning in Small Peasant Resistance and the Politics of Rural Dispossession in Indonesia.* Doctoral thesis, University of Alberta.

Masalam, H., Kapoor, D., and Jordan, S. (2016). Decolonizing PAR in Asia. Paper presented at the 9th International Congress of the Asian Philosophical Association (ICAPA). University of Teknologi Malaysia International Campus, Kuala Lumpur, Malaysia, July 20–24.

Rachman, N.F. and Masalam, H. (2017). The trajectory of indigeneity politics against land dispossession in Indonesia. *Sriwijaya Law Review*, 1(1): 98–113.

Swantz, M.L. (2008). Participatory action research as practice. In P. Reason and H. Bradbury (Eds.), *Handbook of Action Research: Participative Inquiry and Practice.* London: Sage.

7 | PARTICIPATORY ACTION RESEARCH (PAR), LOCAL KNOWLEDGE, AND PEASANT ASSERTIONS IN SOUTHWESTERN BANGLADESH: TAKING BACK THE RIVER IN CONTEXTS OF NGO-LED DEVELOPMENT DISPOSSESSION

Bijoy P. Barua

Introduction

Conventional development has deeper links to capital accumulation in order to "restore the power of economic elites" (Harvey 2005: 19) in the name of economic investment and profit that tends to delink and displace the people from their livelihoods and context through an infiltration of capitalist development in developing countries. In many instances, such an agenda is accomplished via the expansion of market-driven schemes initiated by the larger non-governmental organizations (NGOs) and development agencies in rural areas or what some have referred to as a process of NGOization (Choudry and Kapoor 2013). While implementing development interventions, it fails to include people's knowledge, aspirations, lives, and wisdom in the rural areas of developing countries. Conventional research/ development is inextricably linked to imposition, domination, and colonialism (Smith 1999). In other words, such practice "constantly reaffirms the West's view of itself as the centre of legitimate knowledge ... and the source of 'civilized' knowledge" (Smith 1999: 63) which is essentially considered as scientific/universal knowledge to dominate worldwide (Shiva 2000; Smith 1999).

Participatory Action Research (PAR) simultaneously (in addition to research and popular education as exposition of power) contributes towards local development through democratic practice for social justice and decolonization (e.g. mobilization of small peasants and social context/ecology). As a collective learning process, PAR empowers marginalized social groups (e.g. small/landless peasant and *adivasi* communities) to mobilize local resources (such as land, forestry, environment and nature, regenerative agriculture, collective savings) and to generate people's knowledge for liberation and social action. However, such processes of liberation and decolonization through collective learning and action (PAR) are often challenging to and contradictory with social and political processes due to the consistent penetration of capital accumulation/generation and the imposition of a business-driven approach (model for profit and own organizational growth and sustainability) by larger development actors (e.g. big NGOs) in the country. These intrusions in the name of development are contested by small/landless peasants; a socio-political process in which PAR can play a part.

This chapter will draw upon the author's PAR engagements over two decades while specifically focusing on popular peasant organized attempts to re-assert local knowledge and re-commoning initiatives as in the case of tidal river management (TRM) and as facilitated by a PAR initiative between the author and Uttaran (Transition), a local social action NGO in the southwest region of Bangladesh, and small peasants. This mobilization was an attempt to address flooding and socio-ecological dispossession and dislocation caused by a USAID (United States Agency for International Development), the World Bank, and ADB (Asian Development Bank) Coastal Embankment Project (CEP), the Khulna Coastal Embankment Rehabilitation Project (KCERP) in 1986, and the Khulna-Jessore Drainage Rehabilitation Project (KJDRP) in 1995–1996, utilizing Dutch technology aimed at controlling river flow for industrial development outside the region of dispossession and dislocation (Islam and Kibria 2006). Prior to addressing this PAR project, the chapter will elaborate on current contexts of development dispossession mainly by big NGO-led development efforts, especially neoliberal microcredit initiatives linked to imported (Euro-colonial) conceptions of development and knowledge systems while seeking to dispossess and displace local knowledge systems and valuations of the good life or development.

Current contexts of material and knowledge dispossession and demobilization: development NGOs, neoliberalism, microcredit, and NGOized PAR in Bangladesh

After an initial post-independence history of popular mobilization work in the country, including participation in land-based activism, big NGOs in Bangladesh began to change their approach, strategy, and role in the late 1980s and the early 1990s with the rise of neoliberalism (including in the aid industry) towards a more institutional service provision role (as extensions of the emergent neoliberal and increasingly market-driven state) focused around their own growth and perpetuation, all in the name of participatory research and development in Bangladesh (Barua 2009). NGOs had started to become more investment-orientated rather than people-orientated as the country moved into the ranks of a lower middle-income country. As a result, it is now observed that much of their projects have been confined to commercial business development rather than political mobilization and empowerment. In the words of a development worker that I spoke with:

> Because of such model of development interventions, we are confused with our original commitment and implementation strategies while mobilizing subalterns in rural areas. Of late, we see NGOs tend to shift from original ideological vision as they are occupied with microfinance activities in the country. Over the years, we have realized that the microfinance activities are more concentrated on loan collection and distribution rather than collective learning practice and action in the project areas. We also realize that when we are engaged in the process of learning we are in better condition to reach subalterns and marginalized people, and generate local knowledge on ecology and local economics for sustainable living for social justice. (Personal communication, December 30, 2017)

Similarly, a senior representative of a national NGO opined:

> When we implement the project with the assistance of foreign funding, the donors dictate and impose conditions, and for which we are not able to develop our capacity. In most cases, foreign funded projects neither acknowledge local socio-cultural ecology nor consider people's knowledge for sustainable living. Rather the funds are short term in nature with conditions and impositions. (Personal communication, December 25, 2017)

NGOs today not only promote the neoliberal political-economic agenda but they also accelerate the penetration of a techno-centric

development model and approach for economic growth by ignor-
ing diverse local livelihoods, socio-political-ecological contexts and
epistemic realities of small peasants in the rural regions. Since the
development agencies are over-emphasizing the issue of social business and market, the process of NGOization is deeply engaged in
financial investment as the only solution in the rural areas. The rise
of such a business-driven model of NGOs practically tended to
demobilize a people-centered development approach and the process of PAR in the country. In most cases, these NGOs attempted
to depoliticize and de-radicalize the grassroots-based organizations and social movements in rural areas through the imitation of
Western liberal internationalism and market participation. Because
of the neoliberal approach, NGOs have also proliferated remarkably
as alternative forces of what Harvey (2005: 78) has referred to "as a
separate entity as civil society" in order to mobilize grassroots oppositional politics as a powerhouse outside the state apparatus by the
instigation of international donors in Bangladesh.

While imitating such an approach, the NGOs have also adopted
the method of semi-feudalistic, semi-colonialist, and semi-bureaucratic
management style to fulfill their own aspirations in Bangladesh. On
the other hand, the depoliticization scheme has been engaged in
de-motivating the landless peasant and marginalized group from the
practice of collective learning and social movement, which eventually allowed the NGOs to accelerate their own sustainable economic
growth (through microfinance) in the country. With this process
of action, an appropriation of neoliberal participatory research has
become more dominant in the development sector by the so-called
urban educated experts. In many instances, such people-orientated
research has often been materialized and marginalized "through the
promotion of *aamar kotha aami koi; tore ektu jigaya loi* (I tell you my
own sermon or version; but I ask you for affirmation or verification)" (Barua 2009: 243). In most cases, not only have the bigger
NGOs appropriated the process of PAR for their own benefits,
they have also become dominant actors of the method of participatory rapid appraisal (PRA), which "entailed less extended dialogue
and less ideologically committed" (Chambers 1992: 3) for radical
transformation.

Over and over again, this ideological shift tended to push PAR
into the margin. This ideological shift has grown among the NGOs

disillusioned by the market-driven agenda of the mid-1980s. As a result, the ideological differences were mainly noticed among the larger NGOs. Moreover, similar differences have also extended to the medium-sized and small NGOs in the rural areas of the country. These differences have become more prominent since the 1990s among the NGOs that ultimately jeopardized social movement(s), and which eventually demobilized the rural marginalized groups in the peripheries (Barua 2009). Despite this fact, there is a growing critical debate among the scholars and concerned citizens about the magnitude of NGOs and their roles in transforming rural society in the country in recent years (Lewis and Sobhan 1999). Over the years, it has been observed that larger NGOs are basically situated in the capital/satellite (core) who usually control the peripheries of the country. By contrast, medium NGOs are centered in the semi-periphery (district town), and small NGOs are based in the peripheries (villages) that are socially and politically connected to the people.[1] In such an ideological shift, bigger NGOs often act in parallel to the state for investment and profit-making business instead of collective mobilization and the development of marginalized groups. Because of this divergence, the marginalized people are entrapped by the NGOs in Bangladesh (Barua 2009).

Microfinance, capital accumulation, and dispossession

Since development interventions place greater emphasis on the growth model, due to the "onslaught of neoliberal globalization" (Arens 2014: 8), NGOs have been accelerating the microfinance scheme for social change and progress. This model leans towards the proliferation of financial institutions in order to restore the power of corporate capitalism as opposed to the mobilization of landless groups at the grassroots level. Additionally, the proliferation of financial capital often uses the coercive power of competition within the management of development actors in Bangladesh (Harvey 2005). Such practice(s) of the capitalist mode of development operation(s) ignore(s) participatory action research while implementing microfinance projects in the rural areas. In other words, this profit-driven model virtually ignored the needs of marginalized people in the villages (Barua 2009) as the development intervention of NGOs is mostly guided by multilateral and bilateral funding agencies, in particular the World Bank (Huq 2001). More importantly, this "microcredit model of development intervention by the NGOs reveals not only the capitalist modernizing bent of the development institutions but also lack of concern for the education, health and welfare needs of poor people" (Huq 2001: 15). In this effort, the development NGOs obviously serve the agenda of corporate capital interests while maneuvering the discourse of empowering rural women in the country. Subsequently, the enormous expansion of NGOs and the mobilization of grassroots organizations (such as *samity* – women group) have grown remarkably to ensure microcredit intervention in the rural areas. In this process, the NGOs usually disengage people from the process of collective social movement and the political action (Kapoor 2013) of the poor "in the interest of capitalist control" (Barua 2009: 247) and power by promoting "neoliberalism from below or small-'c' capitalism" (Kapoor 2013: 59) with the cooperation of state-corporate control such as the Microcredit Regulatory Authority (MRA) of Bangladesh Bank and the Palli Karma-Sahayak Foundation (PKSF)[2] in Bangladesh.

For example, state-sponsored agencies such as MRA and PKSF have created a space to build up *public–private partnerships* (Harvey 2005) to expedite microfinance programs in the rural areas. This partnership encourages the notion of "the rational profit-seeking" (Kapoor 2013: 59) model in the peripheries where several smaller NGOs act as agents to demobilize *samity* (group of rural women) without considering the notion of people-centered development in the project areas. Within this endeavor, "NGOs fundamentally serve the economic and political agenda of the world capitalist society" (Barua 2009: 247) in the peripheries. Because of this effort and action, NGOs have been involved in controlling the rural poor through local agents within the *para* (neighborhood) of villages. In this process, "the power of people's movements" (Korten 1990: 124) has been discounted in the field of development as the NGOs (such as BRAC, ASA, BURO, and Grameen Bank) are mainly engaged in capital accumulation/business rather than social mobilization. Such a money-making endeavor would certainly tend to kill a social movement and the spirit of liberation of the marginalized group. Presently, such schemes are being implemented by 19,166 branches of microfinance institutions in Bangladesh, where 239,680 employees are engaged (Credit and Development Forum 2017).

Typically, the NGOs tend to expand this microcredit scheme in the project areas for their own business interests, and for the interest of multinational corporations of Western countries. For instance, BRAC, a Bangladeshi large microfinance organization, sells the products of Monsanto[3] to its group members through microcredit packages as a partner in Bangladesh. Similarly, the Grameen Bank has also been engaged in marketing cellular phones through its microcredit package[4] (Huq 2001). Undoubtedly, the development practices of NGOs often tend to push out the rural marginalized group through a process of dispossession from their land. Their ruthless exploitation of rural poor women is well-known in Bangladesh. Consequently, the rural poor people tend to migrate into the cities from their rural houses for living and survival. This expansion of microfinance decreased the process of collective education, and increased the powerlessness of the people by causing indebtedness to the NGOs. Nazma, a 43-year-old woman, confirmed:

> It was hard to live with our income earlier. In such a situation, I myself joined in a *samity* of microcredit program in our area in 2003. After joining, I took a loan of Taka 5,000 to improve my family income, and eventually I invested said amount to my husband's small business. As I took loan from a microcredit organization, I mostly engaged in paying-back large amount money to the organization to adjust my loan. As a result, we had a difficult time to maintain our family. While encountering such situation, I joined in other organization from where I borrowed Taka 76,000 to boost up my husband's business. Despite this, we had to pay more installments almost every day. While receiving loan money, we neither received proper guidance nor education/training from the organization to develop business; rather, we are overburdened with our loan money. (Field interview, December 2017)

Likewise, another member of a microfinance group, Nasrin, a 38-year-old woman, expressed:

> My husband and myself sell vegetables at Doulatpur village market from 2001. We have three children and we do not have any agricultural land for cultivation. At one point of time, we have thought we could make our lives better if we enhance our income through a small business. To change the family income, we joined local microcredit group and took our first loan in

2006. Although we collected loan, we did not have any proper plan to develop the business. Even we had not received any guidance or training on business operation or plan. In this effort, we just used our loan money for the vegetable selling and paying installments to microfinance institute. Over the years, we spent large amount of money to my daughter's wedding. In addition, some of our capital spent for various cultural programs. At the present, we are in debt of Taka 90,000. In this situation, we are more of defaulters and we do not know what to do.

These narratives clearly signify that women are not able to improve their family income and economic conditions through the micro-credit scheme. Rather, NGOs have been able to create their huge market in the rural areas as a "catalyst of globalization and primitive accumulation of capital" (Ahmed 2018: 8) with the penetration of neoliberalism in the country. For example, the expansion of micro-credit programs by the larger NGOs since late 2007 has had negative consequences (Chen and Rutherford 2013), mainly in the area of participatory learning and research. More specifically, one of the leading proponents of the microfinance program in Bangladesh, Choudhury (2013) clearly mentioned that "Excessive landing into a saturated market could cause a 'train crash' that might cause great sector-wide damage and burden borrowers with debts they did not need" (cited in Chen and Rutherford 2013: 1). Moreover, target participants of microfinance programs have been caught up in the debt repayment trap. This debt trap or train crash of microcredit programs clearly damaged the power of people's movement and collective learning space as it mainly focused on money and material. Similar observation was also made in my earlier ethnographic research in 1998 and 1999 in the southwestern part of the country, where women group members were mostly confined to loan collection and distribution as opposed to group-based collective learning and social action.

Taking the river back: PAR, popular mobilization, and the CEB, KCERP, and KJDRP projects in southwestern Bangladesh

Popular praxis initiates a dialogue and critical analysis to generate knowledge in the process of PAR at the grassroots level for collective mobilization and transformation. This dialectical form of research is inspired by a critical reflection from below in order to make change and initiate social action from the bottom that is not part of dominant discourse. More importantly, it tends to create critical awareness of disadvantaged people for local development. In other words, "people's praxis" encourages reflective learning and practices for community solidarity (Rahman 1993). PAR is politically committed to construct knowledge from daily experiences in order to liberate marginalized people from social oppression as people are "mobilized with PAR techniques from the grassroots up and from the periphery to the center so as to form social movements which struggle for participation, justice and equity without necessarily seeking to establish hierarchical political parties in the traditional mold" (Fals-Borda 1985: 91). In other words, "it is a social action process that is biased in favor of dominated, exploited, poor, or otherwise left-out people for social change and empowerment" (Hall 1996: 187).

> Advocates of participatory action research have focused on their critique of conventional research strategies on structural relationships of power and the way through which they are maintained by monopolies of knowledge, arguing that participatory knowledge strategies can challenge deep-rooted power inequities. (Gaventa and Cornwall 2001: 70)

The central drive of PAR is to create a critical learning environment in order to uphold the popular knowledge that can build the capacity of people to change their social and economic conditions within their own cultural, political, and ecological context. This approach emphasizes critical dialogue where both learners/participants and facilitators/researchers take part in the process of learning while constructing knowledge for people-orientated development to gain control over resources in their own land. It engages people as organic intellectuals to generate their ecological knowledge collectively in order to create transformative social change, and to use local resources for sustainable living. This transformative approach not only engages reflective critical dialogue to construct knowledge within their social location, it also deeply mobilizes the landless farmers for social action and change (Barua 2002; 2009). The dialogical approach creates room not simply for a diverse prospect, "but for advocacy and (social) action based on those views which are not part of the dominant discourse" (Schrivers 1995: 23–24). The goal of dialogical process is to generate indigenous knowledge from below by the marginalized people as stimulated by critical analysis from below (Freire 1970). This form of collective research systematically attempts to understand the issues from the perspective of local people, who construct their knowledge for social action.

The CEB, KCERP, KJDRP, and PAR mobilization with Uttaran for TRM

A Eurocentric model of river and water management was institutionalized by the British colonial administration in Bengal in the 19th century. Consequently, the community-based river governance system was replaced by the colonial power to control water resources in river-basin Bengal. Moreover, the partition of the subcontinent in 1947 affected the farming system as the farmers migrated to India, which eventually disorientated the rural economy in the region. Additionally, the two major floods of 1954–1955 massively devastated life and livelihood in the coastal region of Bangladesh. Despite this, the then government of Pakistan decided to construct embankments on the rivers to control flooding, and increase agricultural production. In this effort, the former Pakistan government invited Krug Mission[5] to visit the erstwhile East Pakistan. As a result, Krug Mission proposed to establish a separate organization, Water and Power Development Authority (WAPDA), and also to initiate structural interventions such as embankments to control water resources. Within this framework, WAPDA implemented the Coastal Embankment Project (CEP) with an objective to convert a brackish water zone to a fresh water zone within the paradigm of *grow more food* in southwestern Bangladesh as funded by USAID and the World Bank in the mid-1960s within the notion of *sabuj biplob* (the green revolution). For this, it constructed, using Dutch technology, 37 compartmentalized polders, 1,566 kilometers of coastal embankment, and 282 sluice gates to delink the floodplains from the rivers and turned wetlands into dry lands with control irrigation. Similarly, the Agricultural Development Corporation was engaged to promote high-yielding varieties (HYVs) of crops and fertilizers in the region (Islam and Kibria 2006). However, this imported technocentric project practically created severe development disaster as the project design failed to realize the ecological consequences of an embankment construction (see Uttaran 2013).

As the region was inundated for several decades, people demanded to resolve the crisis. Accordingly, several techno-centric projects, such as KCERP in 1986 (jointly implemented by the Bangladesh Water Development Authority (BWDA) and financed by the ADB) and KJDRP in 1995–1996 (jointly implemented by BWDA, Departments of Agriculture Extension, and Fisheries, and funded by the ADB), have been designed to construct regulators and cross dams to delink the area from tidal actions without any consultation with the people. However, local communities demanded ecological knowledge-based TRM as opposed to a techno-centric model. In this process of action, Uttaran came forward to mobilize rural landless peasants in the 1990s as a facilitator in the region as the culturally biased project – imposed by the donor-driven techno-centric model – displaced millions of rural inhabitants. Afterwards, Uttaran also mobilized the Panni Committee to establish human rights for peasants through TRM. In the process of collective learning, Uttaran clearly committed to generate indigenous knowledge by ensuring *jonogoner ongshogrohan* (people's participation) in 18 *Upazilas* (sub-districts) (Islam and Kibria 2006). In spite of this ideological perspective, Uttaran believes that

> a participatory learning process could create a space for the million affected people living on the river basins who could identify environmentally sound and economically viable alternatives. As you know, Uttaran has been working with the people and Panni Committee for more than two decades to generate people's wisdom and indigenous knowledge on river management in eleven river basins in order to develop a regional plan of action for community-based river management in the southwest coastal region of Bangladesh. (Islam, Personal communication, January 2018)

As I was inspired by *Freirian praxis* for rural marginalized people, I engaged with Uttaran as young activist through the development forum of Jessore in the late 1980s for social justice. In fact, my commitment to the education and grassroots development for the rural poor/subaltern is as much academic as it is ideological. I believe that development must be constructed from a perspective of local people for sustainable living. In this effort, I have engaged with PAR for TRM since 2016, which enabled me to understand the plight of rural peasants including ethnic minorities who are desperately in need of cooperation to decolonize from colonial imposition and oppression. For example, the culturally biased polder (embankment) project, encouraged by Western donors, not only submerges massive areas for five to seven months every year, it also directly dispossessed a million rural people. The lives and livelihoods of around five million people are under threat in the coastal belt of southwestern Bangladesh (see Uttaran 2013). A 70-year-old man, Imdadul expressed:

> During the early 1960s the river Shaluka used to supply us enough water for our agricultural cultivations. We harvested plenty of rice and vegetables for our consumption. At one point of time the river was drying out gradually. We were perplexed and even, we did not know what was causing the drought. Later, we came to understand that powerful people were placing polder/*bandh* (embankments) with the financial and technical support of *bideshi data* (foreign donor) in the river to convert *brakish water* to fresh water for more crop production and agricultural development. Consequently, this project created water logging, which allowed a section of people to cultivate commercial shrimp farming. These shrimp cultivators (people) were not from our area. They had the political connection and used to maintain relationship with the governmental official. They were farming shrimp by taking lease of *kash* land from the government. While taking lease of *kash* land they also occupied others lands with minimal price. In our area, powerful people (who have political connection and maintain contact with the government official) are engaged in shrimp farming (*chingrigher*) for export and profit. As a result, we lost access to land, water and river.

The Western-biased polder project "was undeniably also about power (politics) and domination" (Smith 1999: 60) for market-driven capital accumulation (Harvey 2005) in the coastal region of the country. This colonial/neocolonial development model denigrated the people's science and knowledge on the TRM system of the region. Consequently, this agenda pushed out peasants/landless farmers from their livelihood and social environment. Dalu clearly expressed:

Unfortunately, Water Development Board built the embankment without any consultation that caused serious disaster in the area. For people, who live close to the river and embankment they lost their agricultural production as the ancestral lands have been submerged under flood water. People lost their livelihoods; and eventually we live in crisis. (Field interview, December 17, 2018)

This form of domination is "generally referred to as 'universal' knowledge available to all and not really 'owned' by anyone" (Smith 1999: 63), which can create environmental disaster and economic crises that are encountered by the rural people in the southwestern region of the country. Nonetheless the Western dominant culture constantly attempts to impose its knowledge as the core or universal knowledge over non-Western countries, despite social and cultural differences. Farid, a community member from Tala Upazila, explained,

River and water was always managed by the local communities in order to maintain natural flow in the pre-colonial time. However, such initiative and process have been replaced by the centralized system since the arrival of colonial power and administration. Despite this, local knowledge on river management and social ecology has been ignored within the framework of colonial agenda and conventional research model and development. The conventional research process never considered our views and opinions. (Field interview, December 18, 2017)

Similarly, Mokadir, a landless farmer, overtly expressed:

The so-called development (mega) project only benefited a few people; mainly investors, shrimp cultivators and politicians who have access to the government officials, whereas landless people like us have encountered huge challenges and problems, including permanent loss of our farmlands, displacement, and severe water logging. There have been many negative impacts on our lives, livelihoods and habitat. (Field interview, December 18, 2017)

This transfer-technology project dehumanized the lives of the rural communities through a process of development violence along the region of Khulna, Satkhira, and Jessore in the southwestern districts of Bangladesh within the notion of "accumulation by dispossession" (Harvey 2005) under the agenda of neoliberal policy. This destructive development not only displaced millions of rural people, it also pushed out the poor landless farmers, sharecroppers, agricultural wage workers, and petty traders from their livelihoods in the coastal region of the country. Rashid, a farmer, reflected:

Dutch technology-based expensive embankment (polder) project disconnected the lakes, canals and lands from the main river streams which created severe water logging in the region. Such unplanned polder displaced millions of people around coastal belt.

This destruction of nature created uncertainty in the area that causes human beings to endure more hardship in the region of the country. Such Euro-biased hegemonic knowledge obliterated the sustainable lifestyles of the people within their ecological context and created material poverty by the "denial of survival needs" (Shiva 1989: 10). Furthermore it tended to ignore diverse cultural knowledge. For example, the construction of polders (embankments) and sluice gate has proven to be disastrous since they cannot generate local economy for the rural communities. Moreover, the polders created a development disaster, and consequently people have turned into environmental refugees in the region. This clearly indicated that "ideas coming from another part of the world cannot be simply transplanted" (Freire 1970: 30). Over the years, the contribution of rural people in the production of knowledge for economic development and social justice was ignored. On the contrary, the conventional research tended to uphold the Western development paradigm which explicitly attempted to undermine local ecological knowledge of the rural community as the method has been imposed by the international development agencies within the framework of a colonial/neocolonial agenda. The Western value-based conventional research/development agenda has been supported by Western bilateral and multilateral agencies to encourage the so-called scientific development program through the assistance of foreign aid and experts. By and large, such conditional aid endangers freedom, and put off self-reliance in the process of development in Khulna, Satkhira, and Jessore, through deceptive tricks. Shiva (2000: vii) categorically mentioned that "priorities of scientific development and R&D (rural development) efforts, guided by a western bias, transformed the plurality (indigenous) of knowledge systems into a hierarchy of knowledge systems".

While addressing the hegemonic development agenda in the context of the local environmental perspective and river basin ecology, Uttaran expresses:

> We believe that community-based river management is inseparably linked to our livelihood in the coastal region. In this effort, we have been able to organize several community consultations and reflective sessions with people and other actors in the region. Over the years, we have initiated more than one thousand informal sessions in the eleven river basin areas with the people in the affected region. Moreover, we have also organized formal community consultation meetings where, technocrats, member of parliament, and government officials of the areas were present to document the voices of the people of the area. We simply adopted an approach of dialogical process as part of learning to generate local knowledge from the people of the region. Through this participatory learning process, people of Beel Dakatia and Beel Bharat Bhaina proved that tidal river management (TRM) based on local knowledge is ecologically sound and appropriate to the local context. In spite of our constant mobilization, the government had to materialize TRM in Kushi and Bhavadha areas to mitigate the development disaster. TRM was developed and managed by the people of the coastal region, not by the donors. It is innovative and profitable for the community. (Islam, Personal communication, January 2018)

Similarly Robin, a community member of Bharat Bhaina, while reflecting on the experience of learning and social action, stated:

> While working and attending the learning session with other people, our experience says that the *jonogoner geayan ebong abhiggota chara unnyan shambhab noi* (development is impossible

without people's knowledge and experience) in the region as the people preserved local ecological and environmental knowledge that provide deeper sense of understanding to make effective plan for the area and community. For the last 25 years we have been struggling to prove it through our experience and participation. I definitely participated in this process of learning with others as part of social action as we live in the region. Our existence and livelihood are deeply connected to the land and nature that helps us to live in peace. We are still struggling to maintain our livelihood and *bashatvita* (homestead). Despite this, we have been able to demonstrate that local knowledge is more environment friendly, appropriate, and acceptable to the people of this region. (Field interview, December 23, 2017)

All the sessions were mainly centered on the process of action-critical reflection-analysis through group learning (see Uttaran 2013). Such reflective community consultation(s) was/were facilitated around open dialogue with circular questioning and experience sharing. Predictably, each session encouraged rural people to use the local cultural media such as proverbs, storytelling, and local wisdom, which are orally available in the villages while generating community-based knowledge on TRM in the southwest coastal region in Bangladesh. Most importantly, the notion of TRM was generated based on local knowledge systems by the people to maintain the river basin at the community for better livelihoods. The objective of TRM is not only to build up or expand the drainage system, but its basic concept is to allow tidal flow into the wetland basin, known as *jowar bhata khelano* (free play of tidal flow), that releases the tidal flow back to the river (Islam and Kibria 2006). This form of knowledge is holistic in nature and inclusive in its epistemological approach as "it gains from the natural environment through a community activity and interaction" (Barua 2004: 102). It is preserved and passed on through an oral record and retained over many centuries within a specific cultural and geographical location for people-centered development and self-reliance (Barua 2004). With this mandate, Uttaran has been engaged in people-centered development since 1985 to generate local knowledge through collective learning and community consultation on community-based river management (TRM) "with a focus on locally defined priorities and local (ecological) perspectives" (Cornwall and Jewkes 1995: 1667) to resolve chronic environmental crises as the people of the rural society of Khulna, Satkhira and Jessore do not consider *bhumi* (land) and *nadi* (river) as capital for investment and profit.

> We regard them as sanctified and holy as the *nadi* brings *poli* (silt) and *bhumi* (land) brings food for their sustainable living rather than disaster and destructive development. In fact, development such as polder/embankment displaced/dispossessed us from our land and livelihood for more than two decades. (Focus Group Discussion, December 18, 2017)

Similarly, a villager, Rashid (50 years old) from *Bhavadha* (December 2017) clearly expressed:

> Our collective learning is to generate local knowledge through the Panni Committee in the region to protect our river, water, livelihood, land and social security. As you know, our river provides water and natural resources for livelihood and food. For protection of river and land, we work collectively to generate knowledge to protect nature and environment in the bank of *Kapotaka* and *Bhavadha*. (Field interview)

Likewise, an activist researcher, Sakkhar, from Jatpur area, of Tala Upazila eloquently expressed:

> The natives of the land have exercised their own form of governance since the ancient times. It was the norm even during the rule of the Mughals. Locals had the control over their own areas and natural resources. Nevertheless, this system changed and became centralized under the British rule. Such process marginalized our indigenous practice and knowledge. There was a tradition of maintaining *Ashsto Mashi Badh* (embankment for eight month) around the coastal region of Bengal by the people in order to control the river water and to maintain irrigation facilities for cultivation of crops. The monsoon was the most appropriate season for cultivation of rice. As the river water used to inundate the lower farming lands with salty water, the

local knowledge on water management was preserved by the people to maintain ecology and environment. (Field interview, December 20, 2017)

Culturally, the land, forest, water, and river are the blessed natural resources that used to promote sustainable living and biodiversity for the livelihood(s) of people in the river-basin coastal region of Bangladesh. People usually respect the river as it preserves culture and biodiversity, and the death of a river could mean a loss of the culture (Haque 2017).

Our rivers cross through countless bends in the belt of southern part of Bangladesh. However, nature does not always determine the twists and turns of these gliding rivers. At times, it is the people who tend to shape pathways of the rivers for their needs and livelihoods which allows the people to use their natural resources for economic and cultural benefit. (Tapan, Field interview, December 2017)

Based on this collective learning, the people of the coastal region tended to mobilize social action to negotiate with the state/government. In this regard, Rashid (50 years old) and Baker (40 years old) of Tala Upazila expressed:

The local people were able to preserve and disseminate cultural knowledge on tidal river management to reformulate polder plan and policy through demonstrations, newspaper and mobilizations of human chains. We organized and mobilized through an action-based research by the Panni Committee with the support of Uttaran, a local non-governmental organization (NGO) to introduce TRM (based on our local ecological knowledge on community-based river management) to protect our lives and livelihoods. The people came out to mobilize anti-polder demonstrations, despite criminal cases and harassments by the law enforcing agencies. (Focus group discussion, December 18, 2017)

As the people constructed knowledge based on their collective experience, they constantly contested the hegemony of economic development to protect their livelihoods along the coastal region of southwest Bangladesh. There were several local movements against large-scale structural violence for over two decades. Specifically, there was socio-political resistance by people against the ADB-funded KJDRP and this movement is known as Beel Dakatia Andolon. Because of such social resistance from Andolan by the people of the region, ADB had to stop its project (Islam and Kibria 2006). This contestation/social action was mobilized against the imposition of multilateral donors, political elite groups, government agencies, and technocrats who tended to legitimize the power of the new economic order under the rubric of a neoliberal agenda. In other words, the mobilization of people for social action – by the multiple actors (such as local community groups, the Panni Committee, and Uttaran) – was organized through an anti-embankment resistance movement to establish TRM along river basins. In fact, several thousand people staged a token hunger strike, and mobilized several rallies to mitigate the sufferings of 1.4 million affected people in Satkhira, Khulna, and Jessore districts and to dredge the Kapatakkha River. For example, they have been engaged in anti-polder demonstrations and protests for local rights and sustainable livelihoods in an approach that retains an equilibrium with the planet and eliminates processes of dispossession, political deprivation, environmental hazard, and inequality in the country. Local people rejected the land acquisition plan of KJDRP, and for this resistance movement people were mobilized with the support of the Panni Committee and Uttaran in the coastal belt of southwest Bangladesh.

Popular peasant anti-dispossession mobilizations: concluding reflections on the role for academics and PAR

Having engaged in the field of participatory learning/action research and community mobilization activities for over two decades as a participatory researcher, community organizer, and development academic for social transformation and change, I observed that the relationship between academics and rural community organizers is distant and remote in the country. The relationship tends to create a binary opposition while mobilizing a grassroots-based program, as the city-based development experts and academics are culturally, politically, and mentally tuned/trained by the Eurocentric model of conventional research and development. Moreover, these professionals/academics are motivated by the market-driven strategy and approach as they are able to accumulate capital through consultancy. Additionally, they are blind towards Eurocentric knowledge production rather than the construction of local ecological and cultural knowledge in contemporary Bangladesh. Interestingly this Eurocentric model failed to uncover people's aspirations, needs, and local ecological knowledge through a conventional approach. Rather it disconnected people from their social context and natural environment.

Similarly, larger NGOs (core) and actors are more concerned to implement business-driven models which tend to demobilize, depoliticize, and de-radicalize the grassroots-based people's organizations and subalterns in the country. Such practice(s) of the capitalist mode of operation(s) ignore(s) participatory research while mobilizing development intervention(s) in the rural areas, although NGOs of the country initiated PAR in the mid-1970s. In most cases, this process tends to jeopardize the initiative of the collective social movements of subalterns through a penetration of a neoliberal economic agenda in the peripheries. Over the years, these satellite/core groups have changed their approach and strategy in the name of techno-centric economic development and social transformation in Bangladesh. Often, this process has been nurtured through the sponsorship of public–private partnerships in the country. In such an ideological shift, grassroots-based community organizations are under constant threat to establish social justice for the rural landless peasant in the villages due to the onslaught of the neoliberal agenda.

However, Uttaran, a rural-based organization, has been actively engaged in the mobilization of rural marginalized/landless people against development violence and dispossession, despite the domination of neoliberal intervention in the southwestern region. For instance, Uttaran has been facilitating PAR in generating indigenous ecological knowledge-based TRM in the southwest coastal region as opposed to the dominion of the donor-driven techno-economic model since the early 1990s. TRM is a community-based initiative and holistic approach generated by rural peasants towards people-centered development as it promotes biodiversity and ecological balance in the region. More importantly, the peasants believe in depoldering the region for their livelihood, and TRM is a necessity for them. Thus, I firmly believe that both academics and professionals could build up a partnership with rural peasants in order to generate

---

location-specific knowledge to counter colonial/neocolonial domin-ion for human rights and sustainable living in Bangladesh, if they are ideologically committed.

Notes

1 I borrowed the concept from Wallenstein's world system theory.

2 PKSF was established by the government of Bangladesh in 1990 to alleviate poverty, and to disburse funds to microfinance institutions (MFIs) and NGOs.

3 There were rallies and protests against Monsanto's aggression in Bangladesh (see *New Age*, May 24, 2015).

4 Simultaneously, NGOs tend to develop partnerships with companies – e.g. Singer, Unilever, and other electronics companies.

5 This mission was initiated by the United Nations in 1957.

References

Ahmed, A.I.M.U. (2018). Contemporary changes in Bangladesh society. Keynote Paper in the First National Conference on Contemporary Changes in Bangladesh Society. East West University, Dhaka, May 12.

Arens, J. (2014). *Women, Land and Power in Bangladesh: Jhagrapur Revisited*. Dhaka: The University Press.

Barua, B. (2002). Participatory research, education and rural farmers: a case study from Bangladesh. Conference proceeding, 22nd conference of Canadian Association of Adult Education. Ontario Institute for Studies in Education, University of Toronto.

Barua, B. (2004). *Western Education and Modernization in a Buddhist Village of Bangladesh: A Case Study of the Barua Community*. Unpublished PhD Dissertation, University of Toronto.

Barua, B. (2009). Participatory research, NGOs, and grassroots development: challenges in rural Bangladesh. In D. Kapoor and S. Jordan (Eds.), *Education, Participatory Action Research, and Social Change: International Perspectives*. New York: Palgrave Macmillan.

Chambers, R. (1992). Rapid appraisal: rapid, relaxed and participatory. Discussion Paper 311. Sussex: Institute of Development Studies.

Chen, G. and Rutherford, S. (2013). A microcredit crisis averted: the case of Bangladesh. Focus note 87. Washington, DC: Consultative Group to Assist the Poor (CGAP).

Choudry, A. and Kapoor, D. (2013). Introduction. In *NGOization: Complicity, Contradictions and Prospects*. London and New York: Zed Books.

Cornwall, A. and Jewkes, R. (1995). What is participatory research? *Social Science and Medicine*, 41(12): 1667–1676.

Credit and Development Forum. (2017). Bangladesh microfinance statistics 2016–17. Dhaka: Bangladesh Microfinance Statistics.

Fals-Borda, O. (1985). *Knowledge and People's Power: Lessons with Peasants in Nicaragua, Mexico and Columbia*. Geneva, ILO, mimeographed (translated from Spanish).

Freire, P. (1970). *Pedagogy of the Oppressed*. New York: Continuum.

Gaventa, J. and Cornwall, A. (2001). Power and knowledge. In P. Reason and H. Bradbury (Eds.), *Handbook of Action Research: Participative Inquiry and Practice*. London: Sage.

Hall, B. (1996). Participatory research. In A.C. Tuijman (Ed.), *International Encyclopedia of Adult Education and Training*. Oxford: Pergamon.

Haque, A.K.E. (2017). River, people and water: a story of alienation. November 24. Available at: https://thefinancialexpress.com.bd/views/analysis/a-story-of-alienation-1511545266.

Harvey, D. (2005). *A Brief History of Neoliberalism*. New York: Oxford University Press.

Huq, H. (2001). People's practices: exploring contestation, counter-development, and rural livelihoods. Community Development Library (CDL), Dhaka, Bangladesh.

Islam, S. and Kibria, Z. (2006). *Unraveling KJDRP: ADB Financed Project of Mass Destruction in Southwest Coastal Region of Bangladesh*. Satkhira: Uttaran.

Kapoor, D. (2013). Social action and NGOization in contexts of development dispossession in rural India: explorations into the un-civility of civil society. In A. Choudry and D. Kapoor (Eds.), *NGOization: Complicity, Contradictions and Prospects*. London and New York: Zed Books.

Korten, C.D. (1990). NGO strategic network: from community project to global transformation.

People-Centered Development Forum, Philippines. November.

Lewis, D. and Sobhan, D. (1999). Routes of funding, roots of trust? Northern NGOs, southern NGOs, donors, and the rise of direct funding. *Development in Practice*, 9(1–2): 117–129.

Rahman, M.A. (1993). *People's Self Development: Perspective on Participatory Action Research. A Journey through Experience*. London: Zed Books and Dhaka: The University Press.

Schrivers, J. (1995). Participation and power: a transformative feminist research perspective. In N. Nelson and S. Wright (Eds.), *Power and Participatory Development: Theory and Practice*. London: Intermediate Technology Publications.

Shiva, V. (1989). *Staying Alive: Women, Ecology and Development*. London: Zed Books.

Shiva, V. (2000). Foreword: cultural diversity and the politics of knowledge. In G.J.S. Dei, B.L. Hall, and D. Goldin-Rosenberg (Eds.), *Indigenous Knowledges in Global Contexts: Multiple Readings of Our World*. Toronto: University of Toronto Press.

Smith, L. (1999). *Decolonizing Methodologies: Research and Indigenous Peoples*. London and New York: Zed Books, and Dunedin: University of Otago Press.

Uttaran. (2013). *People's Plan of Action for Management of Rivers in Southwest Coastal Region of Bangladesh*. Dhaka: Uttaran.

8 | GRASSROOTS-ORIENTED RESEARCH AS POLITICAL ENGAGEMENT FOR SOCIAL JUSTICE: EXPOSING CORPORATE MINING IN INDIGENOUS CONTEXTS IN THE PHILIPPINES

Ligaya Lindio-McGovern

Introduction

My sociological career over the last three decades has been influenced by the idea that research has an important place, if not integral, in shaping action for social justice and transformation. This was partly a result of my experience under Martial Law in the Philippines and my political activism when I immigrated to the US, wherein I continued to fight for human rights and social justice in the Philippines. It was both my intellectual development in graduate school and my engagement as a scholar-activist that has shaped my conceptualization of research as a form of political engagement. During my graduate work for my Master's in the Philippines, I was exposed to debates about participatory research, folk research, and grassroots research that led me to conduct a thesis: *An Exploratory Study Towards the Development of a Possible Method for Folk Research*, which I tried with a squatter (slum) community in Manila, Philippines. My fascination with the literature on feminist research during my doctoral studies in the US led to the evolution of my dissertation: the concept of "organic feminist inquiry" in my study of Filipino peasant women's experience of exploitation, repression, and their forms of resistance. This turned out to be my first book, *Filipino Peasant Women: Exploitation and Resistance*. The fact that there were graduate students who used this book for their own dissertation research has me believing that the concept makes sense. Subsequently, as a professor of sociology, I continued to be motivated in my research to give voice to the marginalized and exploited sectors of society as a form of political action to raise awareness about their conditions. I then conducted fieldwork on the experience of Filipino migrant domestic workers in various sites: Chicago, Vancouver, Hong Kong, Taipei, and Rome, producing the book: *Globalization, Labor Export and Resistance: A Study of Filipino Migrant Domestic Workers in Global Cities*. A common strand in these works is the idea that research can be a medium for giving voice to the voiceless, the oppressed, and the exploited in our societies, whose interests are marginalized if not trampled upon in mainstream social and development policies. Therefore, along with others in the edited volume *Research as Resistance* (Strega and Brown 2015), I believe and argue that research can be a form of political engagement for social justice and human liberation.

But I argue, as well, that not all research lends itself to political engagement. The context and the resistance of the people we choose to study, as well as the political engagement the researcher has had before conducting a research project, play a role in shaping research as political engagement. The context of injustice requiring social transformation embodies relations of ruling and power structures that create the dynamics of oppression, exploitation, and resistance. In such context, one can ask "whose side are we on?" (Becker 1967). Such a question will influence the researchers' questions and research, the process or methods of research, and how the outcomes of the project will affect the struggles of the oppressed. It is in this juncture that research can evolve, as a political engagement, and advance the interest of the oppressed who are so exploited. Grassroots-oriented research seems to lend more towards the concept of research as political engagement for social justice. In this chapter I will discuss the concept of grassroots-oriented research, how it has shaped my study, and my conceptualization of research as a form of political engagement. In addition, I will examine how the context of the people's struggle provided me insights in shaping the products of the research. In the fall of 2017, I received a Fulbright Fellowship from August 15 to December 15 to conduct research on the impact of corporate mining on indigenous people in the Philippines. It is in this context that I discuss grassroots-oriented research as an approach to research that lends to political engagement for social justice, social transformation, and the politics of dispossession of the indigenous communities.

Grassroots-oriented research and the marginalized experience of indigenous people in the Philippines

Political engagement and the standpoint of inquiry

Giving voice to the marginalized and exploited sectors of society and taking their experience as the starting point in one's inquiry is a key component of grassroots-oriented research. The researcher's political engagement and the nature of such engagement can influence such choice. Political engagement is also a way of knowing and understanding the world. I chose to study indigenous communities in the Philippines in relation to corporate mining since they are the most marginalized sector of the Philippine's society from colonial times to the current neoliberal regime. Through my political engagement on Philippine concerns, human rights, and social justice, I came to personally hear the stories of a small group of indigenous people who were on a speaking tour in the United States, and I got a glimpse of their marginalization. They had a stop in Chicago, a three-and-a-half-hour drive from where I lived in another state. Their stories and experiences gave me a glimpse on the politics of marginalization and dispossession in which their lives are enmeshed: marginalization of their experience, knowledge, and meaningful participation in development policies; dispossession both in the material sense (such as right to ancestral land) and cultural sense (such as right to self-determination). Taking their experience as a starting point for inquiry was both a political and a methodological and epistemological choice. It was a political choice because I could have studied corporate mining from the perspective of business, but that would marginalize further the experience of the indigenous people. By starting my inquiry from the indigenous people's experience, I would contribute in de-marginalizing their voice and I could participate in their struggle where my research could be useful in advocacy work for their rights. It was a methodological and epistemological choice because I thought beginning my inquiry from the indigenous people's experience would uncover "relations of ruling" (Smith 1987) behind their marginalization and dispossession, and allow me to contextualize their experience in the broader structures of power that create injustice. As Margaret Kovach (2015: 47) contends, "those who live in the margins of society experience silencing and injustice", so I thought beginning my inquiry from the experience of those who are/were affected by corporate mining would reveal oppressive dynamics of power and even contention. It would also allow me to have a glimpse into indigenous knowledge and views about their relationship with nature, environment, land, development, and extractive mining. It is here where grassroots-oriented research finds some alliance with "indigenous methodologies" (Kovach 2015) in its reference to understanding indigenous knowledge systems. "Organic feminist inquiry", which I developed in my previous work (Lindio-McGovern 1997), posits to begin inquiry about development from the experiences of exploited women. I ensured I also asked questions that would elicit information about how indigenous women are affected by corporate mining from their experience. Therefore, political engagement, methodological and epistemological choices are meshed in my study.

Grassroots-oriented research and the constraints of militarization
Grassroots-oriented research necessitates face to face interaction with those we want to involve in our study. Consequently, it was important for me to conduct fieldwork in the Philippines where I could personally interview indigenous people affected by corporate mining (referring to large-scale corporate mining), participate in some of their activities, and visit at least one mining site; however, the militarization as part of the Philippine government's counterinsurgency war posed constraints. Militarization, which involves the use of Philippine Armed Forces, police forces, and paramilitary forces to violently suppress dissent and opposition to government development policies like corporate mining, has become part of the circuits of oppressive power in the lives of indigenous communities. It is something indigenous women, men, and children experience in their everyday lives. Therefore, in my discussion (later in this chapter) of the circuits of power and relations of ruling that interplay in the politics of dispossession of indigenous people, I include the alliance of the state and its coercive forces with transnational capital. It was in my previous research on Filipino peasant women that I first experienced the issue of militarization and research, and after almost three decades I have experienced it again. Militarization's isolation of indigenous communities from external social networks that can lend support and resources for their empowerment is a form of divide-and-rule strategy to limit the collective power and resistance of indigenous communities.

For instance, an Australian-Canadian transnational mining corporation of Oceana Gold is located in the village of Didipio in the province of Nueva Viscaya. A leader of an indigenous organization informed me that the military in this village instructed him not to bring external visitors to the village and that he should limit his political activities if he valued his life and family – a form of military harassment. Therefore, he explained to me that he would prefer I not be seen with him or ride with him in his van to avoid the risk of me being interrogated by the military about their organization. My indigenous host/contact in the village also instructed me what to do and not to do while in the village; for instance, locking the doors of the unit where I sleep by 6:00 pm and avoiding sitting outside at the start of dusk so as not to be conspicuous as she said she saw a man on a motorcycle sort of scouting around in front of the house. She also told me to be inconspicuous while taking pictures of the mining site because she explained that the mining corporation has informers. Even in the urban area in Metro Manila where I took part in the public mass rallies in which the indigenous people participated, I saw police and military forces using violence to disperse the demonstration, and arrest or block the demonstrators. Therefore, militarization poses risks to the researcher and indigenous people, having implications on knowledge production about their marginalization in development and the courage and risk they take in fighting for their rights. But where there is militarization, research becomes even more important. In such context, grassroots-oriented research in some sense becomes somewhat akin to what Adam Gaudry (2015: 244) calls "insurgent research": research as a form of resistance that contributes to the struggles of the oppressed and marginalized, like the indigenous people, for their collective empowerment and liberation.

Militarization altered my original plan to visit mining sites. When Martial Law was declared in Mindanao and when Palawan was listed among the "security risk" areas, the Fulbright Commission in the Philippines precluded me from going there for security reasons. However, with the assistance the secretary general of KATRIBU (the National Alliance of Indigenous People in the Philippines), who is an indigenous woman herself, I was able to interview indigenous people from these regions and from other provinces who had experienced the impacts of corporate mining in their communities during the Lakbayan 2017 (a caravan) of the indigenous people. Almost 3,000 men, women, and children came down to Metro Manila to publicly expose and protest their oppression and to unite as a force to demand just change. The bulk of them stayed for three weeks in a camp provided by the University of the Philippines and I chose to live close by the camp so I could go there every day. In addition to conducting interviews (both individual and group), I participated in their activities, such as their forums, teach-ins, cultural activities, press conferences, and protest rallies. There were a few occasions when I was invited to speak at these rallies, where I was happy to do so and took it as an opportunity to advocate for the rights of indigenous people while sharing what I was learning about their situation. I viewed my participation, whenever I could, in their forms of collective resistance not only as a research method but also as political action for social justice and solidarity with the struggle of the indigenous people and the ongoing movement for liberation of the whole Filipino people. Taking the risks and the inconveniences made more sense to me by taking this dual role. However, taking a dual role like this had challenges; for example, as a researcher, I had to manage time in order to succeed in recording my observations and information gathered through informal interaction and have some retreat time to reflect, while also trying to be present as much as possible in all the political activities. After the Lakbayan, the secretary general of KATRIBU was able to arrange a field visit to a remote mining site in northern Luzon, the village of Didipio, in Kasibu, Nueva Viscaya, where (as mentioned earlier) Oceana Gold, an Australian-Canadian mining corporation is located. She connected me with two community organizers in the area who could help during my stay and they scheduled for me to stay in the area for ten days.[1] I was able to conduct 15 interviews with indigenous people who were affected by the mining operations and took a view of the mining site. Responding to insights I gained during this field visit, I modified my intentions in relation to the outcomes of the research, such as what kind of publications to produce out of the research. Before I started interviewing, I learned that there were a few who asked how the information was going to be used and how it would benefit them. Consequently, I mentioned during interviews that I would like to produce a short publication that would be useful in educating, organizing, and campaigning in relation to mining and its impact on indigenous people. I showed a sample publication that was done by an NGO and asked if this was something that would be useful for them. They welcomed the idea because they said it would help them in their campaign and organizing work. This experience gave me a new insight on grassroots-oriented research: that while grassroots-oriented research does not preclude publishing with an academic audience in mind, it should extend its reach beyond that circle to include publications that can be useful for the educational and organizational tasks of the grassroots group's social justice work.

Circuits of power in the politics of dispossession of indigenous people

As earlier mentioned, it is important in grassroots-oriented research on marginalized sectors to uncover the relations of ruling or structures of power that are at the roots of their subordination, oppression, and exploitation. At this point it is important to include an examination of the circuits of power that interplay in the dynamics of dispossession beginning from the experience of the indigenous people. The central issue in the experience of indigenous people in the Philippines, in relation to corporate mining, is dispossession. This comes close to what David Harvey (2005) calls "accumulation by dispossession" – a key feature of modern imperialism wherein capitalism expands globally while being entrenched by a neoliberal ideology. Simply put, as transnational corporations accumulate wealth from the plunder of Philippine resources (and of other developing countries), the dispossessed are pushed into immiseration, increased poverty, and food insecurity.

In the process of my research, I came to understand from the experience of the indigenous people with corporate mining that "dispossession" consists of interrelated dimensions. indigenous people have an inalienable right as defined by the UN Declaration for the Rights of Indigenous People (UNDRIP) to ancestral lands. Dispossession from these lands is central in the concept of dispossession of indigenous communities, as it is consequentially interrelated to dispossession of the right to self-determination, right to environment, right to livelihood and sustainable development, right to education and collective ethnic identity, and the right to life. All of these are considered minimum requirements for survival of the indigenous people in the UNDRIP. Therefore, dispossession of these rights threatens the survival of indigenous communities.

The experience of dispossession of the indigenous people as the last frontier of modern imperialism in the Philippines reveals complex circuits of power that involve the interplay of transnational capital as embodied in transnational mining corporations, the state (the Philippine government, its ruling bureaucracy and policies), the military/police or paramilitary forces, and the ideology of neoliberalism. The Philippine Mining Act of 1995 (PMA) was and still is a neoliberal legislative instrument that liberalized the entry of transnational corporations into the mining industry that led to the dominance of transnational capital in this industry. Funded by the International Monetary Fund (IMF),[2] whose structural adjustment policies are promotive of the neoliberal ideology and interest of transnational corporations, the Philippine Mining Act of 1995 has been widely criticized, rightly so, by the indigenous people in their protest rallies as a form of "development aggression". First, corporate mining is rapidly dispossessing indigenous people of their ancestral lands which they have occupied for generations. The majority of corporate mining in the Philippines are in ancestral lands. The loss of their ancestral lands also means loss of their source of livelihood since on their ancestral lands they could engage in subsistence farming and sell what is beyond their consumption need. For example, an indigenous woman who lost her ancestral land to Oceana Gold said,

> when we still had our land to farm we could produce *palay* (unhusked rice) that was more than enough for our own use, the rest we could sell in the market so we had cash. I could have two harvests in a year, I could harvest more than 150 *cavans* (sacks) of *palay*. Now we have to buy rice and life is harder, and sometimes I am thinking of migrating abroad.[3]

The consequent loss of livelihood and increased poverty with dispossession of ancestral land due to corporate mining is a common experience among the indigenous people I interviewed. A *datu* (tribal chief) of a Lumad community (indigenous people from or residing in Mindanao, southern region of the Philippines) even observed that some of his people even resorted to begging in the streets after they were dispossessed of their ancestral land. "I do not want that to happen because it violates their human dignity" (*labag sa kanilang pagkatao*).[4] Therefore, material dispossession and its consequences are viewed as associated with and transgressive of their human dignity. This is dehumanizing – an interconnected rather than fragmented view of the world.

For the indigenous people land and life is so intertwined: "Land is life. Our ancestors have always told us that land is life, so we must defend land".[5] But a tragic consequence of their defense is at times loss of life as the military and paramilitary forces have been used to suppress resistance and opposition to corporate mining. There were indigenous leaders and opponents to corporate mining who were extra-judicially killed. Indigenous communities have experienced harassment and intimidation, illegal arrests, and forced evacuations that clear the land for corporate mining, most especially in Mindanao where mineral resources abound.[6] Mining corporations even have what is called in the Philippine Mining Act of 1995 "investment defense forces" that are utilized to suppress and control opposition to mining. There are instances when paramilitary forces or former members of the state military are hired by the mining corporation as investment defense forces. I view the legitimation of these "investment defense forces" as a manifestation of the "militarization of transnational capital" in alliance with the neoliberal state as part of the manufacturing of consent to capital accumulation by dispossession.

The indigenous community life, which is the source of their collective identity, is also destroyed when indigenous people are dispersed due to dispossession of their ancestral land. But the logic of capital accumulation by dispossession requires destruction of communities that still value the communal concept of land and relations of production – a worldview that runs counter to the logic of capitalist expansion/imperialism. It is in community where sharing of resources is facilitated among members, especially in times of need. It is also in community that communalism in relations of production gets sustained. The violence of dispossession, therefore, is not only physical but also cultural.

Dispossession from ancestral land also has the associated dispossession of the indigenous peoples' inalienable right to a healthy environment, sustainable development, and self-determination. During my fieldwork, I often heard indigenous people say that they have cared for nature, the forest, and biodiversity for generations; they have protected the forests and it has protected them. Yet corporate mining has destroyed the environment which they and their ancestors have maintained for so long. The indigenous people I spoke to in Didipio showed me where their homes and farms once stood, which is now turned into an open-pit mine that only resembles rocks and a large hole, with bulldozers constantly moving around. I saw this from afar through a window in the house of the indigenous woman with whom I stayed. I could feel the polluted air that seemed to stick in my throat when I breathed, that by the end of my stay I almost lost my voice and it was hard for people to understand me when I spoke. My doctor diagnosed an upper respiratory infection which she said I obviously got at the mining site, for which she prescribed antibiotics. She said that open-pit mining emits extremely fine dust particles in the air that do not get trapped in the throat and go to the lungs. The particles contain chemicals and when this dust gets into the water, it goes into people's systems when it is drunk. Long-time exposure can cause asthma. I mentioned to her that while in Didipio, I found out, through government records that some of my informants showed me, that there was a high rate of asthma among the residents. She said she was not surprised and thought that open-pit mining was already banned. An indigenous woman who lost her home and farm land to corporate mining told me that when Gina Lopez was the head of the Department of Environment and Natural Resources (DNR) she suspended the open-pit mining operations of Oceana Gold. However, when she was not re-appointed by President Duterte because of her progressive views on the environment and large-scale mining and replaced with a conservative former member of the military, open-pit mining operations in Didipio resumed. Here we see how a state bureaucracy with a certain ideology comes into the picture in the circuits of power relations in the politics of dispossession.

"Water is gold", a wise saying said by an elderly indigenous man I interviewed in Didipio. He said that before the open-pit mining operations in Didipio began, they had a source of drinkable spring water and they did not have to buy water. Now they have to buy water several miles from where they live. He and others had observed that the spring water source from which they could get water had dried up. They showed me a photo of a spring from which they said they could draw water that was drinkable because it came from deep down in the ground's natural filter and the water was so clear. Now this natural spring that people shared is gone. They also told me about the rivers being polluted since the mine came. Before the mine, they said the animals they raised could drink water from the rivers, but they knew the water had become polluted when the animals died after they drank it. They showed me the tailing dam for the mine's waste that was already overflowing, and when it overflows, they said the water goes to the rivers. Open-pit mining uses abundant water, so their claim of water diminishing and the water getting polluted due to open-pit mining may have some validity unless otherwise disproven scientifically by Oceana Gold who allegedly counterclaims that the mine has nothing to do with such environmental destruction. Corporate publications seem to paint a very different picture than what the experience of the indigenous people revealed to me. Open-pit mining has long been banned in Australia, so Oceana Gold has gone beyond national borders to plunder. That the Philippine government legitimizes transnational plunder and the Australian and the Canadian governments seem indifferent about it illustrates the collusion of transnational capital and neoliberal states in the circuits of dispossession. In this collusion it is the peripheral country that is more on the losing end of the spectrum, and the indigenous people who suffer most the interconnected multi-faceted dimensions of dispossession through corporate mining are the "sacrificial lambs" of the mythical promise of progress of neoliberal development.

The dispossession of the indigenous people's right to sustainable development is consequent to their dispossession of ancestral land for corporate mining. Under the neoliberal ideology circumscribed in the Philippine Mining Act of 1995, corporate mining in the Philippines is unsustainable, not only because of the environmental destruction it brings, but also because it is merely extractive since transnational corporations take the extracted minerals out of the country completely. No related industries to create diverse jobs are developed in the Philippines that will utilize these raw materials. While displaced from their land and livelihood the indigenous people are hardly absorbed in the mining industry, since according to some of the indigenous people I talked to, they were told that they did not have the skills. Some indigenous men who used to earn a living from small-scale traditional mining in their ancestral land find themselves less off than before. The few who may be employed in the unskilled labor of the mine are likely to be contractual without job security. For instance, two (male and female) of the indigenous people in my interview sample in Didipio provided insight to this. The female who worked in the mine was, at the time of my interview, jobless and seeking employment because she said her job contract was not renewed. The male who also worked in the mine, but at the time of interview was jobless, said that he was not informed about why he was not rehired and alleged that he was not given separation pay and had some unpaid work hours. Both were displaced from their ancestral land. Labor contractualization is a national issue affecting workers in the Philippines, which the labor movement is working to halt. In the final analysis, it is the extractive transnational corporations that are reaping the wealth, leaving a more impoverished indigenous community. This runs counter to the United Nations number one goal to eradicate poverty in its 2030 Sustainable Development Agenda.

Associated with the dispossession of ancestral land to corporate mining is also the dispossession of the right to self-determination, which is also connected to the right to sustainable development previously discussed. The indigenous people's experience, that transgressed their right to free-prior informed consent, attests to this. In addition to military violence that meets their resistance to defend their land from corporate grab, the indigenous people in my sample also talked about manipulative tactics, false promises, and deceit to get forced consent to lose their lands to corporate mining. Semblance of consent is not free-prior informed consent. The self-determination of the indigenous people can be conceived as well on the national policy level. That the Philippine Mining Act of 1995 as an instrument of neoliberalism allows for 100 percent of the extracted minerals to be taken out of the country limits the Philippine government's economic sovereignty over the people's resources. But that is part of the logic of dispossession under a neoliberal global political economy. This involves the weakening of peripheral nation-states' economic sovereignty which has a trickle-down effect in limiting and dispossessing the self-determination of local indigenous communities. That is why part of the struggle and resistance of the indigenous people is to transform the neoliberal state, which includes scrapping the Philippine Mining Act of 1995 and replacing it with an alternative policy that will respect the self-determination of the indigenous people and of the nation. In addition, it promotes a national socio-economic development that will guarantee their collective rights to ancestral lands, to sustainable development and healthy environment, within a program of national industrialization and agricultural development that will back local control of resources and patrimony of the nation. That the national liberation movement in the Philippines has integrated in its agenda and demands for change the protection of the welfare and rights of the indigenous people in its proposal for social and economic reforms shines a ray of hope amidst the continuing marginalization of the indigenous people under the neoliberal regimes of the global political economy.

Conclusion

The struggle for social justice must be fought on all fronts, and research that begins analysis of the power structures of oppression from the experience of the oppressed is an important terrain of resistance. Grassroots-oriented research seems to offer such potential and can be explored further in future research with indigenous people and other oppressed groups. Developing an understanding of the complex dynamics of exploitation, oppression, and change is an important task for grassroots researchers and these social groups in the struggle for social justice.

In the brutal context of neoliberal development policies that interplay circuits of power in the dynamics of "accumulation by dispossession", a key feature of modern imperialism, the domains of indigenous people in the Philippines becomes a strategic frontier of the global expansion of capitalism. Central in this violent process of dispossession is the expulsion of indigenous people from their ancestral lands to give way to transnational capital embodied in transnational mining corporations with the alliance of the state, the military, and other coercive forces. The neoliberal policies of supranational structures, such as the IMF and the World Trade Organization (WTO), imposed on nation-states come into play as well. Such expulsion from land has, as well, the consequent dispossession of the indigenous peoples' collective rights to self-determination, cultural identity, sustainable development, and environment that threatens their survival.

Dispossession, as gleaned from the experience of the indigenous people, can be conceived not only in the material sense, but also in the non-material sense as it involves destruction of indigenous knowledge systems. For example, concepts of communalism that created barriers to embedding transnational capital in nation-states, which began in colonial times and continued under the neoliberal regime. National policy change that builds on and protects such an indigenous knowledge system would be one of the ways to reclaim the self-determination of the indigenous people and of the nation. This can be coupled with sustainable development policy alternatives that will protect the rights of the indigenous people, promote their meaningful participation in policy formation, and seriously consider their experience in assessing existing policies.

Notes

1 I refrain from naming persons to protect their identity for security reasons.

2 From my personal interview in October 2017 with Antonio Tujan, Executive Director and Co-Founder of IBON Foundation, an independent think tank and research institution in the Philippines.

3 From a personal interview during my visit at the mining site in Didipio, Kasibu, Nueva Viscaya in October 2017.

4 From a personal interview at the Lakbayan camp in the University of the Philippines, UP Diliman campus in September 2017.

5 From a personal interview of a Lumad from northern Mindanao displaced from their ancestral land by corporate mining, interviewed at the Lakbayan camp in the University of the Philippines in September 2017.

6 From personal interviews of indigenous people affected by corporate mining during my fieldwork in the Philippines.

References

Becker, H. (1967). Whose side are we on? *Social Problems*, 14(3): 239–247.

Gaudry, A. (2015). Researching the resurgence: insurgent research and community-engaged methodologies in the 21st-century academic inquiry. In S. Strega and L. Brown (Eds.), *Research as Resistance: Revisiting Critical, Indigenous, and Anti-Oppressive Approaches*, 2nd edition. Toronto: Canadian Scholars' Press, Women's Press.

Harvey, D. (2005). *A Brief History of Neoliberalism*. New York: Oxford University Press.

Kovach, M. (2015). Emerging from the margins: indigenous methodologies. In S. Strega and L. Brown (Eds.), *Research as Resistance: Revisiting Critical, Indigenous, and Anti-Oppressive Approaches*, 2nd edition. Toronto: Canadian Scholars' Press, Women's Press.

Lindio-McGovern. (1997). *Filipino Peasant Women: Exploitation and Resistance*. Philadelphia, PA: University of Pennsylvania Press.

Smith, D. (1987). *The Everyday World as Problematic*. Boston, MA: Northwestern University Press.

Strega, S. and Brown, L. (2015). *Research as Resistance: Revisiting Critical, Indigenous, and Anti-Oppressive Approaches*, 2nd edition. Toronto: Canadian Scholars' Press, Women's Press.

PART II

**RESEARCH AND URBAN POOR
ACTIVISMS**

9 | COUNTERING DISPOSSESSION THROUGH COOPERATIVIZATION? WASTE-PICKER ETHNOGRAPHY, ACTIVISM, AND THE STATE IN BUENOS AIRES AND MONTEVIDEO

Patrick O'Hare and Santiago Sorroche

Introduction

At the beginning of this century, waste-pickers entered into the public agendas of the local governments of Buenos Aires and Montevideo. Both Argentina and Uruguay had undergone economic crises (2001–2002) that troubled long histories of formal sector employment that stand out among Latin American countries, leading thousands of unemployed men and women to turn to recovering recyclable materials from the garbage in order to get by.

In Argentina, the activities of informal sector recycling and waste-picking had been prohibited since the dictatorship (1976–1983) and incarceration was a regular occurrence for anyone found sorting through discarded materials on the streets. In Montevideo, meanwhile, the ban on exercising the activity had been lifted in 1990, but repression was still common. Activists from different movements, but particularly academics, played a central role in discussions to end the prohibition in Argentina; participation in activities with legislators and open letters to the mass media were the preferred methods. In the city of Buenos Aires, the activity was legalized in 2002, while in the province of Buenos Aires this occurred in 2006. The waste-pickers' new situation demanded new forms of participation that included the redaction of projects, the coordination of workshops in cooperatives, and the accompaniment of waste-pickers in meetings with state agents, a series of activities that we conceptualize here as walking together, drawing on Fernández Álvarez's (2016a) concept of *doing together*, which points to the joint work of the cooperative members in different contexts in Argentina, as they continuously construct their collectives. As anthropologists, we propose a way of working that goes beyond the mere observation of the groups with which we conduct research. For us, to conduct fieldwork is to take part in the daily life of cooperative workers and help them, as much as we can, to improve their living conditions, whether we are designated part of their technical teams or not.

As anthropologists conducting research with waste-picker cooperatives for almost ten years each, we have advanced in that path. After establishing a long-standing commitment to field work, and becoming part of the social world of waste-pickers, the "objective" relations of classical anthropology came undone. Since our discipline was accused – in some cases with good reason – of being a spy of the colonial powers, we want to argue that in Sorroche's Argentine case, as the walk together picked up pace, he might be considered a "spy" on the side not of the government, but of the social organizations with whom he conducts research. In this sense, we want to highlight ways that anthropologists can conduct research within state bodies on behalf of the marginalized rather than with the marginalized on behalf of the state, as has arguably been the case historically (see Asad 1995 [1973]; Price 2000; Walker 2009). O'Hare, meanwhile, discusses his relative disengagement from the state during research with Uruguayan waste-pickers, and explores the possible reasons behind this, and the advantages and disadvantages that it brings.

We consider ethnography, implying a submersion in the social worlds of the groups we study (with), a privileged methodology for taking part and being involved in the daily struggles of working people and activists. As Juris and Khasnabish (2013: 4) have pointed out, an engaged ethnography "is never only to uncover internal conflicts and tensions; the ethnographer also produces critical understandings that can help activists develop strategies to overcome obstacles and barriers to effective organizing". In our case, we have developed research with urban poor who have been in long-term processes of dispossession: from land, when they move from the interior rural zones to the city; from social rights, that were earned in the second half of the 20th century and often lost near the 21st; and even from livelihoods, when waste-picking was banned (Sorroche 2016; O'Hare 2017). This process is, even with the advances we have pointed out above, ongoing, with the private sector and the state still intermittently attempting to dispossess waste-pickers of access to recyclable materials.

In Montevideo and Greater Buenos Aires, waste-pickers are facing down the imposition of large waste incinerators – in the case of Buenos Aires – and the prohibition of working in the streets and entering the sanitary landfill – in Montevideo. A new process of exclusion, enclosure, and dispossession, yet another in a long history, is affecting the urban poor that live from what they recover in the waste stream. This context is demanding us to take sides, even more actively than before, and to mobilize our academic work so as to sustain waste-picker demands and livelihoods. In this chapter, through a series of ethnographic "displacements" in each of our work, the different possibilities and advantages of the national and international researcher are compared. In spite of differences, we argue that the relative and critical objectivity allied to the ethnographic method makes of social anthropology a privileged discipline through which to provide both technical support and activist solidarity to waste-picker collectives.

Walking together (Santiago Sorroche)

In the case of Buenos Aires, Sorroche has conducted research with *cartoneros* – as waste-pickers are called in Argentina – since 2007. All the cooperatives he has worked with are located in Greater Buenos Aires – in the districts of La Matanza, Morón, in the west corridor, and currently in Lomas de Zamora and Lanús, in the south corridor. These last areas represent the historical base of the Movement of Excluded Workers (Movimiento de Trabajadores Excluidos – MTE). His research was conducted for his undergraduate and doctoral theses, and is currently funded by a National Science Council (CONICET) postdoctoral grant.

Working with different Greater Buenos Aires cooperatives, my participation as a researcher has passed through distinct moments. As soon as I began research with waste-picker groups, I started to collaborate in different projects with them, even sharing, in some cases, legal responsibility. The projects, often formulated by NGOs without any consultation with the cooperatives, tend to pass through very disputed processes. The experience that I will discuss here is when I was contracted for the implementation of one of these projects, and my role was to try to reconfigure the project in ways that the cooperative, and I, thought would improve working conditions. A long way from a neutral and distant position, my decision was, from the beginning, to be with and to support cooperatives. *Walking with* them was for me the key element of the project and its development.

This participation was a key way to earn organizations' trust and enable me to become part of the "enclosure" that, in different kinds of research, one often isn't able to enter. Internal meetings, discussions, and everyday problems were part of the world that I managed to gain access to. This wasn't an unreflexive situation. A continuous anthropological reflection was a necessary part of my work and research. For me, being involved and implicated in the struggles of cooperative colleagues kick-started my own academic labor. Being there every day implied not only learning about work, relations between workers and daily problems: it was also a way of taking part in their struggles. Indeed, every week, a new struggle began: against the local government, with the private company that had the waste collection concession, at nationwide or global levels, or against any new proposal that didn't consider the needs and wants of the cooperatives.

Taking part in these struggles while an academic at a national university and a CONICET researcher meant being perceived of, on more than one occasion, as a state agent by many of the waste-pickers, and it demanded a continuous process of taking decisions discussed and agreed with the cooperatives. How should they introduce me to others? What was I able to say or do? How much of my involvement should be made public? Sometimes, when we had a good relationship with a city councilor and met with members of the city hall, this discussion exceeded the bounds of the cooperative and involved more people. In this way, we acquired the native category of "technical team" or more recently, "assessor". To illustrate this last term, I will reproduce a fragment of my field notes:

> We are at the Lomas de Zamora city council. We have a
> meeting with a city councilor who is interested in helping the
> cooperative. They know her from other political relations that
> are spread around the neighborhood. A few days before, we set
> out the strategy. We are trying to get a local regulation passed
> about "large generators" – shops or industries that produce
> more than 500 kg of waste per month. After getting our IDs
> checked, we take the lift to the third floor. I follow María – the
> cooperative secretary – through an aisle until we reach the

office of Daniela, the city councilor. We greet one another, and she introduces their assessor. After that, Javier, one of the cooperative members, introduces me, saying "this is Santiago, he works at the University of Buenos Aires and with the cooperative. He is our own assessor, the cooperative one". (Field note, December 2016)

As we can see in the above fragment, I am considered by the cooperative members as forming part of their own team. After that meeting, the city councilor started to work with me and we redacted four local regulations. Two of them have already been passed,[1] improving not just the living conditions of cooperative members, but also its legal status. This joint work wouldn't have been possible were it not for my academic position in the university. This was one of many times that, when the cooperative introduced me, state officers changed the way that they related to the group. "How was it possible that somebody from the university could be interested in the cooperative?" is a good synthesis of the multiple questions they subsequently posed.

But how did I construct this relationship with the cooperative? I argue that ethnographic research served as a methodological tool that helped me to take part, to become known by every member of the cooperative, and to start new fieldwork with other groups. In particular, I want to show how the *method* of the ethnographic workshop, which we should consider also as a *space*, is not just about research, but can help to establish strong relationships and enable the discussion not just of our ideas but also of our roles. My work and this relation were made possible due to the participation and organization of different workshops in the cooperatives with whom I have conducted research.

When I started my research in 2007, it was through participation in an action-research project that was conducted by a broad group of doctoral students who work at CONICET.[2] Invited by Dr. Maria Inés Fernández Álvarez and Dr. Sebastián Carenzo, I started to take part in the workshops that were conducted weekly at Recycling Dreams (Reciclando Sueños) – a cooperative in La Matanza, the most populated, and one of the poorest, districts in Greater Buenos Aires. That space enabled me to become known, very quickly, by all the cooperative members. But, more importantly, it was an experience which involved learning how to relate to groups which, at least in Argentine universities, are not normally found on the curriculum.

Two years after I started working in the cooperative, the workshops were discontinued due to a number of difficulties that the cooperative faced (Sorroche 2016). Yet the experience remains one of the most formative, intense, and interesting processes of my life. A long time after, I would remember with cooperative members the discussions, problems, and fun that the space condensed for all those who participated. The most interesting thing taken up by the cooperative members and I was the use of the spoken word. Long-term unemployment and subaltern positions had led cooperativists to the false belief that they didn't have anything interesting to say. The work that the group started was a very important way of demonstrating to themselves that unemployment wasn't their fault – a practice that was recovered from the *piquetero* movement.[3] In the same way, they learned that they had opinions that deserved to be heard.

A few years later, after finishing my PhD, I decided to move to another field-site. Postdoctoral research was planned with the Argentine Federation of Waste-Pickers, Carters, and Recyclers (Federación Argentina de Cartoneros, Carreros y Recicladores – FACCyR).[4] A short time before I started work, which I realized would be quite difficult due to the absence of regular and systematic spaces of articulation, I was invited by one cooperative to visit them and to find out how they were working. When I first arrived, I was immediately surprised by the way that they organized work. Trucks entered one after another, filled to the rafters with cardboard and plastic. More than 30 people classified the materials. María, the cooperative secretary, started to explain every moment of the work process to me and, while she was doing that, I was introduced to the members of the cooperative. After the tour, I went into a room, separated from the classification warehouse, sat down, and started to talk. I wasn't really sure what to say: it was a completely new experience for me, and I was completely astonished by the quantities of materials and people working all together. María started to tell me about the problems that the cooperative was facing. Every week, new people began work in the cooperative and through them they had heard about a *popular economy*[5] course that was being dictated by the Confederación de Trabajadores de la Economía Popular (CTEP).

They wanted to take the course and, in order to do so, asked for my help. I returned very surprised but without knowing what to do. We started talking with the "militants"[6] of the federation. They offered me the contents of the course – the materials – and said that, if I wanted, I could impart it on my own. I read, raised my doubts, and started with the workshop a few weeks after.

On another occasion, the workshop served as a great way of not just getting to knowing the cooperative members – who in this case were more than 60 – but also of meeting the cooperatives' needs and of discussing, together, ways of struggling to achieve the recognition of their work. During the workshops and with the whole group taking part, we designed a door-to-door recyclables collection and, having in mind my earlier experiences, I proposed a workshop about environmental awareness. This included some ludic activities, based on role-play, to help them to speak with neighbors. At the same time, after discussing waste regulations and reflecting on local problems, we agreed that a local regulation was needed to advance recognition and payment for their work.

In this way, and as I described above, we developed projects for the regulation of the large generators – that were discussed in the workshop – and soon a local ordinance was passed by the council. Two months later, the cooperative was signing its first contract with a retail store and earning a monthly payment, and all the recyclable materials they produced rebounded in more materials and a cash payment that helped the cooperative to improve their earnings. More interesting still, rumors about the workshop spread throughout the federation. After the biweekly meetings, different groups started to ask me to give the workshops and even to write a manual that could be used nationwide, which I am doing at this moment. The workshop thus became a tool that helped me to contact other groups, get to know them, and discuss ideas about the union organization of waste-pickers. It helped me to connect different groups as we invited leaders of different cooperatives to take part in the workshop, share their experiences in them, and, through their own examples, show others different ways of organizing and improving their living conditions.

The organization of the cooperatives, which looks very impressive and involves multifold relations with state agencies, the creation of new norms, and the handling of hundreds of tons of material, was not a linear, problem-free path. For more than 15 years, organized waste-pickers have been disputing and struggling against the privatization and elimination of their work. When asking the federation's leaders about the movement's victories and how they achieved them, they always said the same: "we were able to achieve all that we have because we didn't lose the streets". "Not losing the streets" has two different meanings that are interesting to note here. One is that they continue to work in the street collecting the materials, against state proposals that try to get them to work in so-called *"plantas sociales"*, social plants. The other refers to them not losing the street as a space for struggle and mobilization.

When the activity was prohibited in 1978, waste-pickers had to develop new strategies to be able to continue with their work. Arrests and bribes were common, and the threat of being dispossessed of collected materials was constant. The privatization of waste services and the landfill system, and payment to companies based on the tons that were collected combined to exclude *cartoneros* from the city. After the crisis of 2001, the activity reemerged and the system was redesigned. This was possible due to the action of individual and cooperativized *cartoneros* struggling together with civil society organizations, academics, journalists, and public servants.

But in order to continue improving their conditions, a daily pedagogic work needed to be carried out. *Cartoneros*, and their organizations, were tested continuously and they needed to reorganize their work. Forming part of the Integrated Solid Waste Management model in the city of Buenos Aires[7] made possible different orders of things that are knotted together: being recognized as workers and improving their conditions, relating with neighbors and organizing their knowledge about waste and its environmental implications. Together, such work helped them to retain access to recyclable materials and, as they formed in cooperatives, to bypass the intermediaries that exploit the *cartoneros*, taking advantage of their inability to amass large quantities to pay them a fraction of the wholesale price paid by industry.

The formation of the cooperatives, and the results they are able to show to different state agencies, what I have elsewhere called a *testimonial politics* (Sorroche 2016), was the outcome of their role in the management of recyclable materials. I understand *testimonial politics* as a form of political work that enables waste-pickers to demonstrate that diversified collection is not only possible but also an environmentally and socially sustainable way of managing waste. This political deployment enables the cooperatives to construct their demands, such as to be considered as public servants. In this way, *walking together* acquired a central role when I was carrying out the workshops, understanding them not only as a methodological tool or a place to test different research questions – as Fernández Álvarez and Carenzo (2012) have shown – but also a space to discuss and advance in the construction of claims, strategies, and methodologies.

Classifying and rummaging together (Patrick O'Hare)

Turning to the case of Montevideo, O'Hare has carried out research with waste-pickers, known in Uruguay as *clasificadores*, since 2009. The first piece of research consisted of an undergraduate thesis which centered on one of the most well-known and successful waste-picker/recycling cooperatives in Montevideo. The core of this cooperative consisted of an extended family who had made a living recovering materials in and around Montevideo's municipal land-fill over the course of several generations. At the time of O'Hare's initial research, the cooperativization of *clasificadores* was being vig-orously pursued by the governing center-left Frente Amplio (Broad Front) coalition, and waste-picking collectives had multiplied across the city.

During my undergraduate research, I accompanied research sub-jects in multiple cooperative courses and meetings with various state agents and bodies. However, the cooperative in question already possessed *técnicos* or assessors who had been working with them over a long period and had helped them to obtain funding and support from various national and international, state and non-state, bodies. Rather than someone who could necessarily assist them to obtain grants or training, I was instead welcomed as something between a curiosity and a comrade. My approach to the waste-pickers had been direct and unmediated by gate-keepers – we initially met at a film screening – and this proved important in laying the basis of our relationship. The exchange that I established – the ability to conduct participant observation in return for my labor in the collection and classification of waste – also prefigured the way that I would conduct anthropological research in the future. Nevertheless, where I could help as an intermediary, using connections to improve the income and working conditions of the waste-pickers, I naturally did so. The key example from this period was my establishment of a *circuito limpio* (clean circuit) in the Humanities Faculty where I was enrolled as a student, enabling the cooperative to collect valuable pre-classified white paper.

For my Master's research in social anthropology, I moved to Greater Buenos Aires where, with the help of Sorroche, I began conducting research at a recycling cooperative supported by the municipal government of Morón. Again, I exchanged the possibility of conducting research for my labor alongside young recycling workers. The cooperative was already supported, and indeed had been founded by, an environmental NGO, and another Argentine social anthropology student served as an assessor who helped in the writing of grants and coordination of workshops. In the cases of both my undergraduate and Master's research, lack of familiarity with the legislative and legal environment constituted a factor that prevented my playing a more active role in the valuable activities of the type Sorroche engages in: helping to develop laws and regulations, aiding in the acquisition of funds and so forth. In both cases, the cooperatives involved already had a team of assessors working with them, and in the latter case the short time frame of my research was an added complication.

If I was largely unengaged in such representational and intermediary activities, what then did the accompaniment of waste-pickers mean in my case? The answer can be illustrated by turning to my doctoral research with a range of waste-picking collectives in Montevideo, from cooperatives to family units, from those entering the landfill clandestinely to those working in formal sector recycling plants. In all of these spaces, I accompanied workers in their labor of rummaging in and classifying the urban waste stream; in consuming from the waste, whether domestic appliances or break-time snacks; in attending the local children's football matches and family birthday parties; and in an innumerable list of other local neighborhood activities.

Such an approach, while welcomed by *clasificadores* themselves as both helpful and humble, did not always go down well with the local actors who engaged with them. On one occasion, I was accused by a civil servant involved in waste-picker policy of "disguising" myself as a *clasificador*, despite the fact that I made it perfectly clear to all those with whom I worked that I was a researcher. This accusation can be fruitful to think through in relation to our discussion of anthropologists acting either as "spies" on behalf of the state or colonial powers, or on behalf of marginalized groups and their organizations. In this case, I was accused by local state actors of engaging in an exercise of pretense, and what mattered was less who I was "working for", than the very fact that I was accompanying *clasificadores* in wearing, eating, and rummaging in, the rubbish. I was, in any case, a rather ineffective "spy", openly giving away my true identity, and betrayed by the Scottish twang to my Uruguayan accent.

Yet my relative independence as a researcher unallied to the Uruguayan state and my objectivity – relative given my closeness to *clasificadores* – allows, I believe, a critical perspective when it comes to considering the cooperativization of Montevidean waste-pickers. Had I been closer to the state, or indeed the trade union movement, during undergraduate research in 2009/10, then I would likely have played a supporting role in encouraging the formation of *clasificador* cooperatives. As it stood, while I am naturally sympathetic to such social formations and helped with group dynamics where possible, I was also able to assess the suitability of the cooperative model proposed for *clasificadores* and the conditions of its implementation. While the cooperative I worked with was relatively successful, other such waste-picker collectives in the city were plagued by problems like the presence of kinship leadership dynamics and dominating male figures (*caudillos*), while the financial and legal benefits of assuming the cooperative form were not always clear. Registering as an official "social cooperative" with the Ministry of Social Development (MIDES) meant the need to pay taxes and limit earnings, while formalization did not always mean that *clasificadores* could more easily sign contracts with large generators for the collection, classification, and disposal of waste. This was partly because other branches of the state, such as the local government (Intendencia) were responsible for granting waste collection licenses, and were much more favorably disposed to disposal than recycling, especially given the conditions under which many *clasificadores* carried out the latter.

A combination of these factors meant that when I returned to conduct doctoral research in 2014, state attempts to encourage the cooperativization of *clasificadores* had largely been abandoned. Instead, what was being proposed was the absorption of many existing *clasificador* cooperatives into municipal plants as part of the Ley de Envases, a packaging law approved in 2004 but whose implementation in Montevideo was delayed by a decade. In an implicit admission that the prior cooperative model had proved problematic for *clasificadores*, the new plants were not managed by the workers themselves but rather by NGOs: waste-pickers became contracted employees with little influence over work-place decision-making. A large part of my doctoral field research consisted of accompanying the disbanding of Uruguay and Montevideo's largest waste-picking cooperative – the Cooperative Felipe Cardoso (COFECA) – and the incorporation of its workers into one of the new recycling plants, the Planta Aries.

There is not the space here to detail the benefits and disadvantages of the move to the plant. Suffice to say that most workers were pleased with the new facilities, a stable if low wage, and the training courses made available, while a minority found management unbearable, were disappointed with a loss of earning *potential*, and returned to working informally in and around the landfill. What interests me here are the links between dispossession and collectivization, whether the latter be through the creation of cooperatives or municipal plants. The origins of the COFECA cooperative can be traced back to 2002, when waste-pickers were expelled from the municipal landfill and subsequently blockaded the gates. This led the municipal government to grant them the right to classify specially selected trucks on a piece of land adjacent to the landfill. This agreement evolved into a stipulation that waste-pickers organize themselves into a cooperative – COFECA – so as to continue receiving waste and permission to work on municipal land. In order to avoid dispossession then, they were forced to collectivize and take on an organizational from that was at that point in vogue with the center-left municipal government. Not all those proposing the model were hopeful that it would work however, with the then landfill director admitting to me that he believed that the waste-pickers would end up fighting among themselves and he could use this as an excuse to evict them from the site.

Fast-forward a decade or so, and history appeared to be repeating itself. While I was conducting participant observation at COFECA, workers were told that their cooperative would be disbanded and that they would be evicted from their site at the landfill. In order to justify the eviction, state actors castigated the cooperative as "not a cooperative at all" given certain discord and the "strong men" dynamics that I have mentioned previously. Working with the cooperative on a daily basis, however, I was able to observe that while this criticism had a certain truth to it, other fundamental cooperative characteristics, such as the equal distribution of income and certain mechanisms of collective decision-making, remained intact. Regardless, workers were told that they should sign up to training sessions to prepare for work in the formal sector plants, or risk being dispossessed of their workplaces and livelihoods.

When both situations are taken into account, waste-pickers appear to be at the mercy of the political winds of governing institutions that favor now this, now that, form of collective organization. The type of organization not favored by the state at any moment, but which happens to be that in which the majority of *clasificadores* work, is that of the family unit, whether nuclear or extended, working at the city landfill or using horses and carts to collect waste throughout the city. State objections to this way of working center on several characteristics including frequent child labor, the use of animal-drawn transport in the city, and the informality of economic activity.

Interestingly, the widespread appearance of horse and cart waste collection in Montevideo emerged in response to two municipal decisions in the 1980s: the temporary ban on *clasificadores* entering the landfill, and the introduction of faster motorized trucks. Pushed out of the landfill and outsprinted by imported rubbish trucks, *clasificadores* living in the peri-urban periphery turned to the low-cost form of transport to which they had easiest access: the horse. Since its inception in 2002, the *clasificador* trade union, the UCRUS, has dedicated itself to both supporting cooperatives and defending the right of waste-pickers to collect recyclables using horses and carts. It carries out case work on behalf of waste-pickers who have had their horses confiscated, and campaigns against animal protection organizations which they accuse of running a racket involved in the expropriation of animals that a large majority of *clasificadores* not only use as work-horses but also care for as members of their families.

Unlike in Buenos Aires then, where cooperatives clearly figure not only as a way of avoiding dispossession but also of improving the income and conditions of waste-picking labor, the Montevidean case is rather less clear-cut. At a particular moment in time, cooperatives could be seen both as a way of avoiding dispossession and as a tool used to dispossess *clasificadores* who did not adopt its organizational form. This situation was apparent to cooperativized *clasificadores*, who in many cases refused to accept trucks or pick-ups (*levantes*) if these were already collected by waste-pickers working in the informal sector. When the political winds changed in the direction of municipal plants, the ethical room for maneuver of *clasificadores* was restricted, since the municipal government rolled out closed, "anti-vandal" waste containers across the city, which were effectively designed so that they could not be opened by street-level waste-pickers. The materials were instead spirited to the new recycling plants, where they were classified by collectivized waste-pickers.

Various issues are at stake in this development. One is the question of what should be considered a dignified livelihood, with many social workers and state assistants operating on the basis that collectivization is about improving the living standards, wages, and health and safety conditions of waste-pickers. But the property status of waste is also in question. Since its inception, the Montevidean municipal state has tried to establish a monopoly over household waste and its collection, and has slowly added other commercial wastes into this equation. Their claim is that as soon as materials are discarded into municipal containers or placed onto the street, they become municipal property. What I argue in my doctoral thesis, however, and what has been advocated by other academics working more closely in the development of public waste policy in Montevideo, is the idea that waste should be considered a common good, or commons. Vulnerable rural immigrants who have arrived in Montevideo jobless have long made their way to the city's waste, exploiting it as a resource in ways comparable to how the English landless poor, for example, had once relied on the rural commons.

To some extent, the process of dispossessing *clasificadores*, similarly to the case of the English commoners, is enacted through processes of enclosure. This includes the fencing and policing of the landfill, which first occurred when the municipal dump was established at Felipe Cardoso in the 1980s. Prior to this, *clasificadores* spoke of the "free landfill" (*cantera libre*), where they could enter freely and recover materials without suffering repression.

Other forms of enclosure include the so-called "anti-vandal" containers which prevent *clasificadores* from accessing materials on the street. The fact that such containment was justified along hygienic grounds, in the sense that it was supposedly designed to prevent inhuman, insanitary, or undignified contact between humans and waste, means that we might designate this form of dispossession as "hygienic enclosure".

To accompany and walk with waste-pickers in such circumstances, I would suggest, involves helping to tear down the fences of enclosure, as the old adage of the commoners movement had it. So, I regularly entered the landfill with *clasificadores* through holes in the fence, crossing a makeshift path over leachates which consisted of dumped tree trunks and car tires, patches of dry ground, and strategically placed ladders. It involved carrying large bags of recyclables on my shoulders over the uneven landfill terrain. It meant being expelled by police on more than one occasion, for not being a familiar face or having proved my mettle to stick it out in the face of threats. Eventually, it also involved embarking on a path also taken by some *clasificadores*: negotiating the possibility of access with the landfill foreman.

Naturally, the transfer of waste and resources from informal to formal sector waste-pickers is a more favorable option than the incineration of all waste. Although the threat of this proposed technology currently looms larger in Argentina than in Uruguay, during my 2014 fieldwork powerful branches of the state were actively working to establish a large and expensive waste-to-energy plant at Felipe Cardoso, which would have spelled disaster for the city's waste-pickers. Luckily, mass opposition was not even necessary because potential costs proved prohibitive and the project was shelved. But rather than work only with the associational forms that aligned or were in vogue with local political common sense, I also worked with those that raised eyebrows, whether the case of the landfill, or that of local families who had squatted land in order to receive, classify, and in some case fly-tip waste. This relational, integrated approach to researching waste-picking in the city meant that I was able to observe when privileged organizational forms might be leading to the dispossession of more vulnerable, informal, and outlawed livelihoods.

Conclusion

To conclude, keeping a distance from the state, whether voluntary or not, conveys certain affordances and disadvantages. It allows the researcher to maintain a critical, independent standpoint, and to avoid complicity in subtle forms of dispossession like those which occur when recyclables are diverted from informal sector wastepickers to those working in cooperatives or municipal plants. Yet even working with the state, Sorroche avoids such complicity by acting within it on behalf of subaltern groups, and promoting policies which further their interests. Recently, O'Hare discovered that the Uruguayan scholar Lucía Fernández, as part of a commission generating new waste legislation, had vigorously pushed for waste to be classified as a public good long before he theorized its consideration as commons in his doctoral thesis. His failure to engage as proactively as Fernández and Sorroche in the development of policies that help mitigate dispossession might be down to his own individual flaws but one suspects that it is also related to the fact that he is an international early career researcher, unfamiliar with national legal frameworks and only present sporadically. While Sorroche and O'Hare have been working with waste-pickers for similar amounts of time, O'Hare's visits have been punctuated by long absences, while Sorroche has been working consistently. The ability to be on hand is, we believe, invaluable when it comes to developing regulatory and legal frameworks, which can often be lengthy processes prone to delay. At the same time, as an international visitor (accurately) perceived as unable to help with authorities in ways that a national researcher could, O'Hare felt more capable of establishing relatively horizontal relationships, living alongside waste-pickers and sharing their private lives, helping to classify waste materials rather than source material aid from the state.

Is important to say that the situations in Argentina and Uruguay differ considerably. As Sorroche shows above, waste-pickers' labor organizations in Greater Buenos Aires fight so as to continue working on the streets and gaining access to recyclable materials. At the present moment, they are struggling to be recognized as a central part of waste management since, as occurs in the metropolitan area of Buenos Aires, they are the only ones who recover recyclable materials. Private companies continue to dispose of waste in landfills that, in recent years, have been denounced by the neighboring populations for the environmental damage they are producing due to the indiscriminate burial that has happened for 40 years. As a researcher, Sorroche has a privileged place alongside cooperatives in the fight against this practice, one which is strengthened by being an assistant professor and researcher in a national university. This has allowed him to take part in workshops and to play a central role in the discussion of the local norms that enable the cooperatives to improve their conditions. In that sense, and as we have shown in this chapter, the different conditions in which, as researchers, we are implicated, allow us to strengthen relations with waste-pickers. The time that one is able to be in the field partly determines the ways that one can get involved and come to know the social worlds in which the cooperatives are embedded. As such, ethnography is a key methodology that lets us immerse ourselves not only in the lives of waste-pickers but also in their struggles.

Forming part of particular social worlds and learning from new ones allows us to help cooperatives in different ways. In Sorroche's case, this allowed him to act as a "spy" on behalf of social organizations he worked with. He was able to meet and convince public servants and NGO workers that what he and his colleagues decided with waste-picker cooperatives constituted a better proposal than whatever the former had designed at a desk far away from social realities. Social anthropologists thus do not only transmit information from the state or NGOs, we also work as translators and authors of ideas and projects that help them to improve their work and organization. *Walking together* does not only mean to take part as a technical advisor or helper: it is to experience the lives of our research subjects in all their diversity, as in the case of O'Hare. The fact that someone would come from afar and be interested in their lives, hopes, and desires is also important for a population that is continuously left behind and persecuted. To take an interest in the lives of others can constitute a way of improving waste-pickers' self-esteem and helping them to gain more confidence in their capacity to think, speak, struggle, and win.

Notes

1 The ordinances that passed were quite different. The first was oriented to the political, and obliged the city council to segregate recyclables and give them to cooperatives. The second was inspired by a provincial regulation (due to the federal character of Argentina, the provincial or national government

isn't able to coerce municipalities into waste policy because this is the prerogative of local government). Thus in 2013, the provincial government made a resolution that gives priority to cooperatives for the collection of waste from industries and commercial enterprises that produce more than 500 kilograms per month. But due to the political structure explained above, the regulation didn't have any impact except in the case of some companies, who mostly didn't pay for the service. In this way, the local ordinance gave the municipality the power to make inspections and to fine the companies that didn't have a waste management program and the segregated disposal of recyclable materials. At time of writing, the cooperative had already signed three contracts and five more are being negotiated.

2 For more information about this process, see Fernández Álvarez and Carenzo (2012).

3 The *piquetero* movement arose at the end of the 1990s. Organized around unemployed people, they demanded the creation of jobs and the implementation of social policies to coordinate and organize different activities between the movement. For more information, see Manzano (2014).

4 The federation was driven by the Movement of Excluded Workers

(Movimiento de Trabajadores Excluidos – MTE) and took part in the foundation of Popular Economy Workers Confederation (Confederación de Trabajadores de la Economía Popular – CTEP). The Confederation tries to represent, as a union, all informal workers or, as they call them, "Popular Economy Workers".

5 Popular economy is the way that the different organizations that take part in CTEP define their work. In other places, this is commonly called the informal economy: the distinction is political and is related to the demands of the Confederation, in recognizing all these people as workers, and to show that they are not separate from the broader labor force (see Fernández Álvarez 2016b).

6 This is a distinction that is made inside the federation. Most of the militants are young people that took part as a political decision taken to help the organization in administrative, political, and organizational tasks.

7 In Greater Buenos Aires the struggle is to be recognized in similar ways as in the City of Buenos Aires. Last year, some advances were made, such as the regulation of large waste generators, the recognition of waste-pickers as workers, and the acknowledgment that they should be paid for their labor.

References

Asad, T. (Ed.). (1995 [1973]). *Anthropology and the Colonial Encounter*. London: Penguin Random House.

Fernández Álvarez, M.I. (2016a). Introducción. In F. Álvarez and M. Inés, *Hacer juntos(as): Dinámicas, contornos y relieves de la política colectiva*. Buenos Aires: Editorial Biblos.

Fernández Álvarez, M.I. (2016b). Experiencia de precariedad, creación de derechos y producción colectiva de bienes(tares) desde la economía popular. *Revista Ensamble*, 3(4–5): 72–89.

Fernández Álvarez, M.I. and Carenzo, S. (2012). Ellos son los compañeros del CONICET: El Vínculo con organizaciones sociales como desafío etnográfico. *Publicar en Antropología y Ciencias Sociales*, 10(12): 9–33.

Juris, J.S. and Khasnabish, A. (2013). Introduction: ethnography and activism within networked spaces of transnational encounter. In J.S. Juris and A. Khasnabish (Eds.), *Insurgent Encounters: Transnational Activism, Ethnography and the Political*. Durham, NC: Duke University Press.

Manzano, V. (2014). *La política en movimiento: movilizaciones colectivas, y políticas estatales en la vida del Gran Buenos Aires*. Rosario: Prohistoria.

O'Hare, P. (2017). *Recovering Requeche and Classifying Clasificadores: An Ethnography of Hygienic Enclosure and Montevideo's Waste Commons*. Doctoral Thesis, University of Cambridge.

Price, D. (2000). Anthropologists as spies. *The Nation*, 271(16): 24.

Sorroche, S. (2016). *Gubernmentalidad global y vernacularización en la gestión de residuos. Análisis etnográfico desde la experiencia de cooperativas de cartoneros en la Gran Buenos Aires.* [Global governmentality and vernacularization in waste management. Ethnographic analysis from the experience of waste-picker cooperatives in Greater Buenos Aires]. Doctoral Thesis, Universidad de Buenos Aires.

Walker, M. (2009). Priest, development worker or volunteer? Anthropological research and ascribed identities in rural Mozambique. *Anthropology Matters*, 11(1): 1–12.

10 | HISTORIANS, GUERRILLA HISTORY, AND CLASS STRUGGLE IN ARGENTINA

Pablo Pozzi

When I started studying history, back in 1971, Argentina was undergoing a surge of left politics. Only four years earlier Che Guevara had been killed in Bolivia, and the Uruguayan Tupamaro guerrillas, with their "Robin Hood" style actions, were popular. It was then that one of my professors forced me (literally) to read a book with an incredibly boring title: *Primitive Rebels* (Hobsbawm 1968). It was written by a guy with an unpronounceable name; and I was convinced that, as an Englishman, he was an agent of imperialist penetration: Eric Hobsbawm. As my students would say nowadays: it blew my mind. It turned out that not only was he not an imperialist agent, but his history was good, relevant, and, most of all, it contributed to understanding the Latin American struggles that fascinated us. Later we read E.P. Thompson, and we began to understand that left politics and intellect could be fruitfully joined together. These historians, and a few others, became a role model for most of my generation, especially those we considered the more intelligent and committed among us. Many became social historians and regarded our profession as a militant contribution to what we considered the national and social liberation of Latin America. And so, myself and many of my colleagues regarded our role as having a social function that combined academe with "going out into society". At the same time, we discovered that people in general were eager to discuss history and sought in its lessons answers to present-day problems.

For instance, many years ago several metallurgical union activists invited me to participate in a labor history workshop. The workshop was carried out in Propulsora Siderúrgica, a large factory with a very militant tradition. I arrived ready to teach them since I was the one who "knew" history and walked into a discussion of Hobsbawm's *Workers: Worlds of Labor* (1979). They were fascinated with Tom Paine; the discussion on labor aristocracy seemed (to them) useful to understanding present-day Argentine unions; and the traditions of English workers suggested numerous things as to their activism in the factory. I will never forget a worker who said that Propulsora was a "a hellish grey factory as the English guy says". What to me was an academic study, was to them a book that made them think about life, that made imagination fly, and especially that was "for them". Ken Worpole (1984: 115) pointed out that it was tragic that academe had become increasingly separated from labor politics, so that neither exerts any kind of influence on the other. In the case of the historical profession this threatens to destroy its *raison d'être*: there is little money and power in being a historian; if you do not want to contribute to improve society, then why be a historian at all? Hobsbawm, Thompson, and the workers at Propulsora taught me that you could be a serious historian, and politically committed at the same time. Also, I discovered that it was much harder to make complex ideas understandable in a way that an educated worker can read, empathize, and learn from. It makes no difference if you are sharing 20th century or 16th century history, a good historian must combine knowledge with the experience and questions of a determined social group to be relevant and understood.

This article will examine the role of an activist historian as a researcher in four different instances: as a columnist and advisor in radio *La Voz del Sur*; as technical advisor for a group of metalworkers writing an oral history of their union local; as an academic coordinator to one of the popular *asambleas* during the 2001–2002 crisis; and as "resident" historian to the labor rank and file newspaper *Nuestra Lucha*. Though all are linked in terms of being "bottom up" experiences, each one was a very specific product of the moment and of the social sector that gave it life. The metalworkers were part of the opposition to the national leadership and sought to understand their own history and use it as an organizing tool. The *asambleas* arose out of the December 2001 collapse, and organized people into barter clubs, helped set up small-scale wheat mills and bread-baking ovens, and carried out round tables and conferences as a tool for dealing with popular desperation and, through debate, to find new ways to deal with the crisis. Last of all, *Nuestra Lucha* (Our Struggle) was the labor paper organized and funded by the Zanon Cooperative under Worker's Control. Between 2004 and 2007 it distributed thousands of copies, free of charge, at factory doors. Its goal was to educate, and to raise consciousness among workers, while at the same time generating a vehicle for sharing experiences.

The premise underlying this piece is that there is an important, though unrealized, linkage between social sciences and society at large that is realized through the academic activist. The key notion is that academics have a social function, beyond serving the state or dominant sectors. At the same time, this social function not only contributes to common people's civility and democratic tendencies, but it also helps to renovate academic thinking, hypothesis, and approaches. Once upon a time Eric Hobsbawm criticized E.P. Thompson for "wasting his time in theoretical debates and in political activism" (Anderson 2002: 7). Thompson, possibly the greatest historian of the 20th century, was better known as the public face of the Campaign for Nuclear Disarmament in Britain. In truth what is posited here is that Thompson's contribution as a historian cannot be separated from his activism, and vice versa. At the same time, the academic's contribution to political activism infuses politics with a measure of critical thought that might otherwise be lacking in politics. Last, but not least, the basic notion is that our reason for being can be found in the contributions we can make to develop critical thinking among the average citizen.

Radio "The Voice of the South"

Since the 1930s Argentina has been an unusual Third World nation. Economically it had a strong industrial base geared mostly towards consumer products for a protected domestic market. Argentine industry fueled its growth with the foreign currency obtained through agricultural and beef exports produced by a few large landowning families. Industrial growth created a large working class, organized in strong unions. Culturally many of these workers leaned to the left expressing their anti-imperialist and laborite feelings through Peronism. Still, the organized left included a sizeable Communist Party and smaller Trotskyist groups; with some influence within the working class. From 1969 to 1975, the various left groupings (including the Peronist left) had grown to the point that there seemed to be a possibility for an anti-imperialist and anti-capitalist revolution. The response, from the right, was the 1976 *coup d'état*. The 1976–1983 dictatorship unleashed a wide repression, affecting all of society and especially labor and its organizations.

In 1983 Argentina returned to a democratic form of government after a long and harsh seven-year dictatorship. Raúl Alfonsín, a leader of the center-right Radical Civic Union (UCR) was elected president on a progressive platform. After 1985 Alfonsín had mostly caved in to economic pressures, and adopted a neo-conservative outlook to his economic policies, including wage freezes and the privatization of the state sector. However, labor opposed this, and carried out 13 general strikes. In 1989 he was forced to hand over his office six months earlier to his successor, due to hyperinflation, riots, and economic bankruptcy. His successor, Carlos Menem, from the center-left Justicialist (Peronist) Party carried out a whole series of neo-conservative economic and social policies which were very similar to those implemented by the dictatorship. The results have been immense changes on an economic and social level, and a political crisis.

This was the historical context wherein, many years ago, I was approached by two workers from the Pedró Hermanos Meatpacking Plant, deep in Monte Chingolo, Buenos Aires Province. They were union activists who were also active in their neighborhood. Both lived in Villa Obrera, in the Lanús District, a traditional and very combative working-class community that had been hit very hard by the economic policies of the 1976 dictatorship. Villa Obrera had witnessed one of the 1981–1982 uprisings against the dicta-torship, that had thrown out three mayors, based on the *Sociedad de Fomento* (neighborhood association) and led by a Peronist and two communist activists. The workers who contacted me were the two communists. They were running an illegal radio station based in their neighborhood association and wanted a historian to help them out with their "History for *Vecinos*" program. The radio station, called *La Voz del Sur* (The Voice of the South), had thousands of listeners, no salaried employees, and no advertising. Suddenly I had to create a ten-minute history segment every week that was interesting, accessible, and taught some lesson about peo-ple's empowerment. It was hard work, and it also reconciled me to academe as it made me feel useful.

Though the radio station was illegal, it was certainly not clandes-tine. Thousands would call every day to comment on programming, or to request an announcement (a typical one was: "José, María says lunch is ready"). Listeners debated anything and anyone and loved to participate. This generated not only listeners, but a lot of support. The radio antenna was built by the metalworkers at a nearby factory. The furniture was contributed by several neighborhood carpenters. Families would organize bake sales to help out. Once, the police raided the station and carried away most of the equipment. The next day several street gangs showed up to ask what was needed to return to broadcasting. We never asked where they got the equipment they offered.

Since I had no idea of how to do radio journalism, the process of creating a radio segment was a question of trial and error and of paying close attention to what callers and visitors said. In a sense, it was a cultural experience as to popular perceptions of history. It reminded me of an Argentine version of Sellar and Yeatman's *1066 and All That* (Sellar and Yeatman 1993); most comments would start the same way: "I can tell you know a lot about history. Now, let me explain to you why there was a military coup in 1955". Or: "I disagree. Argentina is not a great country, because we threw out the British when they invaded in 1806 and 1807". Most people were fascinated by history; just like they had been bored by it in secondary school. And most had a good knowledge of anecdotes and facts. This arose from a long-standing tradition of the Argentine working class: "if history is written by the victors, that means there must be another history; that of the people", as Pete, a construction worker, explained to me. As such, seemingly gossipy questions took on meaning. For instance, people would ask if Liberator General José de San Martin was a spy for the British, or if it was true that Bernardo de Monteagudo, one of the revolutionaries during the struggle for independence from Spain, was a *mulatto*. If you were willing to listen, these were opening remarks to a lengthy discussion on racism or on British domination of Argentina. This meant that, eventually, we settled on a format that relied heavily on peoples' interests. The segment would start with an anecdote, then give it a wider context, to end up discussing some issue that was relevant to the listeners.

This was much harder than it sounds. Not every anecdote (or story) was interesting to our audience, and relevancy was hard to gauge. What we would do was rely on anecdotes that flew in the face of received and established historical knowledge. Then we would open with a question: for instance, why is the United States a world power and not Argentina? After suggesting a few reasons, we would take callers and let them take us in the direction of their interests. This was quick, and accessible (after all it was only ten minutes of commentary with a short question and answer period of no more than ten minutes). People would come by the station to continue the discussion. It was fascinating; I loved it.

La *Voz del Sur* went on for a couple of more years (from 1985 to 1990), reaching almost 600,000 listeners, until the commercial stations in the area began copying the format and stealing the programming. However, I learned several things from it. First that history was important to the average person; then that many Argentines had more than just a notion of the subject; and last that the problem with making it relevant lay with academics, and not with the average folks. As such, the way we communicated knowledge was crucial. Not only did it have to be accessible, but we had to learn to listen to be able to teach. There was no separation between the public and the private, between experience and academe, between knowledge and everyday life. People would overtly link history and present-day problems.

The steelworkers' "history group"

While doing the radio segment, I also taught at the Unión Obrera Metalúrgica (UOM: metallurgical workers union) Quilmes Local school for activists. The old, traditional Peronist leadership had collaborated with the dictatorship, and had just lost an election. The new leadership was a mix of former guerrillas, left Peronists, progressives, and Trotskyists. One day several metalworkers had listened to my show at La *Voz del Sur*. That day we had been speaking about the *Semana Trágica* (Tragic Week) of 1919 and how it had started as a result of the police massacring striking metalworkers. The lesson was that the workers had a proud and heroic history, and it was important to know what their contribution had been to make a better life for us all. My listeners went to the union leadership and suggested that I should write a history of how they had thrown out the old, collaborationist, leadership. The leadership thought it was a good idea, with many possibilities for propaganda and legitimizing their existence.

The one who was not happy with the whole thing was me. I was interested in doing something that was useful to the workers, and not just an individual piece of research that nobody would use.

After discussing it with my student workers, we decided that for this to be useful it should be a team effort. We would ask for volunteers to research and write this history. The whole task would be of the workers, and my role was to function as "technical advisor", teach them how to research, and supervise the writing.

Eventually the "history group" was eight workers and myself, who would meet after work hours. We started by discussing what they wanted to say, and why this might be important. Then they suggested reading a few articles on labor history (they hated most of them) and discussing what they knew of UOM history. At some point, the decision was that history needed "papers"; and the word was put out among the Local's 5,000 members. The next month people showed up with all sorts of things: newspaper clippings, photos, flyers, some letters, and even some old union ledgers. But what they brought with them was memories. Many workers came to "tell us" how it had been. We concluded that we needed to do oral history, and interview as many workers and their families as possible.

In the Argentine case, the problems of "doing" oral history are linked to the issues derived from repression and dictatorial regimes. To ask an interviewee for their written authorization automatically implies that you generate doubts as to what the historian is going to do with the interview. Self-censorship on both sides, as survival techniques when faced by cruel repressive governments, has become deeply ingrained in the testimonies, the memory, and the subjectivity of the participants. The techniques to evoke a remembrance or to achieve a response are not (and neither can they be) the same as in societies whose repressive levels are lower. At the same time, the possibility that what a participant declares in an interview can be used towards ends never imagined by the historian is an ethical and practical problem that is not dealt with in any oral history textbook written by Europeans or North Americans.

Still many of the interviews done by the team were fascinating, revealing a strong workerist tradition. Raymond Williams defined "tradition" as "an oral handing down ... a general word for matter handed down from father to son" (Williams 1985: 319), which presupposes an eminently oral form. He also specified that all tradition is "intentionally selective of a configured past and present, which then results to be powerfully operative within the cultural and social process and identification that constitute subaltern subjectivity"

(Williams 1980: 137). One of the key elements, besides testimonies, to trace the subaltern subjectivity through generations, is that of oral traditions handed down from parents to children which conform popular culture and lore. Our metalworkers told us their story, and unconsciously transmitted a tradition. As such, they were concerned with being as precise as possible; or rather, what they thought was factual precision. Most mixed personal experience with what could be termed the "official history" of the union. Many were concerned with correcting what another had said. And all tried to transmit a pride in what they saw as a history of struggle and dignity.

Initially the interviews were poor. I had given the team a couple of articles on oral history and we had discussed the mechanics of interviewing. And yet, the interviewers tended to get involved in discussions with those interviewed; did not let them finish an answer; and all questions tended to lead to a certain response. They wanted responses they agreed with. So, after the first few interviews, we stopped and organized a workshop on oral history, where we discussed the various interviews and sought how to improve them. In addition, we had each team member interview another, and then discuss the results. Then we interviewed many of our original subjects. These were much better. At the same time, they generated a new problem. Many of those we now interviewed really liked the experience of being a part of history and did not want the interview to end. They would come back time and again with "something I remembered", or "I forgot, and this is important". For most of them history was something that "important" people (usually rich white-skinned males) did; not them. Our problem now was how to stop interviewing a person, without giving offense. At the same time, I learned that often without thinking about it, or realizing it, our practice as academics was imbued with prejudice even in the very small things.

The results were fascinating in terms of describing solidarity networks, cultural criteria, class traditions and perceptions, as well as a wealth of facts that had escaped most history books. It revealed a labor culture in Argentina, grounded in a traditionally strong perception of us versus them, where the employers have been identified not only as different but as an antagonist. This does not imply any kind of "revolutionary" criteria, but rather a series of traditions, customs, and uses that are translated into a dispute over control of the point of production.

The research went on for six months and mobilized many union members and their families. Eventually the team wrote the results and published them as a booklet for union members. Though the members were happy with the results, the union leadership was dissatisfied. The research showed that the Quilmes metalworkers, though politicized towards the left, did not belong to any political party, and that included Peronism. This meant that one of the questions posed by many of those we had interviewed referred to the issue that if the union members had all sorts of political opinions, then why did the union leadership tend to align itself almost exclusively with Peronism? They asked: shouldn't the union represent all the members, even those who are conservative? The leadership felt that the history team had become a problem for them. As Worpole (1984: 117) pointed out, there is "potentially subversive nature in historical knowledge". At the same time, the research generated problems with colleagues at the union school. First, it showed that an average worker, with at most a secondary education, could produce an original piece of research. In addition, it changed the role of the academic, from producer (and controller) of knowledge, to that of a facilitator and a fulcrum for collective endeavors in public history. Both leadership and school coordinators decided that "the experience had not been fruitful" and we were "just playing politics in the union". But for me it was a fascinating experience where a collective effort broke new ground in historical studies and posed new questions. And it was the perspective and experience of the eight members of the team (and one historian) that contributed to knowledge in a way that could not have been made by the academic alone. At the same time, it also starkly revealed to me that knowledge empowers common folks and is felt as dangerous by those in positions of power.

Teaching history to deal with the 2001 crisis

Some 20 years later, the Argentine economy and society went into technical collapse at the end of 2001. On December 19 the government announced the new budget with a US$6 billion cut back, over 50 percent more than the original announcement. It included massive layoffs, wage reductions, rollbacks in pensions, and cutbacks in teacher incomes. Thousands of people turned out to demonstrate and demanded food from local supermarkets. In Córdoba City municipal workers attacked City Hall and literally wrecked it. In Mendoza, Buenos Aires, Tucuman, Rosario, Corrientes, and Neuquén, people sacked supermarkets and battled the police. By the end of the day there were several dead, over a hundred wounded, and hundreds arrested. On December 20 the toll of dead and wounded had doubled, and President Fernando de la Rúa, finding himself isolated and repudiated by the population at large, presented his resignation.

The result was that by 2002 Argentina had collapsed with hundreds of thousands of unemployed and underemployed. In its wake arose an unemployed workers movement with tens of thousands of members. This movement organized barter clubs, mobilized to stop housing evictions, and struggled to obtain government aid and jobs. The millions of unemployed began meeting in what were called *"asambleas populares"*. These *asambleas* debated what to do, set up soup kitchens and bread ovens, set up small businesses selling bread or the members' skills, and carried out political education. Every Saturday the *asamblea* for an area (or zone) would meet to conduct business in the morning, then they would hold "classes" (usually from about 11:00 to 13:00), and then would serve lunch. The classes dealt with myriad different subjects, including biochemistry (how to make soap or cleaning fluids), agronomy (how to set up your own vegetable garden), and history (how did we get here?). Many of the classes were practical (applied), but the history class was supposed to be the linchpin around which the others revolved. History was thought to provide an explanation of what was happening and to combat anomie, to raise consciousness, and as entertainment; that it was a way to keep people coming to the *asamblea*. As such classes were supposed to be entertaining, accessible, participatory, and serious.

Early in 2002 some of our students at the Universidad de Buenos Aires, whose families had been hard hit by the crisis and who participated in several *asambleas*, asked several of us to organize a series of history classes (they were very specific that they were not to be lectures). Two of us began participating in the *asambleas* of the Buenos Aires neighborhoods of San Telmo, Almagro, and Caballito. We organized a series of courses based on previous experiences with trade union schools: basic economic history, labor history, Argentine history from 1955 to the present. We used several booklets designed for union work, which were handed out for free to all participants (we had the university union print a run of about 3,000).

Class would start with the teacher (us) posing a problem/question, opening a discussion, writing a gist of the responses on the board, and then back to a short lecture, to again open the floor for discussion. Taking a page from Alessandro Portelli's militancy in the *Circolo Gianni Bossio* (Portelli 1997), we relied heavily on songs, poems, jokes, anecdotes to keep the flow of the class moving along, and as an incentive to participation (people tended to add their own as a response to a song or a poem or a joke). This tended to break the divide between professor and student: for instance, they would plead that I not sing (it seems I cannot hit a single note).

It seemed easy, as by now we were veterans of popular education. And yet, it was very complicated. The unemployed included workers, middle sector employees, professionals, housewives. Their educational level was very varied, as were their cultural references and abilities to communicate. Suddenly you had unemployed bus drivers, together with bank tellers, teachers, pharmacists, and autoworkers. It reminded me of David Montgomery (1997: 28) saying: "our taxes finance death squads throughout America; and look at the talent they are bringing us". I would look at the *asamblea* and think "it is incredible, how capitalism's destruction has led to new types of anti-capitalist activism and sharing of experiences". This sharing was not easy as there was a lot of prejudice and racism, especially between professionals and factory workers, and between those who had an activist past and those who were brand new to militancy. For the class to work (and for the *asamblea* to function) this had to be dealt with without antagonizing the participants. Sometimes the exchanges were very offensive; but rather than quash them, and sending them underground, we would explicitly build the class around them. We tended to do this by overtly inciting the discussion and admitting there was a lot of prejudice: were the workers who carried out the October 17 mobilization and later the *Cordobazo*,[1] a bunch of *negros* bent on washing their feet in park fountains? Were they dark skinned? What is a "negro"? Why do dark-skinned rich folk consider themselves whites? How come most Argentines believe they are not Latin American, but rather European? Each question generated a controversy: for instance, one student said, with a straight face, that "there are two things I do not like, racists and niggers", while some responded with cat calls, others tried to explain that that was racist. Since many Argentines believe that there is no racism in Argentina, these exchanges were eye opening to most participants. Considering the wide variety of professions and social sectors of the unemployed, the responses fostered an interchange between people who would normally never interact, much less consider the other's point of view.

Classes would go on for two hours, and a basic premise was that though we had a syllabus we were not constrained by it. Students could suggest subjects, or even change topics if they had the consensus of their comrades. This tended to make classes entertaining and relevant, and attendance kept up at over 80 percent of those who showed up for the first class. The results were interesting: people would approach us with all sorts of ideas – some practical, some not – for classes, for readings, and even for ways on how to re-organize the Argentine Republic. For instance, out of one class on the struggles of the unemployed in the 1930s, there arose the proposal to get in touch with metalworkers and engineers to make a small, portable, flour mill. At the same time, a delegation was sent to farmers in the provinces to buy 20 to 50-kilogram bags of wheat to be milled in the new flour mills. Suddenly, by cutting out the middle man, they lowered the price of flour to a fraction of the cost while improving the earnings of the farmer. In addition, it broke class barriers between people who had never even thought of relating to one another. Finally, history seemed to come alive with practical applications derived from past human experiences.

By mid-2003 the social and economic situation in Argentina had stabilized, though unemployment remained at around 30 percent, and underemployment was rife. This meant that the *asambleas* died out, and so did our role in them. But many of the workers who participated learned from the experience and spearheaded new labor initiatives in the following years such as the Movement of Recovered Factories (MRF).[2]

The paper Nuestra Lucha

With the MRF, the left and thousands of new younger working-class activists became energized, and a new rank and file movement developed. One of the more important worker-controlled factories, Zanon Ceramics, together with a sector of the left, set up a newspaper for these activists: *Nuestra Lucha* (Our Struggle) came into being in 2004, and distributed thousands of copies at factory gates throughout Argentina.

Nuestra Lucha relied on unpaid worker correspondents through-out Argentina, and some intellectuals like the economist Eduardo Lucita, and historians such as myself. It functioned in zonal col-lectives (for instance, in Córdoba City, the collective was about 30 persons and myself as the only non-industrial worker) that debated the paper, contributed with articles, decided what was newsworthy in their area, gathered finances to keep it going, and distributed it early every morning and afternoon, when workers either went to work or left the factory. We handed out, free of charge, thousands of copies, and had a heady response. Most people gave us a few coins or a bill or two (to us it was very significant because not only did we not ask for contributions, but worker salaries were very low), some gave us their phone number and asked us to get in touch, and a few just asked when and where did we meet. We would hand out 2,000–3,000 copies in our area, every week; and many would wait for us a week later to let us know what they thought of the different articles or give us information and suggest new subjects to write about.

My role, besides participating in general, was to write a regular column on history. If truth be told, it was more of an opinion piece, the subject to be determined by the collective, and geared towards explaining diverse issues. For instance, they were interested in an explanation of the rank and file movement "*clasismo*", or why did the armed forces overthrow elected governments, or how did the labor union bureaucracy arise. The catch was that the explanations had to be accessible, short (no more that 45 lines), and lead with an anec-dote to catch the readers' attention. A major problem was that the language and tone of the pieces was not what was acceptable to the average militant; they tended to see history as a lesson in Marxism, whereas many in the collective thought of it as a lesson in ethics, morality, and most of all worker pride. There were endless discus-sions as to the paper's role: should it "raise consciousness" or "bring all workers together?" I believe that a working-class newspaper should reflect the needs and concerns of all those who participate in it, no matter how contradictory. And that the main criteria should be that, as David Montgomery said, "this could only be done if your discussions and analysis were as thoroughly down to earth as you could possibly make them" (MARHO 1976a: 171). These types of initiatives could only survive and become fruitful if they stuck very close to the working class; and that could only be done by carrying out the broadest possibly democratic practices. The result could be considered chaotic, or a true reflection of worker interests.

In the end, *Nuestra Lucha* carried articles for all tastes, though most of the "historical" pieces emphasized the kind of moral lessons that arise out of the concept of common people "making history". These pieces worked well and were one of the most read parts of the paper. For the historian this was complicated, partly because the worker members of the collective had a lot of respect for me (in other words they expected me not to say silly things), and at the same time they expected that I would shut up when I could not contribute something useful. They really valued that I was the only academic participating in the collective; but they had no intention of considering me as anything more than one of the *compañeros* whose opinion was as good (or as bad) as anyone else's. After a lifetime of being a professor, and holding a chair at the University of Buenos Aires, it was hard to get used to not being "the fount of wisdom". In addition, it was complicated, not only because I had to learn a journalistic style, but also because I had to get used to writing collectively with people who were not part of the profession and had very definite ideas as to what they thought I should say. Lucky for me I could fall back on my experience, two decades earlier, at the UOM Quilmes; and yet it was not easy. Still, no matter how complicated, it was fun, and it taught me many things about Argentine society. For instance, once we held a meeting at my house. The neighbors seeing many dark-skinned, humbly dressed people hanging around the block, quickly called the police. Though many Argentines will insist that it is an egalitarian society, the reality was that class and racial discrimination is a reality that workers suffer every day. Also, the collective really liked having me there. I always felt that I liked history and not historians who tended to encase themselves in the marble halls of academe. *Nuestra Lucha* made me value history and historians again. And when you separate all the wheat from the chaff, you realize that history is the only teacher that workers have.

By 2007 a new leadership was elected at Zanon under workers control. After some soul searching, they decided to discontinue the paper and use the resources for other, more urgent, needs. Thus, the paper came to an end, but not before it had become an example to others. Once it stopped publishing, several of the collectives put out their own papers based on this experience. Monthlies such as *El Roble* (in northern Buenos Aires), or *El Mortero*, came into being generating a small rebirth of worker publications.

"Guerrilla history"

I participated in these initiatives because I enjoyed them, because they made me feel useful, and for a selfish reason: because it gave me a fresh perspective from which to rethink history. But I also had a political objective: I believe that if the average person is able to think for him or herself, then they will be that much harder to dominate. Our job is to aid people in throwing off the shackles imposed by an education geared towards justifying the status quo. This means that we do not tell them how to think but provide the tools so that they can think for themselves. As Montgomery explained, "if, as radical historians, we are doing work that has some sort of meaning to politics and to the daily lives of working people, then it's got to be shared with them" (MARHO 1976a: 180). The catch is that we might not agree with, or even like, what they think as a result of becoming free thinkers, but the idea is not to impose our thoughts on them, but to contribute to having them think for themselves. At the same time, it also recognizes that we intellectuals are not impartial, objective observers, but rather we are part of society and thus have a responsibility towards it. Staughton Lynd called this type of historian someone who does "guerrilla history". That is "a way to break through the methodological impasse of being an observer, a way of ceasing to be an eye and becoming also a hand" (MARHO 1976b: 151). This is an interesting concept, with the underlying premise that history is subversive only if the historian "is only a catalyst, an organizer, the one who creates the occasion for ... people to share their experiences" (MARHO 1976b: 152). I think I contributed to working-class subversion, and yet I was never a catalyst or an organizer, but I put in my grain of sand to others who were. My contribution was important, but it was clear to me that it was not determinant.

At the same time, the experience of participating over four decades in various worker initiatives, being involved in struggles, contributing what knowledge I had, educating and learning from them, convinced me that many of the things academics had written about Argentine workers were simply not true. They are considered as very conservative, passive, and with a low cultural level. Many colleagues believe that what historian Milcíades Peña wrote years ago was true: Argentine workers are "*pancistas*" (meaning "concerned with only filling their stomachs") (Polit 1964). The same could be said for the perception that all Argentine workers are Peronists. This is not my experience. Indeed, many are Peronists, but also many others belong to other political parties, and a majority cannot be said to be politicized except in a very general, cultural sense. In general, I found workers to have initiative, curiosity, and a permanent desire to understand the world to be able to change it.

This experience tended to pose a challenge to my research as an historian. I quickly found that to explain what were to me existing phenomena, I had to delve into other disciplines: anthropology, sociology, discourse analysis, oral history, cultural studies, and many others were useful. I needed methods, perspectives, and theories that were external to history to understand highly complex and contradictory social processes. Perhaps, my worker students forced me to become an interdisciplinarian, breaking down boundaries between disciplines. Am I still an historian? I am more concerned with trying to explain how Argentine workers perceive themselves as part of a class (and reproduce cultural patterns and traditions that can only be considered as belonging to a class), than with professional labels, or theoretical niceties. For instance, Argentina has been considered a "hot bed of leftist activity"[3] from the 1870s until today. Why have leftist ideas gained such a strong following among Argentine workers? My work suggests that these ideas are more of a class tradition, a culture in the sense of Raymond Williams (1980), than an ideology. At the same time, to be able to study this, you have to consider its historical evolution, while having recourse to other disciplines to suggest some answers. Undoubtedly, my experience as an activist historian has had an influence on my work as an academic.

"We made history together"

These past few decades have been terrible for the Argentine working class. We have gone from full employment in 1975 to 30 percent unemployment, and an untold percentage of underemployment. Unionization has fallen from 82 percent in 1973, to under 35 percent in 2015. And yet, my feeling is that the old slogan of the Córdoba Fiat "*clasista*" autoworkers is still very much alive: "To struggle, to fail, to struggle again until final victory, that is the history of the working class".

The great historian and activist Howard Zinn (2001: 34), many years ago, wrote:

> And so I have no right to despair. I insist on hope. It is a feeling, yes, but it is not irrational. People respect feelings, but they still want reasons. Reasons for going on, for not surrendering, for not retreating into private luxury or private desperation. People want evidence of those possibilities in human behavior I have talked about. I have suggested there are reasons. I believe there is evidence. ... What we choose to emphasize in this complex story will determine our lives. If we see only the worst, it destroys our capacity to do something. If we remember those times and places – and there are so many – where people have behaved magnificently, this gives us the energy to act, and at least the possibility of sending this spinning top of a world in a different direction.

I felt these words expressed what was in my heart as a person, and what I wanted to be as an historian. I was lucky enough to be able to contribute throughout my life to the Argentine working-class movement. At the same time, I was fortunate that my work as an historian was never a product of individual work, rather it was the product of questions and perspectives posed by hundreds of *compañeros*. As Staughton Lynd said: "this is guerrilla history" (MARHO 1976b). In Argentina we call it "militant history". This history might be good or bad, just like the more traditional history might be well done or not; the difference is that this history tries to be relevant to the average person. This has been, at least for me, a learning process over many years, while I tried to contribute in different working-class initiatives. I believe that our participation was important to them, just like it was to us. And I believe that together we made history.

Notes

1 October 17, 1945, was the date when masses of workers came from the Buenos Aires suburbs into the center of the city to successfully demand that Juan Perón be freed. The *Cordobazo*, on May 29, 1969, was a popular (worker-student) uprising in the city of Córdoba that forced the resignation of military dictator General Juan Carlos Onganía.

2 Movimiento de Fábricas Recuperadas. By 2008 about 10,000 businesses that had either gone bankrupt or whose owners had declared bankruptcy had been taken over by their employees.

3 "While Federal and State authorities in the United States were shutting down the union-organizing activities of the Industrial Workers of the World (IWW), American officials were uncovering what they believed were equivalent and related dangers in Argentina ... believed that Communists were crawling all over Buenos Aires ... identified the working-class Boca district of Buenos Aires as a hot bed of leftist activity" (Sheinin 2006: 50).

References

Anderson, P. (2002). The age of EJH. *London Review of Books*, 24(19): 3–7.

Hobsbawm, E. (1968). *Rebeldes primitivos*. Barcelona: Ariel Quincenal.

Hobsbawm, E. (1979). *Trabajadores. Estudios sobre la clase obrera*. Barcelona: Editorial Crítica.

MARHO. (1976a). Interview with David Montgomery. *Visions of History*. New York: Pantheon Books.

MARHO. (1976b). Interview with Staughton Lynd. *Visions of History*. New York: Pantheon Books.

Montgomery, D. (1997). El movimiento sindical: historia y perspectivas. *Taller, revista de sociedad, cultura y política*, 2(4): 13–29.

Polit, G. (1964). El legado del bonapartismo: conservadurismo y quietismo en la clase obrera argentina. *Fichas de investigación económica y social*, 1(3): 70–80.

Portelli, A. (1997). Memory and resistance: for a history (and celebration) of the Circolo Gianni Bossio. In A. Portelli, *The Battle of Valle Giulia: Oral History and the Art of Dialogue*. Madison, WI: The University of Wisconsin Press.

Sellar, W.C. and Yeatman, R.J. (1993). *1066 and All That: A Memorable History of England*. London: Sutton Publishing.

Sheinin, D. (2006). *Argentina and the United States: An Alliance Contained*. Athens, GA and London: University of Georgia Press.

Williams, R. (1980). *Marxismo y literatura*. Barcelona: Ediciones Península.

Williams, R. (1985). *Keywords*. New York: Oxford University Press.

Worpole, K. (1984). Implicaciones políticas de la historia local del movimiento obrero. In R. Samuel (Ed.), *Historia popular, historia socialista*. Barcelona: Editorial Crítica.

Zinn, H. (2001). ¿Por qué tener esperanzas en tiempos difíciles? In P. Pozzi and F. Nigra (Eds.), *Huellas imperiales. Historia de los estados unidos 1929–2000*. Buenos Aires: Editorial Imago Mundi.

11 | PUBLIC SOCIOLOGY AND SCHOLAR-ACTIVISM IN THE US-FILIPINO LABOR DIASPORA

Robyn Magalit Rodriguez

In this chapter, I discuss "politically engaged research" projects I worked on in collaboration with other Filipino scholars and Filipino migrant worker organizations in the San Francisco Bay Area in California, a region that has been a major destination for immigrant (and migrant) workers from the Philippines. I will highlight two different case studies: the establishment of the Critical Filipino and Filipina Scholars Collective (CFFSC) in the early 2000s and the CARE Project, a community-engaged research project conducted in 2012 on the working and living conditions of low-wage and undocumented Filipino caregivers.

I choose to discuss these two projects because they represent two very different forms of "politically engaged scholarship". The first might be characterized as "scholar-activism" in the sense that it was academic institutions within and against which we directed our political work. The second might be best characterized as "community-engaged" research as it involved collaboration with a community-based organization and the research aims of the project were driven primarily by the organization. Each came with different kinds of challenges that can be instructive for those interested in "politically engaged research". Critical reflections on these projects can form the basis of a decolonial Filipino migration research agenda, which is crucial for Filipinos in the diaspora who are increasingly joining the ranks of the US academia. Given the history of the American university in the colonization of the Philippines as well as its role in legitimizing different forms of exclusion for Filipinos in the United States, a decolonial Filipino migration research agenda is important for members of the diaspora interested in knowledge production for justice.

Background on the Filipino labor diaspora in the United States

As a consequence of its colonization by the United States in 1898 with the signing of the Treaty of Paris at the conclusion of the Spanish–American War, the Philippines emerged as a major source of migrant workers for American capitalists at the turn of the 20th century. The growing US economy required agricultural laborers, particularly on the west coast. Though employers had relied on low-wage workers from other Asian countries, including China and Japan, US workers and other white supremacist forces, feeling threatened, waged campaigns, often-violent ones, to stop their entry. With two key sources of labor cut off, labor recruiters soon looked to the Philippines. As a colony of the United States, the Philippines became a convenient source of labor since Filipinos, considered "nationals" of the United States, were exempt from immigration restrictions (Baldoz 2015). Labor recruiters actively sought laborers, especially young men, from the Philippines and by the 1930s, more than a hundred thousand Filipinos would make their way to the fields of California (Mabalon 2013). The American colonial education system played a key role in the mobilization of Filipino colonial subjects for labor in the United States and its territories (Hawaii and Alaska). As Filipino-American writer and labor activist Carlos Bulosan put it "America is in the Heart" (Bulosan 2014).

Filipinos continued to work as farm laborers into the 1960s, even after Filipino immigration was effectively put to a halt with the passage of the Tydings–McDuffie Act of 1934. Filipinos, like the Chinese and Japanese before them, were seen as a threat to US workers. They were also seen, like the Chinese and Japanese before them, as a cultural menace. Indeed, Filipinos were often the target of terrible acts of white supremacist vigilante violence like in Watsonville, California.

By 1965, with the passage of the Immigration Act of 1965 in the United States, Filipinos would come to the United States as professional workers or through family sponsorship. During roughly the same period, the Philippine government had introduced a policy of emigration and emerged as a kind of "labor brokerage state" which would facilitate the export of Filipinos not just to the United States but globally (Rodriguez 2010). The US-established educational system would continue to supply labor to the United States and the world such that the Philippines would emerge as having one of the largest labor diasporas in the world. Increasingly, Filipinos engage in a form of serial migration that takes them to different destinations around the world over the course of their lives for a series of contractual jobs; then many make their way to the United States where they become low-wage and often undocumented migrant workers (Francisco and Rodriguez 2014). For instance, a Filipino may work first on contract in Saudi Arabia and then on to a contract in South Korea until finally making their way to the United States.

The broader history of migration from the Philippines to the United States has necessarily shaped the presence of Filipinos in American universities. Indeed, Filipinos' first formal insertion into higher education institutions in the United States was as part of the American colonial project. The first cohorts of Filipinos brought to the United States in the first decade of colonization were *pensionados*, individuals selected from among the Philippine elite to play a role as collaborators in the colonial project by being schooled in US institutions then returning to the Philippines to assume roles in the colonial government.

At the same time, Philippine higher education was created by the United States. Notably, University of California, Berkeley scholars and administrators were among the key architects. This is a crucial point because the one case study of scholar-activism that I discuss in this chapter was led by Filipino scholars (including myself) who were all completing doctorates in Filipino studies at the University of California, Berkeley. Indeed, a good majority of us were housed in departments located in Barrows Hall, named after an especially important designer of public education in the Philippines under colonial rule. William H. Taft, president of the Philippine Commission appointed Barrows to serve as the superintendent of schools for Manila in 1900. He would later become chief of the Bureau of Non-Christian Tribes of the Islands. An anthropologist, Barrow's work in the Bureau included reconnaissance of the little-known areas of the Philippines. By 1903 he was appointed general superintendent of education for the Islands and completely reorganized the educational system. It was ultimately under his charge that Thomasites, American teachers who were recruited to do the work of "Americanizing" the Filipinos, were imported into the Philippines en masse. They took up where the soldiers had left off. If the military had been successful in brutally eliminating Filipino revolutionaries during the Filipino-American war, the Thomasites mission was to work on capturing the hearts and minds of those who remained. Teachers became the new "army of occupation". Paradoxically enough, David Barrows' papers, housed in the UC Berkeley library, would draw succeeding generations of Filipino scholars to the campus.

Filipino scholar-activism

In the late 1960s, Filipino students, recognizing American academia's complicity with US imperial projects, participated in the Third World Liberation Front (TWLF) and went on strike first at San Francisco State University then later at UC Berkeley, demanding what would later be termed "ethnic studies". Filipinos and other descendants of Asian immigrants were actively involved in the struggle for ethnic studies which emerged from the convergence of the civil rights movement, the anti-war movement, and the interracial labor solidarity exemplified by the founding of the United Farm Workers (UFW) led by Larry Itliong along with Cesar Chavez.[1] After a tense and violent struggle on both campuses, students were successful in making their respective university administrations respond to their demands for a curriculum that was responsive to their individual and collective experiences with the creation of "Ethnic Studies" programs (Okihiro 2016).

The movements for ethnic studies offered very distinctive definitions of the purpose of knowledge and knowledge production that were different from the mainstream academic departments. This is exemplified, for example, in the statement by the Pilipino American Collegiate Endeavor (PACE), one of the student groups involved in the TWLF:

We, the Filipinos, have come to the realization, along with our Third World brothers, that the struggle for self-determination is the struggle of all Third World peoples; that the neutrality, a neutrality which for the most part kept our community from progressing in this racist society, can not be tolerated or practiced any longer. There have been too many situations in which our people have denied to themselves the rights and opportunities to determine their future. There have been too many situations in which our people were given jobs as busboys, clerks, and janitors even though they may have had college degrees. It is therefore evident to Filipinos at SF State that racism is not only levelled at our Black brother, but at us as well, when we consider the prevailing inadequacies (small number of Filipinos in college, opportunities denied to Filipino professionals in this country, exploitation of Filipino farmworkers in Delano working for a few dollars a day). Seeing that these inadequacies should and must be eliminated for the betterment of our community, We demand that there be established within the School of Ethnic Studies, a Department of Filipino studies, and that within that department individuals who comprise the Department of Filipino studies will have complete control of its business including faculty practices and course material.[2]

Here, PACE offers an outline for what I would come to shape as the two case studies of focus in this chapter. First, PACE calls for an end to "neutrality". It suggests that knowledge and by extension knowledge production cannot be passively consumed (or in the case of scholarship, passively produced), but that it ought to incite members of the community towards critiques of systems of power – particularly white supremacy and the system of capitalism. As E. San Juan argues, the birth of ethnic studies was animated by an "activist impulse" (San Juan 1991: 468). Second, it calls for more access to the university as part of a project for addressing issues of injustice. Access to the university includes increased admissions, as well as the development of curricula and research through the establishment of a Department of Filipino Studies. That the students called for a Department of Filipino Studies as opposed to a Department of Filipino American Studies is also important. It suggests that the students of PACE were critical of what Filipino studies scholar, Oscar Campomanes, calls the "contributionist" approach to ethnic studies, an approach that seeks Filipino inclusion into a liberal multiculturalist project and fails to critique the "imperialist moorings" of this approach (Campomanes 1997). Much of my personal inspiration to become a scholar-activist derives from the ethnic studies struggle. This struggle also inspired the colleagues with whom I worked.

Case study 1: the critical Filipino and Filipino scholars collective

The events of September 11, 2001 (9/11) had tremendous impacts on Filipinos in the United States as well as the Philippines. In the United States, heightened surveillance of immigrants of color came through the rise of the "homeland security state", which included the expansion of the state's immigration enforcement apparatus and led to increasing immigration apprehensions and deportations. Filipinos were not exempt. At the same time, when US President George W. Bush declared his "global war on terror", he called on allies to join his "coalition of the willing", and the Philippine government of Gloria Macapagal Arroyo was the first in Asia to heed his call. Indeed, the "homeland security state" is the domestic counterpart to the global war on terror: war at home was just as important as war abroad.

Filipinos in the San Francisco Bay Area experienced this in direct ways. For instance, only a few months after the 9/11 attacks, Congress introduced the Aviation Transportation Security Act (ATSA), ostensibly to tighten security at the nation's airports. ATSA federalized the hiring process of airport security screeners and required that they be US citizens. Previously, airport screeners had been hired through private contractors who profited by employing mainly low-wage immigrants. In the San Francisco Bay Area, airport security screeners were predominantly Filipino immigrants. ATSA would effectively put thousands of people out of work.

Under the regime of homeland security (exemplified by the folding of the Immigration and Naturalization Service and the erection of the Department of Homeland Security), which continues to govern immigration enforcement in the United States, the state's technologies of surveillance and its apparatuses of policing immigrants have expanded in unprecedented ways. Not only do they aim at barring the entry of "illegal" immigrants, or merely tracking down "illegal" immigrants who have slipped into the interior of the nation-state. Distinctions between legal and "illegal" immigrants have become practically meaningless as the immigration regime has also expanded the range of activities that would render those who are legal, illegal. In the years following 2001, numerous cases of immigrant apprehensions and deportations racked the Filipino community nationally. In 2002, the so-called Absconder Apprehension Initiative was launched to target immigrants who had overstayed the terms of their visas (i.e. "absconded") and were thus "illegal" and subject for removal. Of those targeted, 12,000 were Filipino. By 2003, that list was revised and 85,000 were estimated to be undocumented.

Filipinos along with many others took to the streets to protest the global war on terror and its domestic counterpart, the homeland security state. Coalitions like the Filipinos for Global Justice Not War played a prominent role in organizing and mobilizing these protests, often leading chants calling, "from the Bay to the Philippines, we've got to stop this US beast". Included among the protestors was a critical mass of Filipino graduate students like myself. Many were pursuing PhDs or doing research at the University of California, Berkeley, as mentioned above. Others were based in universities just outside the San Francisco Bay Area (like the University of California, Santa Cruz). Still, others were relatively new instructors at area colleges and universities. We often marched together under the banner "Filipino Scholars" or "Filipino Educators Against the War". We recognized that we occupied a specific social status in our community as scholars and educators and with that status, a particular responsibility to speak out about the injustices facing our community (indeed humanity at large). We decided to form the Critical Filipino and Filipina Studies Collective (CFFSC) in early 2003.

Our work as a collective was two-pronged: first, it attempted to organize in and from the spaces of academia to address urgent issues of the day and second, it sought to support on-the-ground transnational struggles of Filipinos by leveraging our status and our skills as scholars. This is captured in our working mission statement:

> As an activist-scholar group, the Critical Filipina and Filipino Studies Collective (CFFSC) seeks to organize educators and scholars to interrogate and challenge histories of Western imperialisms (Spanish and US imperialisms), ongoing neocolonial relations in the Philippines, and their relationship to past and present Filipina/o migrations. We claim our roots in the anti-imperialist and anti-fascist struggles of the Filipina/o people from which a critical nationalist Philippine Studies was born and the student movements of the 1960s in the US that gave rise to Ethnic Studies. We propose that the field of Critical Filipina/o Studies focuses on the relationship between the history of Empire and the Filipina/o diaspora.

As interdisciplinary scholars in the fields of Asian American and Pacific Islander studies; Philippine studies; political economy; critical globalization studies; and race, gender, and sexuality studies, the members of CFFSC are dedicated to political activism and social criticism through teaching, research, and scholarship. Our academic work highlights the histories and continuing legacies of Empire for Filipinas/os in the Philippines and in the global diaspora, the struggle of Filipinas/os against the colonial ideology of white supremacy, neocolonial conditions in the Philippines, and global capitalist expansion. CFFSC supports and works with Filipinas/os for Global Justice and FOCUS (Forwarding Opportunities through Community Upliftment and Service) – community and grassroots organizations for people's rights that provide a people's agenda for the advancement of livelihood, dignity, respect, and empowerment for Filipinas and Filipinos in the Philippines, the United States, and in the global diaspora.

It is important to note how we explicitly traced our genealogy to both the ethnic studies struggles of the 1960s and 1970s in the United States as well as the anti-fascist struggles of the 1970s to 1980s in the Philippines. Indeed, while my own personal path to scholar-activism as a US-born Filipino can be traced to the ethnic studies struggles led by groups like PACE, many of my colleagues who were immigrants from the Philippines had come to scholar-activism by way of the anti-fascist movement and organizations like the Congress of Teachers/Educators for Nationalism and Democracy (CONTEND). The CFFSC engaged in numerous interventions in those early years. With respect to organizing in and from our academic spaces to weigh in on urgent issues of the day, we successfully organized to get the Association for Asian American Studies (AAAS), a professional association in which many of us were active, to pass an anti-war resolution. Not only did we encourage our colleagues to condemn the "global war on terror" as it manifested abroad and among working-class Filipino immigrants at home, but we called on our colleagues to engage our students on the issue and to devote scholarship to it as well. We also collectively wrote and generated a petition among other Filipino scholars in the diaspora to condemn specifically the Philippine state's complicity in the "war on terror" and circulated it in the ethnic Filipino media in the United States as well as major media outlets in the Philippines. However, our first collective research project was to chronicle the impacts of post-9/11 policies expanding the government's immigration enforcement apparatus and to highlight the organizing to resist deportations. That research resulted in the publication of the "Resisting Homeland Security" report in 2004.

The report was prompted in large part by a highly publicized case of impending deportation that hit the local Bay Area media. Dale Cuevas, a young man in his early twenties, "came out" as undocumented, making a highly public plea for Filipino community support to try to stop his family's deportation. Dale and his sisters, Donna and Dominique, had arrived in the United States with their parents, Delfin and Lily Cuevas, when they were very young children. The United States had been their home for nearly 20 years by the time they were made aware of their undocumented status. Their parents had entered the country as tourists having fled the Philippines during the martial law period. Since the United States and the Philippines were allies during most of the Marcos dictatorship, Filipinos fleeing the regime could not readily apply for political asylum and often had to resort to other means for entry. For the Cuevas parents, it was on temporary tourist visas. Of course, their intention was to stay in the United States permanently and hence once their tourist visas expired. With enhanced and expanded surveillance technologies, the Cuevas family's visa lapse was discovered and they were slated for deportation. Their family's imminent departure came as a surprise to the Cuevas children who were entirely unaware of their undocumented status. The media appeared to be especially drawn to the Cuevas children's plight as numerous Bay Area and even national news outlets told their story (Chadwick 2004; Estrella 2004).

Members of the CFFSC as well as local Filipino immigrant rights activists, including members of FOCUS (Forwarding Opportunities through Community Upliftment and Service), a Filipino community organization based in the San Jose area, caught wind of the Cuevas family's plight and immediately took steps to contact them to support their deportation fight and to help them galvanize further support from the Filipino community as well as the broader public. The only recourse available to the family to avert deportation was the sponsorship of private legislation by either of California's

US senators, Dianne Feinstein or Barbara Boxer. We all knew that private legislation would not be easily forthcoming, especially in the years following 9/11 when both houses of Congress were generally in support of increased immigration enforcement, but we proceeded to strategize to secure the senators' support anyhow. Members of the CFFSC helped to organize public forums in the Filipino community not only to highlight the Cuevas family's struggle but to link it to Bush's "homeland security" approach to immigration enforcement as well as to historicize it to earlier moves towards more aggressive forms of immigration enforcement that pre-dated 9/11. We spearheaded a signature campaign, specifically focusing on getting official organizational support from Filipino community organizations, other immigrant rights groups, trade unions, and more to demonstrate to Feinstein and Boxer that there was widespread moral support for the Cuevas family among their traditional base. We organized delegations to the senators' offices, then pickets in front of their offices when they failed to receive us. In short, members of the CFFSC worked as community organizers, doing labor that is most often done by immigrant rights' activists and perhaps less the practice of university academics.

At some point, however, we realized that there was some importance in applying our skills as researchers and writers as well as leveraging our status as PhD students to chronicle the impacts of post-9/11 immigration policies on our community as more and more cases of detention and deportation came to our attention due to our on-the-ground organizing work. Community forums we organized to help raise awareness of the Cuevas family's plight emboldened more undocumented Filipinos to come forward with their stories and we helped to create a support group for them. Moreover, after our unsuccessful bid to stop the deportation of the Cuevas family, we believed it would be important to analyze the lessons of the campaign. The readership for the report we wanted to produce was primarily members of the Filipino community in the United States with specific focus on immigrant rights activists. In other words, our intention was not to engage in academic debates in the scholarship on immigration. By partnering with FOCUS, we hoped the report would be a document that could spark political consciousness and organizing in the Filipino diasporic community as well as offer important lessons for more seasoned organizers. Indeed, some members of FOCUS (including myself) were also CFFSC members. Though I can't speak for others, I felt it important to commit myself to FOCUS because much of its work was centered in the communities where I had grown up and I felt that it was important for me to engage in that space even as I was organizing with the CFFSC.

The research and writing of the report involved a smaller subset of the CFFSC in collaboration with members of FOCUS and members of organizations linked with the National Alliance for Filipino Concerns (NAFCON). Among the scholars, we were roughly divided between scholars trained in the social sciences and the humanities. Some of us had recently completed our PhDs, others were graduate students at the beginning of their PhD studies. Upon the report's completion, it was circulated through the NAFCON network as well as our own. Though it's difficult to assess the impact of the report, we know it has been widely cited and it continues to be a political education piece for NAFCON organizations, nearly 15 years since its original publication.

CFFSC exists to this day but one challenge we have experienced is that nearly all of the original members have not sustained their work in the collective. This is mainly due to the fact that once we were all complete with graduate work, we secured jobs as tenure-track faculty all around the country. We had few opportunities to meet on a regular basis to coordinate our efforts. Also, we faced the challenge of trying to secure tenure, a difficult feat for scholars of color who do work on the topics we do (race, empire, diaspora). Indeed, our very existence as a group, inasmuch as it was formed in response to the immediate post-9/11 political moment, was also rooted in struggles to fight for the hiring and tenure of Filipino studies scholars on the UC Berkeley campus. We all realized that tenure was no guarantee for any of us and that it would require a singular focus.

After many years away from the work of the CFFSC, those original members would remain in the collective's ambit but not central to its functions. I alone remained to carry on the work of the CFFSC alongside graduate students I was mentoring. It is beyond the scope of this chapter, but it is important to note how challenging it can be to maintain scholar-activist, politically engaged work within the context of the neoliberal university without a community of like-minded scholars in close proximity to support that work. Academic work is inherently isolating. The CFFSC does offer a model of what can be possible for radical scholars and the need for us to continue to create spaces of collectivity to devise new forms of academic praxis or what Moten and Harney (2004) call the "undercommons".

Case study 2: the CARE Project

A second project discussed here is one done in collaboration with my former student, now colleague, Valerie Francisco and in partnership with the Filipino Community Center (FCC) of San Francisco. Called the "CARE Project", it was aimed at documenting San Francisco-based Filipino low-wage and undocumented caregivers' living and employment experiences. However, as Francisco describes it, the CARE Project's "ultimate objective was to use community-based research to develop a core of caregiver-organizers and migrant leaders" (Francisco 2016: 214). The FCC, located in a San Francisco neighborhood – the Excelsior, has a high concentration of Filipinos. Immigrants from the Filipinos often stop in to the FCC seeking assistance on housing, health, legal and employment issues, among others. The issue of wage theft among caregivers became an especially significant matter for FCC as several individuals came to the center seeking support in pursuing lawsuits against their former employers. Together with non-profit legal organizations, the FCC managed to win back thousands of dollars of back wages for several caregivers. Organizers with the FCC realized, however, that litigation would only be effective for a small handful of people. They believed that helping support the building of a migrant worker-led organization would offer better assurances that migrant workers' rights would not be violated. The organization could ensure that migrants understood their rights and collectively press for the protection of their rights at the local, state, and national levels. Indeed, successful campaigns for the protection of domestic workers' rights in other states (and internationally) as well as a growing state-wide struggle for a California domestic workers' "bill of rights" that would also extend to caregivers, bolstered FCC staff resolve to support caregivers' self-organization. Francisco's previous experience in conducting participatory action research for her dissertation (now book) among Filipina domestic workers in New York offered a model of good practice that FCC staff believed could be replicated in San Francisco (Francisco-Menchavez 2018). Francisco's research was successful in helping to expand the membership of a Filipina domestic workers' organization based in Queens and it was hoped that under our joint leadership, a migrant workers' organization – with caregivers at the helm – could be built in the Excelsior.

The initial cohort of caregiver-researchers-organizers recruited to participate in the CARE Project included 15 migrant workers – mostly caregivers – who underwent a nearly six-month training process. These migrant workers were individuals who were already FCC regulars including the few who had successfully won (or were actively pursuing) wage-theft claims as well as others who participated in other FCC social activities. They would later take a lead in helping collect 50 interviews of their peers and establishing their own organization. Before I discuss the CARE Project in more detail, however, I think it's important to note how the work of the CFFSC in the early 2000s connects with the work in the CARE Project in the 2010s.

Francisco was an undergraduate student at San Francisco State University when we first met. In fact, we met in connection with the immigrant rights organizing I was part of through the CFFSC and FOCUS. She was a student leader in PACE at San Francisco State University (SFSU), at the same time, she was getting trained in participant action research (PAR) by a faculty member in the Department of Sociology there. However, in the CFFSC's work, she saw a different model for community-engaged research and sought mentorship – my own – in her development as a young scholar-activist. Though she was not able to study directly with me at Rutgers University (where I worked immediately after graduate school), she went on to study at the City University of New York (CUNY) graduate school and I was able to serve on her dissertation committee. Her dissertation was a PAR project with a Filipina domestic workers organization in Queens, New York. Throughout graduate school, meanwhile, Francisco helped to maintain the work of the CFFSC, constituting the second generation of that organization. Francisco's work has thus been deeply shaped by multiple genealogies of Filipino scholar-activism from her membership in PACE at SFSU to her mentorship by me as a founder of the CFFSC.

Francisco has already written about our work in the CARE Project, particularly with respect to the ways PAR helped support migrant worker organizing and leadership development among the Filipino caregivers connected to the FCC. She discusses, for example, the ways we used "theater of the oppressed" games to develop the interpersonal dynamics among caregivers. Even though the objective of organizing is to mobilize individuals to come together collectively to address shared issues and struggles, the "glue" that holds them together is the sense of connection and community they feel in a group. The games helped build connection and trust among the core group of worker-researcher-organizers. At the same time, the games were designed to help demonstrate how the research process works (Francisco 2016).

What I want to highlight in this chapter, however, are two points with respect to the university rather than the community side of community-engaged (university-linked) research. First, inasmuch as our (Dr. Francisco's and my) commitment was to centering and validating the knowledges of the caregivers themselves as opposed to our own expert knowledges as academics, the significance of the university imprimatur on the CARE Project is something we could not take for granted. From the very start, we were committed to decentering our roles as academics. This was the objective, for example, of the very first training module we conducted, which was entitled "Right to Research". The opening activity of the module was called, "The Doctor Is In". On a large butcher paper with a drawing of Albert Einstein, we asked participants to write or draw out answers to the questions: "Who holds knowledge?" "Where does knowledge come from?" "How do people collect data?" The point of the exercise was to demonstrate how too often people believe that knowledge is only in the hands of and can only be produced by the highly educated or experts. Instead, we encouraged them to see that they are the best people to produce knowledge about the conditions they and other members of our community face; they are the best people to determine what sorts of questions need to be asked and they should ultimately determine what kinds of action ought to be pursued given the information their knowledge (i.e. research) produces.

If our aim in this module was to challenge the hierarchies between researcher and researched or "the town-gown" divide, the hierarchies were inescapable and in fact, paradoxically enough, it is very likely what helped support worker organizing and thus worker empowerment. I would argue that it was precisely the prestige that our university affiliations bestowed on the CARE Project that helped pique initial interest and more importantly workers' dedication to the project. The CARE Project required a high level of commitment.

We were clear from the onset with the core group we gathered that participation would require up to six months of their time. Though we discussed workers' capacity for meeting on a regular basis and used their schedules to help determine the frequency and duration of the meetings, we emphasized, nevertheless, that the project was going to take time. We also assured the workers that they would be "rewarded" for their commitment by concluding the project with a "graduation ceremony" where they could share their research findings with the broader community. Workers' commitment was certainly due to their desire to organize but I think the opportunity to affiliate with a university-led project and to gain skills sets from university professors were also important incentives. Many of the workers had no college degrees. Among those who had secured college or university degrees in the Philippines, they had been working for a long time as low-skilled and low-status workers and appreciated the chance to be intellectually challenged by participating in a research project. Certainly, many were also drawn to the idea of gaining "official" certification (after all, project participants would be participating in a graduation ceremony and awarded certificates of participation) that they might be able to include in their resumes and use for jobs outside of care labor. Finally, participation in the CARE Project allowed workers to be linked to prestigious institutions (which colleges and universities are often considered).

Though I cannot verify my observations (I have never formally asked the workers what they felt about the CARE Project's university connections), I can attest to the ways workers would underscore my role as the "doctora" or "professora" in the Project or their references to me as a "mentor" despite our attempts at diminishing or at least de-emphasizing and decentering our university status and affiliations. Over the course of several months of working on the CARE Project, however, it became clear that the social relationships that workers built with one another is what would keep them coming back every week for six months, but I would argue that the CARE Project's university connections played an important and unique role in drawing them together and getting them to initially commit to the Project.

The second point I want to underscore about our work in the CARE Project – and this was also true for the CFFSC report – is that the research was not meant to advance scholarly knowledge or to inform political debates and conversations that take place largely in the space of academic journals or other academic publishing platforms. For all of its attempts at democratizing knowledge production, I would argue that PAR is still something that is driven primarily by scholars and their (university-centered) imperatives. Alternatively, the research process for the CARE Project (and the research outcome in the CFFSC report) was intended primarily to help initiate and bolster social justice organizing in the Filipino diasporic community. PAR was seen as a tool for organizing, not for data collection. Though Francisco and I would later publish a few pieces based on the interviews collected though the CARE Project, it was not necessarily our aim in working on the project to publish the data to advance the scholarship on immigrant working-class communities. Indeed, until now, nearly seven years since the Project commenced, we have yet to fully transcribe the interviews because while the transcriptions might have been important for us as researchers, it was less urgent for the organizing.

In many ways, the research process was more important than the research findings. The primary objective of the project was to use the research process as a way to consolidate a core of caregiver-organizer leaders. We provided the caregiver-organizer-researcher core with training and skills to carry out research of the issues facing their peers. We hoped that the caregivers (both the organizer-researchers and their "subjects") would be politicized by the process as they gained perspective on their shared struggles with others. Through the process of research, organizer-researchers would, moreover, be able to build contacts among caregivers and form their own organization. This objective was met with the launching of Migrante San Francisco (Excelsior) in 2013. Migrante San Francisco was the very first chapter of Migrante International to be established in the United States. Migrante International is a transnational Filipino migrant workers alliance that is affiliated with a broader alliance of Philippine militant left organizations, BAYAN (Bagong Alyansang Makabayan).

However, I think that because we didn't complete the transcriptions and thus do further analytical work on the research findings (work we are well-trained to do as academics), we may have failed to help shape the future trajectories of Migrante San Francisco's organizing efforts. Though the research process was successful in getting the migrants together and spurring them to form Migrante, processing all of the data and discussing our findings with the workers – in short, doing our jobs as academics – might well have helped Migrante expand its organizing efforts as well as better participate in different policy reform efforts.

Concluding reflections

The case studies I offer in this chapter are examples of two forms of scholar-activism where research and/or writing – the key tasks of all academics, even when they think of themselves as "politically engaged researchers" – are merely tactics aimed at advancing organizing among the dispossessed, specifically low-wage, and undocumented migrant Filipino workers. Academic publishing, which is, I would contend the ultimate aim of research that draws on PAR methods, was secondary if not irrelevant to the process.

The work of CFFSC illustrates a way that scholars can partner with dispossessed communities by using their research and writing skills to lift up the work of movements but in a non-academic venue to ensure more immediate circulation. Moreover, though discussed only briefly here, the CFFSC, in its work at organizing within academic spaces, such as their/our work in securing the passage of an anti-war resolution by the Association for Asian American Studies (then later leading the passage of a Boycott, Divestment and Sanctions resolution making the Association the very first US academic association to do so), illustrates a form of scholar-activism through which we can create an "undercommons" in the university and academic institutions. The CARE Project, meanwhile, illustrates how scholars can partner with dispossessed communities to use the research process not simply to advance academic understandings of their issues and concerns but rather to use the process as a means of consciousness-raising among migrant workers and helping them to come together collectively.

It is important to underscore the very distinctive genealogy that informs the scholar-activism that I describe here. My formal training is as a sociologist so it seems appropriate to start there to highlight a different iteration of "politically engaged scholarship". Michael Burawoy, faculty member in the Department of Sociology at the University of California, Berkeley, spelled out his definition of "public sociology" during his presidential address to the American Sociological Association in 2004. For Burawoy, public sociology broadly defined, "brings sociology in conversation with publics, understood as people who are themselves involved in the conversation" (Burawoy 2005: 7). His call for public sociology is in response to the threats that neoliberal globalization poses not only for scholars but for our world at large. It is sociology's role, for Burawoy to defend the "interests of humanity" (Burawoy 2005: 24).

Burawoy's intervention is important in several ways. On a basic level, Burawoy's intervention was personally significant for me as it affirmed the work I was doing during the course of my graduate studies. Interestingly, I was a student of Burawoy's (he was my dissertation chair). Though a crucial reason for why I was compelled to work with him was precisely for his own track-record of politically engaged scholarship – Burawoy had long-worked in support of the anti-apartheid struggle in South Africa – we never discussed "politically engaged scholarship" or "public sociology" in any formal way. Indeed, I was rather oblique when it came to discussing my activist work with him. I kept our discussions strictly professional as if my research questions were merely academic, informed only by debates and conversations in the field, when in fact they were very much driven by my embeddedness in and commitment to Philippine left diasporic politics. Burawoy's intervention was also important for occurring at a particular historical moment. It was a year after the war in Iraq had been declared by President George W. Bush in the early period of the long, not-yet-concluded "global war on terror". The San Francisco Bay Area had been awash with waves of anti-war protests and new forms of activism, including the formation of the CFFSC, of which I was a founding member. It was a crucial time for all scholars – not just sociologists – to critically reflect on our role in society and to be decisive about positioning in defense of humanity.

Part of my purpose in noting the different genealogies and iterations of "politically engaged research" – one located in a traditional discipline like sociology and another located in the fight for ethnic studies – is to center ethnic studies as a field of study. Over the course of its now 50-year history, ethnic studies continues to be attacked and maligned, as well as undermined and devalued in the university and beyond.[3] Interestingly, while the field has had to fight to survive, many universities have increasingly embraced "community-engaged research" as it has become a new metric by which they can be measured and valued.[4] However, a decolonized community-engaged research agenda – of which ethnic studies is part – is especially vital for migration scholar-activists. As ethnic studies scholars Ramon Grosfoguel, Laura Oso, and Anastasia

Christou argue, "Knowledge is not detached from 'racial/colonial domination'". Hence to decolonize migration scholarship, requires the centering of critical scholarship and thinking "from below". According to Grosfoguel, Oso, and Christou:

Critical decolonial thinking is the epistemology that emerges in colonial situations where the hegemonic perspective is subverted by the cosmologies, languages, and epistemologies of the subaltern. It is a new form of epistemology that emerges in the "in-betweenness" of two languages, two cosmologies, two epistemologies, and in which the subversion of hegemonic knowledge is produced from the subaltern's geopolitics of knowledge. There are minority intellectuals/ activists who are "colonial racial/subjects of empire" and migrant intellectuals who are "colonial immigrants" and who are implicated in the production of critical decolonial thinking inside metropolitan centers. (Grosfoguel, Oso, and Christou 2014: 647)

The approaches to research and writing discussed here forms the basis of an emergent research agenda for Filipino scholars in the diaspora who, like me, are committed to directing our work towards supporting and uplifting the on-the-ground struggles of our people around the world. Given the history of higher education in both the Philippines and key institutions in the United States and its role in the colonial project, it becomes important for Filipino scholars in the United States, in many cases the descendants of Filipino immigrants and migrant workers, to deploy a decolonized approach to migration scholarship.

Revisiting the work we did through the CFFSC and the CARE Project is especially important now in light of the rise of the Trump administration to highlight one mode of academic intervention that may prove to be productive in this political moment. These cases moreover offer an alternative to public intellectualism that today is done primarily through social media and on an individualist basis.

Notes

1 See http://welgadigitalarchive. omeka.net/ for primary source material on Filipinos' contributions to the farmworker movement.

2 www.pacesfsu1967.com/aboutus.

3 http://articles.latimes.com/2012/ feb/20/opinion/la-oe-rodriguez-ethnic-studies-20120220.

4 www.carnegiefoundation.org/ newsroom/news-releases/carnegie-selects-colleges-universities-2015-community-engagement-classification/.

References

Baldoz, R. (2015). *The Third Asiatic Invasion: Empire and Migration in Filipino America, 1898–1946*. Quezon City: University of the Philippines Press.

Bulosan, C. (2014). *America Is in the Heart: A Personal History*. Seattle, WA: University of Washington Press.

Burawoy, M. (2005). For public sociology. *American Sociological Review*, 70(4): 4–28.

Campomanes, O.V. (1997). New formations of Asian American studies and the question of U.S. imperialism. *Positions: East Asia Cultures Critique*, 5(2): 523–550.

Chadwick, C. (2004). Siblings raised in U.S. threatened with deportation. Available at: www.npr.org/templates/story/story.php?storyId=1639013 [Accessed September 1, 2018].

Estrella, C. (2004). Adult kids face deportation to land they don't know after 19 years in U.S., Filipino parents nearly out of legal options. Available at: www.sfgate.com/bayarea/article/Adult-kids-face-deportation-to-land-they-don-t-2813069.php [Accessed September 1, 2018].

Francisco, V. (2016). Migrante, Abante: building Filipino migrant worker leadership through participatory action research. In A.A. Choudry and M. Hlatshwayo (Eds.), *Just Work?: Migrant Workers' Struggles Today*. London: Pluto Press.

Francisco, V. and Rodriguez, R.M. (2014). Globalization and undocumented migration: examining the politics of emigration. In L.A. Lorentzen (Ed.), *Hidden Lives and Human Rights: Understanding the Controversies and Tragedies of Undocumented Immigration*. Santa Barbara, CA: Praeger.

Francisco-Menchavez, V. (2018). *The Labor of Care: Filipina Migrants and Transnational Families in the Digital Age*. Urbana, IL: University of Illinois Press.

Grosfoguel, R., Oso, L., and Christou, A. (2014). "Racism", intersectionality and migration studies: framing some theoretical reflections. *Identities*, 22(6): 635–652.

Mabalon, D.B. (2013). *Little Manila Is in the Heart: The Making of the Filipina/o American Community in Stockton, California*. Durham, NC: Duke University Press.

Moten, F. and Harney, S. (2004). The university and the undercommons: seven theses. *Social Text*, 22(2): 101–115.

Okihiro, G.Y. (2016). *Third World Studies: Theorizing Liberation*. Durham, NC: Duke University Press.

Rodriguez, R.M. (2010). *Migrants for Export: How the Philippine State Brokers Labor to the World*. Minneapolis, MN: University of Minnesota Press.

San Juan, E. (1991). Multiculturalism vs. hegemony: ethnic studies, Asian Americans, and US racial politics. *Massachusetts Review*, 32(3): 467–478.

12 | THE BHOPAL STRUGGLE AND NEOLIBERAL RESTRUCTURING: RESEARCH, POLITICAL ENGAGEMENT, AND THE URBAN POOR

Eurig Scandrett and Shalini Sharma

The Bhopal gas disaster in historical context

Union Carbide India Limited, a subsidiary of the US transnational Union Carbide (UC) Corporation, established an insecticide factory in Bhopal in 1969 at around the same time as the Communist Party of India (Marxist-Leninist) launched its armed struggle in the aftermath of the bloody conflict of Naxalbari, an insurgency that continues to this day.

In 1975, the year Indira Gandhi suspended constitutional rights and declared a State of Emergency in India, UC obtained from Madhya Pradesh state regulators, the relevant permissions to adapt its factory for the manufacture of ingredients for the insecticide, including storage of the highly toxic methyl isocyanate, in contravention of regulations (Hanna, Morehouse, and Sarangi 2004).

In 1984, the same year in which Indira Gandhi was assassinated, an explosion at the UC factory caused 40 tonnes of methyl isocyanate to leak into the environment, killing and maiming thousands of people.

The correspondence of these dates is coincidental in any causative sense, but gives an indication of the political context in which the world's most devastating environmental disaster occurred.

The period in question can be understood as an interregnum, in which Nehru's project of state-planned, rational economic development based on democracy, secularism, and socialism had almost certainly been defeated, yet the new neoliberal economic regime driven by inward private investment and governed by repressive Hindu fundamentalism had yet to be born (Corbridge and Harriss 2000). An interregnum is a time when "the old is dying and the new cannot be born; in this interregnum a great variety of morbid symptoms appear" (Gramsci in Hoare and Smith 1971: 276), when factions and interests take advantage of opportunities afforded by the collapse of the dominant order, as new, as yet unknown alliances form. The Bhopal gas disaster may be understood in this context: a vacuum filled with economic opportunity by remote corporate board members in the United States; as a foretaste of the emerging neoliberal regime with its dispossession of livelihoods; but also as a place where new forms of resistance to these trajectories emerge, are devised, and experimented with. The interaction between intellectuals of the urban poor and radical intellectuals through such mechanisms as participatory action research is an example of this.

Chatterjee (2008) describes the early post-independence development of Indian capitalism as that of a "passive revolution". The British colonial administration's policies of governance created or reinforced structures of landowner power and cellular social organization, and thereby constrained the development of an independent Indian bourgeoisie. By independence, the industrial bourgeoisie were in the ascendancy, but dependent on an alliance with the landowning class in order to impose the conditions necessary for the development of capitalism.

The green revolution in the 1960s employed large state subsidies to increase agricultural production and stimulate agrochemical production in India. This created highly uneven rural development favoring larger landowning interests and squeezing small farmers. It led both to an increase in the power of a rural landowning class and a general movement of people from the villages into urban areas seeking casual labor. By the 1970s, the city of Bhopal's growth was fed by increasing numbers of poor migrants seeking work and settling in informal *bastis* (settlements) in the industrial north of the city around the UC factory, which produced insecticides for the agricultural industry.

The seeds of the world's worst industrial disaster were planted in the fertile soil of a major shift in class alliances, in which competing interests were taking advantage of a declining post-colonial settlement. The main beneficiary of the disaster was the transnational capitalist class, whose opportunistic investment decisions have taken advantage of state subsidy for profit making and weaknesses in systems of state protection. The victims were the urban poor, dispossessed from the villages and attracted by the prospect of industrial employment. The Bhopal industrial disaster can be understood as a herald of neoliberalism in India – declining state regulation or support, expanding opportunities for capital invest-ment, dispossession of the most marginalized, minimal corporate accountability, and maximum profit.

Post-colonial neoliberalism is accompanied by what Harvey (2006) has called "accumulation by dispossession", which consti-tutes a logic of expropriation of resources from the poorest and most marginal to the advantage of the rich and powerful who own the means of expropriation. Distinctively, those exploited by neoliberal-ism are not just the workers in profiteering industries, but also all those whose livelihoods, environments, health, bodies, futures can be expropriated for profit. This leads to a more diverse and dis-connected class of victim compared with industrial capitalism, and consequently a more fragmented class of resistance. As global neo-liberalism takes its course, the organic intellectuals of dispossessed classes seek to interpret their conditions, explore the opportunities for allies, and develop mechanisms of opposition. Politically engaged research such as activist ethnography has an opportunity to engage in this historical process of the emergence of an intellectual function from among the class of the dispossessed, and has played a role in the Bhopal movement since its beginning.

The survivors' movement and its campaigns

The survivors of the Bhopal disaster and their supporters have sustained an over-30-year campaign for justice including for com-pensation, economic rehabilitation, environmental remediation, health care, and punitive, exemplary sanctions against UC and Dow Chemical, who acquired the company in 2001. Using a range of legal challenges, industrial dispute, street protests, direct action, civil disobedience, creative publicity stunts, and alternative provision, the movement has demonstrated a considerable flexibility and ingenu-ity against formidable enemies (Bhopal Survivors' Movement Study 2009). "Survivors" is a term used for those who were alive in 1984 and faced the gas leak; children who were born after the gas leak and inherit the affects; and people affected by groundwater contami-nation who grew up in the movement. At the time of writing, the main sections of the survivors' movement are the Bhopal Gas Peedit Mahila Udyog Sangathan (BGPMUS), with roots in a women's trade union, the communist-affiliated Bhopal Gas Peedit Sangharsh Sahayog Samiti, and the International Campaign for Justice in Bhopal (ICJB), an alliance of five local organisations (Bhopal Gas

Peedit Mahila Stationary Karmchari Sangh – a women's trade union, Bhopal Gas Peedit Mahila Purush Sangharsh Morcha – a community rights group, Bhopal Gas Peedit Nirashrit Pension Bhogi Sangharsh Morcha – working for welfare of the destitute, Children Against Dow-Carbide, and Bhopal Group for Information and Action), with other national and international solidarity groups.

In the 1981 census, literacy rates in Madhya Pradesh were 34 percent (19 percent for women), among the lowest in India, with the non-literate sector primarily among the poorest, including those living in north Bhopal around the UC factory. Many of the Bhopal survivors are not literate and have received no or minimal formal education. While some of those in leadership roles tend to be better educated and in some cases outsiders who came to Bhopal in 1984 and stayed, the vast majority of activists, including many leaders, organic intellectuals, and much of the mobilizing cadres and rank and file activists are local gas- and water-affected people, mostly poor, village born, (formally) uneducated women.

Objectively, with respect to the movement's primary aims, it has yet to achieve significant success. Legal cases for compensation have failed repeatedly: UC Corporation claimed that the settlement (without liability) reached with the Indian government in 1989 for US$470 million, partially disbursed according to questionable criteria of victimhood, annuls any requirement for compensation. The Bhopal Memorial Hospital has been plagued by corruption, and health care has consistently been inadequate.

Economic rehabilitation initiatives were established soon after the disaster by state and non-profit enterprises. In a long-running campaign, Bhopal Gas Peedit Mahila Stationery Karmchari Sangh (Women's Stationery Workers' Union) eventually won an employment tribunal case which determined that the wages paid to workers in the stationery production workshop established for economic rehabilitation was unlawfully below the wages paid at similar state employment facilities. The factory site remains contaminated, polluting local water courses, and attempts by survivors' groups to involve international oversight to any rehabilitation of the area have so far been unsuccessful. Chairman and chief executive of UC at the time, Warren Anderson, who was briefly arrested while in India after the disaster but released after government intervention, died in 2014 after the United States repeatedly refused to honor extradition requests from Indian courts.

While there is no doubt that there has been benefit to survivors from the campaign, there is no question that, at the time of writing, it has fallen well short of the demands of the movement for universal benefit to the survivors, and the major beneficiary has been the corporation. Indeed, the Bhopal story has been a textbook case of corporate avoidance of liability. UC immediately dissolved and exported all Indian assets that could be accessed by Indian courts; reached a settlement with the Indian government in 1989 without assent from the survivors; was absorbed into Dow Chemical in 2001, which merged with DuPont in 2017. The corporate veil has been used effectively to obfuscate any legal sanction against those responsible for making boardroom decisions which led to the disaster, and has helped to neutralize any legislative barriers to accelerating inward investment in India's growing economic boom.

There have also been material achievements of the movement. The provision of piped water to neighborhoods dependent on groundwater contaminated with toxins from the factory site was the result of a concerted local campaign. However, while the core campaign objectives appear no nearer to being achieved, there is a strong case that the cultural-epistemological achievements of the movement as a locus of cognitive resistance to the wider trends towards neoliberal orthodoxy have been significant. This constitutes far more than the "plucky underdogs" fearlessly standing up to global corporate power and state complicity (although this trope certainly has been unapologetically employed). Rather, the survivors constitute an analytical and epistemological resistance to global neoliberalism, which constitutes elements of the development of an emergent organic intellectual function. This generalization from the concrete specificity of the movement, has provided a reservoir of collective good sense as a resistance to the prevailing common sense of neoliberal Hindu authoritarianism. As Amir, the 17-year-old activist in Children Against Dow Carbide stated in 2008:

> What has happened has happened and we can't change that but we will keep on fighting. We want to stop another Bhopal happening elsewhere. Even when we get justice we will keep fighting so that no company feels it can do what Union Carbide did, and nobody else will have to experience what Bhopal has. (Bhopal Survivors' Movement Study 2009: 216)

Participatory and action research of various kinds have been present in the movement since its beginning, including lay autopsy, people's health action, healthcare assessments, and treatments incorporating medical traditions based on diverse epistemologies, drawing on lay expertise as well as international advocacy and solidarity research accountable to the survivors' movement (Fortun 2001; Dinham and Sarangi 2002). A considerable amount of research has been based on relationships of equality between survivor-activists and activist-intellectuals, among whom the figure of Satinath Sarangi is central (Sarangi 1996; Dinham and Sarangi 2002). The activist ethnography described in this paper should be seen as part of this tradition.

Activist research with the survivors' movement

The movement includes many, including in leadership roles, with very little education and limited functional literacy, often displaying considerable communicative and analytical literacy in political praxis. For activist researchers, this is an important consideration which requires the foregrounding of oral narratives and non-literate symbolism in movement-relevant research (Bevington and Dixon 2005).

The Bhopal Survivors' Movement Study (BSMS) sought to engage with the analytical and strategic approaches of the movement, especially its non-literate activists, in order to contribute to its documentation and to reflect back to the movement itself, while the Remember Bhopal project transformed the memories and moral witness of the survivors in the form of a co-curated museum. Both projects drew on oral narratives and methodological insights from Freire's *Pedagogy of the Oppressed* (1972) as a mechanism for generating a dialogue between the knowledge of Bhopal survivors engaged in struggle and the theoretical resources of researchers committed to solidarity with the movement.

At the heart of Freire's pedagogy, and the participatory action research methods derived from it, lies a dialectical conception of knowledge. Knowledge is generated and becomes critical consciousness through its own dialectical tensions – between concrete and abstract, specific and general, practice and theory, action and reflection, or the "word" and the "world". In Freire's methods, this can be stimulated through "the coding of an existential situation" and collective engagement in a process of decoding: "the critical analysis of the coded situation" (Freire 1972: 77). Codes, in the forms of artifacts and narratives, play an important role in both the Bhopal Survivors' Movement Study and Remember Bhopal Museum.

The Bhopal Survivors' Movement Study

The Bhopal Survivors' Movement Study (BSMS) 2006–2009 made use of a blend of ethnography with participatory action and activist research as a means of conducting research in solidarity with the survivors. The research team comprised two academics, Eurig Scandrett and Suroopa Mukherjee and two research assistants, Dharmesh Shah and Tarunima Sen, all of whom had some involvement with solidarity action with the Bhopal movement. The team sought to capture and build on the survivors' own analytical understanding of their social context developed through praxis. In order to ensure that literate and non-literate activists could all contribute to the analysis, visual and oral methods were employed in preference to textual.

Ethnography generally employs methods of participatory observation and interviews. In this study, researchers were engaged in the "participatory observation" of solidarity activism, including participating in protests, planning meetings, and public events alongside the survivors and also accountable solidarity activities away from the survivors in India or Britain. In this process, researchers reflected critically on their own involvement – as non-Bhopalis, literate, educated, and relatively affluent (and in the case of the principal investigator [Scandrett], white, British, and non-Hindi speaking).

The research team needed an interview method in which data could be analyzed by interviewees alongside interviewers without reliance on textual literacy. Video dialogue is a participatory action method based on Freire's methodology. The research assistants were embedded within the communities of north Bhopal close to the remnants of the factory site, while the academics made regular visits. The researchers' experience of solidarity work with the Bhopal struggle and other social and environmental justice campaigns provided a knowledge base from which to build, and also a bank of goodwill with which to build trust. The research team agreed that we could not be neutral in the face of a struggle for justice between the survivors and their powerful adversaries.

Time was spent meeting survivors involved with the movement, building trust with the various factions, gatekeepers, and individuals, and learning about key issues and concerns in the community. During this process, opportunities for codes were identified in preparation for the interview phase, which included photographs, newspapers, campaign materials, or personal effects of survivors or deceased loved ones. These artifacts were provided by the survivors during the informal process of "coding" and subsequently used both as prompts to stimulate discussion in the interviews and as "codes" to represent elements of the social context for decoding.

Thirty-eight semi-structured interviews were conducted by the research assistants focusing on the dynamics of the movement process and the learning, knowledge generation, and analytical development occurring through engagement with the movement. The interviews were videoed from a static video camera behind the interviewer. The videos of the interviews were then copied to disk and given to the interviewee. As data from interviews accumulated, a summary of the interviews was translated into English and discussed by the research team, who identified themes that were arising across interviews. Themes were inductively selected that were "generative" in Freire's sense of having the potential for further, deeper, and more critical analysis, including deriving abstractions from concrete situations: what critical analytical tools are being used by the Bhopal activists to interpret their social context? Such generative themes are largely implicit in survivors' narratives, and their generative capacity tested as they were used in a second round of interviews referred to as "video diaries".

These follow-up interviews took place with around half of the initial interviewees, usually between one and three months after the first. This period was regarded as close enough for events not to have changed perceptions significantly, yet sufficiently distant to allow interviewees to come to the material fresh. In the "video diary" interview, the interviewer and interviewee jointly watched the video of the first interview, decoding it and extending the opportunity for critical analysis. Utilizing Freire's methods of decoding, the interviewers used the generative themes that had emerged from across the movement to provide progressively more analytical questions on the issues raised in the first interview. Both the initial interviews and the video diaries were subsequently transcribed for further thematic and discourse analysis by researchers. In this way, interviewees, including those without literacy skills, provided critical analysis of content emerging from across the research.

As generative themes were revised and explored through the video dialogue method, they were presented in focus groups with survivor-activists for further analysis. This involved visuals in the form of sketched pictures or PowerPoint designs, which served to shift attention away from speakers towards content, and participants could be prompted to imagine alternative ways in which these ideas could be presented. Through these collective processes, meta-analytical themes derived from academic (literature-based) theory were re-interpreted back to the survivors collectively who assessed, used, or selected from them for the purposes of their own meaning-making and reflective analysis.

Thematic analysis therefore followed through several stages of iteration and included the survivors in identifying, exploring, and constructing themes drawing on their own analytical resources and learning new ones for the benefit of reflection on their movement. The emphasis was on participation in dialogue, on the dialogical construction of knowledge in the context of social struggle. It was educational as well as research – new knowledge was generated, assessed, and applied by researchers and participants alike for the primary benefit of the movement's struggle for justice.

Scandrett and Mukherjee (2011) and Mukherjee et al. (2011) argue that through a dynamic process of leadership by organic intellectuals and "discursive encounters" (Baviskar 2005) with other movements, the principal movement groups adopt parallel and somewhat complementary analytical approaches which broaden the influence of the movement. At the time of the research, Bhopal Gas Peedit Mahila Udyog Sangathan identified itself as a poor-people's movement, focused on economic rehabilitation and compensation, and built primary alliances with landless, Dalit, Adivasi, and other poor-people's movements in India. On the other hand, the International Campaign for Justice in Bhopal (ICJB) identified itself more as an environmental justice movement, focused on health impacts and socio-economic rehabilitation; remediation of environmental pollution, contaminated land and water; and built primary alliances with environmental justice movements, NGOs, and international environmental rights groups. Another group, the

Gas Peedit Nirashrit Pension-Bhogi Sangharsh Morcha, which primarily organizes among the most destitute – the elderly and disabled – adopted a social welfare frame. It was independent at the time of the research but has since joined the ICJB alliance.

Moving beyond the leadership is a tier of mobilizers who interpret the knowledge for a wider group of rank and file and peripheral participants. While narratives around knowledge in initial interviews often focus on the interviewee's position in a hierarchy – claiming status in the movement because of, or despite educational achievement – this can be more reflective in video diary interviews as the complexity of the roles that people play in the movement is analyzed. Lave and Wenger (1991) have emphasized the important role of legitimate peripheral participation to a movement, and the learning processes which enable such transition into movement activists. While the distinction between responsibilities is not clearly defined or exclusive, there is a sense of division of labor within the movement on the basis of knowledge. Noting Gramsci's insight that "All men [*sic*] are intellectuals ... but not all men have in society the function of intellectuals" (Gramsci in Hoare and Smith 1971: 9), this research has facilitated a critically nuanced analysis of and by the organic intellectuals of the movement to contribute to their collective self-reflection.

Researchers' participation in solidarity with the movement was a core component of the activist ethnography of the research, but also sustained after the data collection was completed, thereby contributing to the dialogical relationship initiated through the BSMS. Following a decision of the ICJB's annual strategy meeting, two survivors who had participated in the research undertook a tour of Britain and Ireland, organized by Scandrett in conjunction with the Bhopal Medical Appeal and others, during 2012, the year of the London Olympics, of which Dow was a sponsor. The tourists were: 18-year-old Safreen Khan from Children Against Dow Carbide, a daughter of gas-affected activists and herself affected by water contamination, she went on to work with the Remember Bhopal Museum, and Balkrishna Namdev, a gas-affected former union organizer who works with Gas Peedit Nirashrit Pension-Bhogi Sangharsh Morcha, which had recently joined the ICJB coalition. A visit to the Scottish Trade Union Congress led to a raft of conference motions and a solidarity delegation of Scottish trade union activists (including Scandrett from the University and College Union) to Bhopal for the 30th anniversary in 2014. A delegation comprising 11 rank and file trade union activists representing seven trade unions and union organizations marched alongside the survivors, expressed solidarity alongside activists from other dispossessed communities across India and a few other international environmental justice campaigners, and met with Indian trade union activists in Mumbai and Delhi as well as Bhopal, mobilized around the common commitment around the environmental and occupational protection of workers and the dispossessed.

Collective curation of memory in the Remember Bhopal Trust and Museum

The necessity to develop an enduring, community-curated, accessible, three-dimensional public space for preserving the memories of Bhopal triggered the Remember Bhopal Museum Project (RBM) in 2010. Such collective memory curation was required to counter the state–corporation collusion that sought to sanitize the narratives of injustice. Survivors wished to assert their moral right to memory. They also wished to demonstrate that they are perfectly capable of creating a museum template that proves how.

Indeed, having been betrayed several times by their own government, the survivors were committed to protect their memory against any appropriation by the state–corporate nexus. From shrines created by individuals in memory of loved ones to community-led projects such as the *Statue of Mother and Child* and the "Yaad-e-Haadsa/Memories of a Tragedy" Museum, the survivors had been pro-active in initiating independent, organic memory projects. Survivors regard themselves as moral witnesses, yet had been neglected by most chroniclers of the Bhopal disaster including media and scholars. They were seen as subjects of pity, not as thinking people. The narratives collected and used for media/academic projects largely remained inaccessible to survivors – they were the subjects, not the audience.

The RBM was a movement project that sought to address this ongoing violence and placed the right to tell their own stories with the survivors: by restoring survivors' voice in a live museum; by enabling their interpretation of their own memories of disaster/ movement; by adopting their articulation of the museum's purpose, the RBM aimed to become a space where the survivor is both a storyteller and a visitor; a space that doesn't dilute the story of the world's worst industrial disaster or render it apolitical in the name of catharsis. This was an ambitious, unconventional goal.

First, at the time, in India there were no museums on social movements. There were no representations of social movements within existing national museums. To have a social movement theorize itself into a museum was path-breaking for a country where the state is primary custodian of museums and collective memory. Second, the existing museums were either personality-centric or celebratory. To have a museum tell the story of the ongoing Bhopal disaster(s), the brutality of state capitalism and modern bureaucratic government, was fundamentally unveiling an India that is far from "shining". But, most of all, a museum that tells the story of the larger India in telling the story of Bhopal would ensure that remembrance is not reduced to ritualistic tribute; rather it challenged India's ruthless transition into the 21st century.

But, can a museum be a critique of state capitalism not just in its message but also in its character? Can a museum house the diverse experiences of a growing community of survivors? Can a museum be developed using the expertise of the community of survivors, activists, and their supporters? These questions, slowly simmering within the movement for a long time, provided the backdrop to the RBM project, but the museum was brought to life through a series of events that heightened its necessity as well as the movement's ability to build it.

Rama Lakshmi, a trained museologist, had covered the Bhopal issue for years as a *Washington Post* journalist, while Shalini Sharma was an ICJB activist before embarking on a PhD on media–movement relations. It was during Sharma's fieldwork in India in 2010–2011 that they met at the ICJB's office where Lakshmi explained her idea using oral histories for collective curation, extending the template of community museum *Yaad-e-Haadsa* built on Satinath Sarangi's suggestion in 2005; both shared the movement's concerns about the state's effort to convert the UC factory into a memorial complex overriding survivors' demands for the clean-up of toxics buried in the factory premises that over the years led to groundwater contamination. The government had solicited Space Matters, a Delhi-based architect firm, for designing the memorial complex through a public competition without consulting or informing survivors. Soon, the architect firm was also being consulted on options for toxic-waste remediation. Meanwhile Dow Chemicals was continuously lobbying the Indian government to get it off the legal hook. Therefore, when the Madhya Pradesh government took a renewed interest in the museum issue – which they had ignored for over 25 years – and tried to open the contaminated factory for tourism, the movement actors grew suspicious (Sharma 2014). The state's Bhopal memorial project was seen as an effort to convert the unsafe zone of the UC factory into a safe zone urging people to move on and seek closure, in spite of pending justices (Sharma 2014). There was a sense of urgency within the movement to set up a people's museum that situates Bhopal both as a lesson and as a deterrent. Lakshmi offered help with the museum curation and Sharma agreed to help with research and coordination of the RBM Project. This voluntary, solidarity-based, collaboration between a museologist-journalist and an academic-activist with the Bhopal movement provided an engaged, yet objective blueprint to the museum.

The RBM project used participatory approaches from ideation to research its inception. The reflexivity and solidarity within the movement fostered it. The movement actors were determined to keep the museum secular, inclusive, and democratic. To reclaim their story survivors and activists stressed the need to control the content. Lakshmi proposed an oral-history-based museum collectively curated by a community of activists and survivors. Accordingly, Remember Bhopal Trust (RBT) was established with survivors, long-time Bhopal activists, and movement supporters as members. In keeping with the movement demands, the RBM was to be completely free of any state or corporate funding. The seed fund was raised through public donations. This meant that the ground research, content development, and other professional services required for developing the museum had to be done on a strictly voluntary basis.

The RBM was envisaged to be "an unmediated, unfiltered, community-curated public space" which prompted staging of oral histories at the center of the institution for preserving, consolidating, and fortifying people's memories in Bhopal (Lakshmi and Sharma 2018). In doing so, the RBM showcased how oral-history-based museums are a "public intervention strategy in post-colonial historiography" (Lakshmi and Sharma 2018). Harvesting oral narratives of survivors and activists, which had effectively countered the state–corporate-controlled memory-making processes, was seen as crucial to ensure inclusion in the museum by restoring voice and dignity.

The research and content development for the museum was a slow, organic process. Lakshmi and Sharma met leaders of each survivor-led organization in Bhopal and subsequently attended their weekly public meetings to explain the RBM project to the survivors and seek their participation. The different Bhopal groups came on board after the researchers' assurance that the museum will reflect the voices and demands of the movement at large. Sharma's long-term familiarity with survivor groups; Lakshmi's insights into the storytelling potential of the museum; and the survivors' ability to articulate their stories enabled the snowballing process to collect oral histories as well as objects.

In situating oral histories as a central curatorial strategy, the RBM project de-academized and de-eliticized the curatorial process. Breaking away from conventional curatorial approaches, the RBM team did not begin with locating the object, researching its context, and then finding the person behind it. The oral history method gave the content control to people who were directly affected by the industrial disaster but who were often by-passed by the scientific experts, scholars, etc. People's stories led to objects. And people selected the stories they wanted to share. While telling their stories people shared experiences that hadn't been previously revealed and identified an object that made the stories more salient – often surprising the two researchers whose trained eyes might have missed these connections. For instance, the oral histories brought to the RBM:

- a pink sari that Bano Bi never wore but held dear as the last gift from her husband who died on the night of the gas leak;
- a hammer and sickle that Dr. Satpathy, a forensic expert, used to break open the skull of the dead in lieu of the non-existing technology to deal with mass deaths;
- a mobile phone that didn't exist at the time of the gas leak, but reminded Saeeda Parveen of the last years with her ailing husband;
- a broken red bangle that had nothing to do with contaminated water that Nafeesa Bi lived with in Bhopal, but reminded her of women's struggle with police in Delhi.

This ensured that the Bhopal saga does not start and end with the 1984 gas leak, rather the museum presents it as what it really is – the many disasters that are still unfolding and people's ongoing struggle to reclaim their lives. The RBM oral historians took particular care to go beyond the template of "what happened that night?" – a template popular with media and academics – and explored the lives of survivors/activists before the disruptive event as well as how their relationships changed over the years. This strategy helped to both recognize the common templates of social remembering that allowed the movement to subvert official memory narratives as well to breakthrough the script-like, replica memories and bring the diverse voices to the fore (Lakshmi and Sharma 2014; 2018). The oral histories generated hidden/new aspects providing "more history" of the disaster, built "anti-history" to the narrative of the powerful, and brought to center-stage the "real history" of the people with first-hand experience of the disaster and the justice movement (Frisch 1990). We also recorded protest songs, poems, and slogans to capture the organic literature that emerged in the movement. Together these helped to "bring to light the existence and impact of non-violent organizing where it has not been commonly noticed" (Bartkowski 2013: 1).

Fifty oral histories were recorded in Hindi and English. This allowed the people to tell their stories in their chosen language. But, operating on a shoe-string budget the researchers could not afford to record interviews in the sanitized space of a studio – rather interviews were recorded in homes and offices of survivors/activists. During sweltering summers windows were closed and fans were switched off; women were requested to remove all jewelry barring a bangle (in respect of local culture where married women are required to wear bangles at all times). A rich collection of oral histories is generated, but recordings are not noise free.

The funding limitations made RBT explore creative ways to generate material often relying on the solidarity networks of the movement. This facilitated participation of digitally connected supporters to record the translation in their voice using their mobile phones, which is displayed alongside the original in the museum. The museum visitors only need to pick one of the two phones to listen in the language of their choice. It also made the museum an unmediated space free from a tour guide or interpreter or any specific chronological walk-through. In the museum, it evoked an illustration of cross-cultural solidarity and, to some extent, reduced barriers such as literacy, language, age, gender, and class.

This oral-history-based museum is temporarily housed in a residential colony of survivors at a walking distance from the UC factory. It has been deliberately kept free of entry fees, making it accessible to working-class survivors as well as blue-collar professionals and government officials including foreign diplomats.

The museum has gone beyond the RBT's expectations in terms of new personal experiences it generates. Three days after the museum's inauguration in 2014, a frail woman stood at the gate curious to see who the new occupant is. She worked as a domestic help in the nearby areas. Sharma invited her inside the museum. The woman went from one phone to another. Speechless she sat down at the museum stairs and broke down. She told Sharma, the stories were exactly how her father had described the night of the gas leak to her. She never went to school or heard her school-going kids talk about the disaster. But, she found her life story being told through the many different voices. She rushed out to bring first her children, then her husband, and then her neighbors to the museum. She kept repeating to them: Listen, this is what happened. Do not forget.

Another powerful episode three years on: a troupe of local dancers entered the museum for some respite from heat at the insistence of Safreen Khan and Tasneem Khan, the museum caretakers. The drummer in the troupe stared blankly at the black-and-white photograph of a woman on the wall. Then, he broke down, cried inconsolably for several minutes. He told the caretakers that the picture was that of his dead wife who had gone missing after the night of the gas leak. He hadn't seen her dead body, nor did he have any photograph of her. After 33 years, he saw his wife again on the museum wall (Lakshmi 2017).

The encounter with oral histories in the museum's safe space is cathartic, uncompromising. It is raw, emotional, yet liberating, and solidarity affirming as diverse trauma, lived experiences, and memories connect.

The oral histories are also mobile – other activists have used the oral histories alongside their vernacular translations such as in Tamil. This, to some extent, made the museum accessible to those who could not physically visit it while also providing pedagogical opportunities to resilient communities facing environmental injustices. Students and researchers, both from India and abroad, frequently request excerpts of the oral histories for their projects and events.

Many contribute through their scholarly, artistic, and other creative projects. Rob Edwards of the National Union of Journalists, on the trade union delegation with Scandrett, covered the museum's opening in the British press (Edwards 2014). Connections such as these have helped widen the variety of ways in which inter-generational and international engagement and knowledge building continues.

The museum research remains an ongoing project. The RBM was built to run free of state and corporate sponsorship. The museum requires a weather-controlled environment: in its current setting, keeping objects safe against heat and humidity is a daily battle. The RBM team designed physical learning activities but could not implement them due to space constrictions. RBM is still struggling to find sustainable non-toxic preservatives to keep objects safe. These challenges are related as much to funds as to existing resources. Raising enough public donations without tax benefits, at a time when the government is increasingly harsh against the organizations that challenge its plans for "development" and "ease of business", is a Herculean task. In the meantime, the museum acts as a holding space for the memories and wounds of the survivors who are under constant pressure to move on. In doing so, it continues to poke at the consciousness of the emerging India with the question: What will be the cost of forgetting Bhopal?

Conclusions

The early stages in the development of neoliberalism constitute not so much a rupture involving the emergence of an entirely new class, but rather a distinctive phase of capitalism in which we would expect to see shifting class alignments with new class factions emerging and a renegotiation of hegemony. Such class factions will gain more or less degrees of cohesion and class consciousness as an organic intellectual function establishes itself. During its development, these organic intellectual functions are likely to be contested.

The Bhopal Survivors' Movement, emerging in the violence of the early phases of neoliberalism, are starting to make sense of their experience in coherent political terms. What has been documented (and facilitated) by these examples of activist ethnography is the process of formation of an organic intellectual function from the fragmentary experience of neoliberal chemical capitalism.

What we as researchers have engaged with – the Bhopal Survivors' Movement Study documenting knowledge production and analysis; the Remember Bhopal Trust and Museum materializing knowledge articulation and dissemination – may be understood as a tentative process towards "an organic cohesion in which feeling-passion becomes understanding and thence knowledge" (Gramsci in Hoare and Smith 1971: 418).

The Bhopal Survivors' Movement is part of that process of organic intellectual formation, emerging with neoliberalism among one of its earliest victims and making partial alliance with other victims in over 30 years of struggle. Elements of the formation of the collective organic intellectual formation can be glimpsed, comprising traditional intellectuals committed to the movement as well as grassroots mobilizers with no education and non-literate communication skills. In a single generation, many of the survivors were thrust from peasant to proletariat to dispossessed. In so doing they have been part of a social process in which participatory research may make a small contribution, encouraging comments from the sidelines of a struggle with which researchers only barely participate.

Abdul Jabbar Khan, a Bhopal gas survivor and leader of one of the movement groups, BGPMUS, argues that the traditional intellectuals who have supported the movement become problematic for it:

> For the first 10 years of the movement it seemed like a good idea to involve intellectuals just as they were active in the NBA [Narmada Bachao Andolan]. Now such people think very lowly of the Bhopal gas movement, they think it's a nuisance. They never have it in them to struggle. I feel that they could not connect to the problems of the common man because their experience was all book based.
>
> …
>
> During the British rule most of the intellectuals were in important positions in the system and they were the main hindrance to the freedom movement. It has been the same with the French revolution and the Russian revolution. The intellectuals are always with the rulers. So I would say that the uneducated people who do not possess "literary" knowledge are the ones who can bring justice, much more than the educated. (Bhopal Survivors' Movement Study 2009: 78–79)

Jabbar's comment was made to camera as part of the activist ethnography research in the Bhopal Survivors' Movement Study, a process clearly and explicitly involving traditional intellectuals. By contrast, as explored earlier, the role which Satinath Sarangi has played has facilitated a great many studies in which traditional intellectuals and survivors have closely collaborated to benefit the movement. It is this ambiguous role which activist researchers seek to play (including the authors of this chapter), embracing both the worlds of traditional intellectual and organic intellectual – playing a small role in developing the latter function among the emergent class of dispossessed, and often, in the increasingly neoliberal university, marginalized from the former.

Acknowledgments

This research was funded through grants from the following sources, to whom we are very grateful: the Bhopal Survivors' Movement Study was funded by the Barry Amiel and Norman Melburn Trust; the British Academy; the Carnegie Trust for the Universities of Scotland; the Lipman-Miliband Trust; the Nuffield Foundation.

The Remember Bhopal Trust and Museum acknowledges the many private donors and different chapters of the Association for India Development who have helped build and run the museum.

References

Bartkowski, M.J. (2013). Recovering nonviolent history. In M.J. Bartkowski (Ed.), *Recovering Nonviolent History: Civil Resistance in Liberation Struggles*. Boulder, CO: Lynne Rienner.

Baviskar, A. (2005). "Red in tooth and claw?" Looking for class in struggles over nature. In R. Ray and M. Fainsod Katzenstein (Eds.), *Social Movements in India*. New Delhi: Oxford University Press.

Bevington, D. and Dixon, D. (2005). Movement-relevant theory: rethinking social movement scholarship and activism. *Social Movement Studies* 4(3): 185–208.

Bhopal Survivors' Movement Study. (2009). *Bhopal Survivors Speak: Emergent Voices from a People's Movement*. Edinburgh: Word Power Books.

Chatterjee, P. (2008). Democracy and economic transformation in India. *Economic & Political Weekly*, 43(16): 53–62.

Corbridge, S. and Harriss, J. (2000) *Reinventing India: Liberalization, Hindu Nationalism and Popular Democracy*, second edition. New Delhi: Oxford University Press.

Dinham, B. and Sarangi, S. (2002). The Bhopal gas tragedy 1984 to ? The evasion of corporate responsibility.

Environment and Urbanization, 14(1): 89–99.

Edwards, R. (2014). The agony of the Bhopal toxic gas disaster 30 years on. Available at: www.robedwards.com/2014/12/the-agony-of-the-bhopal-toxic-gas-disaster-30-years-on.html [Accessed February 23, 2018].

Fortun, K. (2001). *Advocacy after Bhopal*. Chicago, IL: University of Chicago Press.

Freire, P. (1972). *Pedagogy of the Oppressed*. London: Penguin.

Frisch, M. (1990). *A Shared Authority: Essays on the Craft and Meaning of Oral and Public History*. Albany, NY: State University of New York Press.

Hanna, B., Morehouse, W., and Sarangi, S. (Eds.). (2004). *The Bhopal Reader*. Goa: The Other India Press.

Harvey, D. (2006). *Spaces of Global Capitalism: Towards a Theory of Uneven Geographical Development*. Oxford: Oxford University Press.

Hoare, Q. and Smith, G.N. (Eds.). (1971). *Selections from the Prison Notebooks of Antonio Gramsci*. London: Lawrence and Wishart.

Lakshmi, R. (2017). The lazy way to remember the Bhopal gas tragedy. Available at: https://theprint.in/2017/12/02/wrong-way-remember-bhopal-gas-tragedy/ [Accessed February 23, 2018].

Lakshmi, R. and Sharma, S. (2014). Remembering Bhopal: voices of survivors. *Social Justice*, 41(1–2): 28–37.

Lakshmi, R. and Sharma, S. (2018). Building a safe space for unsafe

memories: the Remember Bhopal Museum. In K. Holmes and H. Goodhall (Eds.), *Telling Environmental Histories: Intersections of Memory, Narrative and the Environment*. New York: Palgrave.

Lave, J. and Wenger, E. (1991). *Situated Learning: Legitimate Peripheral Participation*. New York: Cambridge University Press.

Mukherjee, S., Scandrett, E., Sen, T., and Shah, D. (2011). Generating theory in the Bhopal Survivors' Movement. In S.C. Motta and A.G. Nilsen (Eds.), *Social Movements in the Global South: Dispossession, Development and Resistance*. Basingstoke: Palgrave Macmillan.

Sarangi, S. (1996). The movement in Bhopal and its lessons. *Social Justice*, 23(4): 100–110.

Scandrett, E. and Mukherjee, S. (2011). Globalisation and abstraction in the Bhopal Survivors' Movement. *Interface: A Journal for and about Social Movements*, 3(1): 195–209.

Scandrett, E., Mukherjee, S., and Bhopal Research Team. (2011). "We are flames not flowers": a gendered reading of the social movement for justice in Bhopal. *Interface: A Journal for and about Social Movements*, 3(2): 100–122.

Sharma, S. (2014). The politics of remembering Bhopal. In P. Davis, I. Convery, and G. Corsane (Eds.), *Displaced Heritage: Responses to Disaster, Trauma and Loss*. Woodbridge, Suffolk: The Boydell Press.

13 | PRAXIS-ORIENTED RESEARCH FOR THE BUILDING OF GROUNDED TRANSNATIONAL MARRIAGE MIGRANT MOVEMENTS IN ASIA

Hsiao-Chuan Hsia

Capitalist globalization and marriage migration

Parallel to the trend of labor migration, marriage migration has become another significant form of forced migration whereby women from poorer countries migrate to richer countries through cross-border marriages (Hsia 2015b). These transnational marriages are particularly significant in East Asian countries, including Japan, South Korea, and Taiwan, more ethnically homogenous than most countries in the world (Iwabuchi, Kim, and Hsia 2016). Of the three East Asian countries, Taiwan has experienced the most rapid increase in transnational marriages. Beginning in the mid-1980s, and growing rapidly in the 1990s, according to official statistics released in 2002, one in every four new marriages was between a citizen and a foreigner, although the percentage decreased after 2003 and hovered between 12 and 20 percent of all marriages registered annually. In 2017, 15.3 percent of all newly-wed couples were Taiwanese nationals and foreign spouses, among whom 75.7 percent are female foreign spouses.[1] The vast majority of foreign spouses are women from Mainland China and Southeast Asian countries, including Vietnam, Indonesia, the Philippines, Thailand, and Cambodia.

Elsewhere I have argued that this phenomenon of marriage migration is the by-product of capitalist development – one way that marginalized men in the core and semi-peripheral countries and poor women in the peripheral countries find their survival in these cross-border marriages (Hsia 2004). Moreover, marriage migration as a form of forced migration reveals the "reproduction crisis" at the present stage of capitalism (Hsia 2015b), as summarized in the following.

As capitalist globalization intensifies, the welfare state is in crisis and many social services are eliminated. Rising living costs combined with the lack of a comprehensive social welfare system lead women in the more developed countries to seek cheaper surrogates to take care of household needs while they work to provide income for their households. Therefore, many countries have established policies of importing migrant domestic workers to resolve the crisis of reproduction which leads to the "restructuring of reproduction" (Hsia 2008b), in which women from the peripheral states migrate to perform reproductive labor for the core and semi-peripheral states – that is, in the reverse direction to the restructuring of production.

However, these policies serve only as "Band-Aid" solutions, especially as fertility rates in core and semi-peripheral states continue to drop with rapid increases in the costs of childrearing. Moreover, although middle-class families can resort to hiring migrant domestic workers, farmers and working-class families cannot afford to hire this type of labor. Consequently, men of working-class and farming families in the core and semi-peripheral states follow the flight of capital to neighboring less developed countries in search of brides (Hsia 2010).

Most marriage migrant women decide to marry Taiwanese men because they hope to escape poverty and turbulence in their home countries, intensified by capitalist globalization. Yet, they often end up in economic stress because their husbands are mostly from small farming and working-class families, devastated by capitalist globalization (Hsia 2004). In addition to economic stress, other precarious conditions of marriage migrant women in Taiwan include lack of social network and support, social discrimination, and obstacles to obtaining formal and substantive citizenship (Hsia 2010). The severe discrimination they had faced is reflected in the term "foreign brides" commonly used to refer to them.

However, while the trend of marriage migration is paralleled to that of labor migration, issues of marriage migrants have not received as much attention as the issues of migrant workers, not only from researchers but also from activists. The dominant discourse about marriage migrants has painted them as victims, particularly of sex trafficking. However, despite all precarious conditions, marriage migrant women in Taiwan have been transformed from being isolated "foreign brides" to migrant activists. With support of local activists, marriage migrant women in Taiwan have succeeded in changing laws and policies. They have also been engaged in transnational networking and the establishment of the Alliance of Marriage Migrants' Organizations for Rights and Empowerment (AMMORE) to advocate for marriage migrants' rights and welfare on regional and international platforms. The development of the movements for marriage migrants started from Taiwan and later expanded to the Asia Pacific region and is partly attributable to my long-term praxis-oriented research since 1994 (Hsia 2015a; 2018).

Praxis-oriented research and the building of grounded transnational movements

This praxis-oriented research has lasted for more than 20 years with the aims of empowering stigmatized "foreign brides" to speak for themselves and developing a social movement for their rights and welfare. I use the term "praxis-oriented" research instead of the more commonly used term "action research" because as I elsewhere argued (Hsia 2006a), "action" in sociology does not necessarily involve personal and social transformation and "action research" often ends up being appropriated by policy makers who want efficient – rather than fair – outcomes. "Praxis", on the other hand, as a central concept of Marxism, draws attention to the social construction of economic and social institutions and the possibility of changing them – enhancing humanity's capacity for freedom, which cannot be achieved entirely at the individual level. In other words, "praxis-oriented research" does not merely encourage the participation of research subjects, but more importantly, the research gears itself towards the material world, analyzing the contradictions in societies, and pinpointing the possibilities of changing them.

This long-term praxis-oriented research began in 1994, when I learnt that not being able to write Chinese and speak Mandarin was a primary barrier in the everyday lives of these Southeast Asian women who married Taiwanese men in the rural community, Meinung, in southern Taiwan. These women were then called "foreign brides" and perceived as the cause of social problems not only in the media by also by the governments and general public. I began to offer free Chinese classes to several Indonesian women who were married to their husbands in Meinung. After a few classes, I discussed with the community activists in Meinung about the significance of the classes as part of community activism and therefore decided to expand it as the "Chinese Literacy Program" for all "foreign brides" from different Southeast Asian countries in Meinung, whose opening class was held on July 30, 1995, the first program designed specifically for "foreign brides" in Taiwan.

From my fieldwork, I learnt that many of these Southeast Asian women were confined to the home because of the language barriers, so by learning Chinese, I believed that these women could be freer from constraints, and further enabled to form a mutual support network and advocate for their own rights and welfare. In essence, the objective of the "Foreign Brides Chinese Literacy Programs" was, via learning Chinese, to empower the so-called "foreign brides" to speak for themselves and form an organization to fight for their rights.

When we initiated the programs, we always added quotation marks to the name of the program as a reminder of the ideology embedded in our common parlance. First, these women were not illiterate. Rather, the problem was that their native languages and capacities are deemed useless in Taiwan. This language program is thus titled "Literacy Program" to stress the difficulty they face in Chinese-language-dominant Taiwan. Second, the term "Foreign Brides" reveals discrimination implying that these women are not only seen as foreigners forever but also as subordinates to Taiwanese men.

While being aware of the ideology embedded, we did not invent a new term as a replacement, because we believe that naming itself reflects power relations and we did not want to speak on behalf of these women. It was not until 2003 when these women were empowered to speak up for themselves and collectively decided on a new term (in Chinese), "new immigrant women". By collaborating with the Awakening Foundation, the leading feminist organization in Taiwan, we organized the "Let New Immigrant Women Speak for Themselves Writing Contest", where the foreign women married to Taiwanese men were invited to express their feeling of being called the "foreign brides", and how they would name themselves alternatively if they disapprove of this term. "Foreign Brides" were requested to vote on names suggested by the entries of the writing contest, and "new immigrant Women" received the highest votes.

Since then, "foreign brides" have been seriously criticized and "new immigrant women" become more popularized (Hsia 2015a).

After many trials and errors, the community activists and I eventually incorporated the principles and methods of the *Pedagogy of the Oppressed* (Freire 1970) and the *Theatre of the Oppressed* (Boal 1979) to facilitate the Chinese programs, which were expanded from Meinung to Tapiei County (Hsia 2006a) and had helped the new immigrant women transform themselves from being isolated in their households and silent in public, to being publicly engaged. Finally, after eight years of empowering the new immigrant women, "TransAsia Sisters Association, Taiwan" (TASAT) was officially established on December 7, 2003, the first grassroots organization in Taiwan initiated and run by the new immigrant women themselves. To ensure the leadership of the new immigrant women, TASAT's Constitution stipulates that migrants from Southeast Asian countries should occupy more than two-thirds of the elected board members. Until the present, all the programs and projects are collectively discussed, decided on, and implemented with active participation of the new immigrant women.

In the same year of its formal establishment, TASAT networked with other organizations concerned with the rights and welfare of im/migrants to form the Alliance of Human Rights Legislation for Immigrants and Migrants (AHRLIM) to advance the movement for immigrants' rights in Taiwan (Hsia 2008b). AHRLIM is Taiwan's first alliance specifically campaigning for the rights and welfare of immigrants. After years of AHRLIM's struggles, several significant policy changes have been achieved, including amendments to the Immigration Act in 2007, the Statute Governing the Relations between the Peoples of the Taiwan Area and the Mainland China Area in 2009, and the Nationality Act in 2016, the three most crucial laws affecting new immigrant women in Taiwan. More importantly, in every campaign launched by AHRLIM, the new immigrant women organized by TASAT play significant roles, including speaking at rallies, forums, and press conferences, lobbying legislators, and participating in AHRLIM's internal discussion and dialogues with governmental officials (Hsia 2008b).

Spearheading the immigrant movement in Taiwan since 2003, AHRLIM is composed of actors with diverse backgrounds, including grassroots im/migrants' organizations and domestic movement organizations of women and in the labor and human rights sectors. In essence, the movement for immigrants' rights and welfare spear-headed by AHRLIM is "transnationalism within the nation-state" since participants are of different nationalities, including immigrants originally from various nation-states and the native citizens concerned with the issues of migrants. As the movement expands, the transnationalism within Taiwan has crossed the borders and developed to become "transnationalism beyond the nation-state boundaries" as the Action Network for Marriage Migrants' Rights and Empowerment (AMM♀RE) was formed in 2008 and later formalized in 2017 as the Alliance of Marriage Migrants Organizations for Rights and Empowerment (AMMORE). Through various efforts of AMM♀RE and AMMORE, the issues of marriage migrants have been brought to regional and international movements for migrants and immigrants, including the term "marriage migrants" being accepted as the replacement to "mail-order brides" or "victims of human trafficking", even in some of the documents of UN institutions. This transnational advocacy network (TAN), spearheaded by AMMORE, in turn helps advance campaigns and policy changes at the national level in Taiwan and other countries (Hsia 2018).

Roles of the praxis-oriented researcher

As a praxis-oriented researcher, the ultimate goal of my research is to empower the marginalized people and advance grassroots movements rather than simply completing my short-term research "projects". Many community-based participatory research efforts initiate changes in the community through community interventions; however, most changes are not sustainable once the research funding ends. As mentioned, my praxis-oriented research has lasted more than 20 years and is still ongoing, through which the once highly stigmatized "foreign brides" have been empowered and organized, and transnational movements for their rights and welfare have been developed. In this long process, I have played three major roles, including knowledge production, networking, and movement building, to be illustrated in the following.

Knowledge production

As Choudry and Kapoor (2010) point out, knowledge production within social movements and activist contexts is very rich and significant, yet often overlooked not only in scholarly literature but also by those in the movements. My long-term praxis-oriented research has demonstrated that knowledge production is crucial for activism geared towards social changes and movement building.

First, my study on the situations faced by "foreign brides" led to my entry into the long process of empowerment through offering classes to fulfill their basic needs, starting with learning Chinese language. To further identify the long-term direction towards structural changes, analysis of the root causes of the "foreign brides" phenomenon was necessary. To develop and advance the movements for marriage migrants' rights and welfare, my praxis-oriented research also needed to analyze how to debunk the hegemonic discourses, overcome organizational barriers, and expand the scopes of the movements from local and national to regional and international levels. In the following, my illustration of the importance of knowledge production will focus on two aspects: identifying root causes and countering hegemonic discourses.

Identifying root causes as the basis for agenda-setting

When I began to explore issues of the so-called "foreign brides" in the early 1990s, I noticed that both public and governmental discourses portrayed them as causes of social problems. While there was basically no research on this topic yet, a few researchers expressed the same concerns through media interviews or newspaper columns. However, such "social problems" discourse only revealed the surface, rather than addressed the root causes of the problems, which is critical for social praxis that aims at changing social structures.

Since my analyses reveal that the root causes of the "foreign brides" phenomenon are capitalist globalization and the resulting unequal development at both global and national levels (Hsia 1997; 2004), I perceive both men and women in these cross-border marriages as victims of the unequal structures struggling to find their way out through such marriages. In other words, I do not perceive those men marrying "foreign brides" simply as evil-doers, and my initial action was to organize the Chinese classes for these women to break away from isolation.

Since the "foreign brides" phenomenon has clear gender implications, when it caught public attention, gender had been the focus for many feminists and gender-sensitive scholars and experts. Ironically, their portrayals of these "foreign brides" were often not much different from the mainstream media's construction of them as "social problems" (Hsia 2008a).

This perception of the "foreign brides" often led scholars sympathetic to women's issues to view them as victims of domestic violence. To raise public awareness of the problems, these scholars often highlighted the helplessness of "foreign brides" while demonizing their husbands. Most women's groups shared this view, especially when they first became aware of such transnational marriages.

I personally experienced disapproving views when I initiated the Chinese Literacy Program in 1995. A few months after the program began, one of the leading feminists wrote an article criticizing the literacy program, claiming that it served to perpetuate Hakka[2] culture, because it encouraged more Hakka men to buy "foreign brides" while creating better living conditions through such programs.

In the first two years after I initiated the Chinese program, I contacted two major women's organizations in Taiwan and asked if they could hold public hearings on the issue of "foreign brides". One of their leaders told me that their organization's idea of action was to find ways to send "foreign brides" back to their home countries, because they believed that these marriages were merely a form of trade, encouraged by a patriarchal system. I could not at all accept such proposed action planning by this women's organization, because my analysis of this "foreign brides" phenomenon directed my action towards addressing capitalist globalization as the root cause of the problems. Although it is true that transnational marriages are commodified, it was not at all clear that sending these "foreign brides" back to their homelands was in their best interest, since these women engaged themselves in the cross-border marriages for the purposes of escaping poverty and turbulence in their home countries. Therefore, my initial action to address the problems was to empower and organize these "foreign brides" with the long-term objective of building movements for immigrants, which would later be linked to the global movements addressing issues of capitalist globalization. Without thoroughly analyzing the politico-economic structures of transnational marriages, these feminists oversimplified issues of marriage migration and dismissed them as a mere reflection of patriarchy in which men in these cross-border marriages were the sole evil-doers.

Furthermore, the analysis of root causes of marriage migration also helps expand the movement from Taiwan-focused to regional and global movement for migrants and immigrants. As previously mentioned, issues of marriage migrants have not been as recognized as those of migrant workers. To overcome the lack of recognition within the global migrant movements, I have been trying to frame issues of marriage migration as part of the global phenomenon of forced migration, so that it can become comprehensible to the TANs for migrants and issues of marriage migrants can be taken up by the international migrants' movements. One of my efforts was the naming of "foreign brides" in the global context.

In September 2007, TASAT and AHRLIM co-organized the International Conference on Border Control and Empowerment of Immigrant Brides. I raised the issue of naming in the session on action planning and shared TASAT's experiences of naming campaigns as mentioned above. Additionally, as the co-organizer of the conference, I explained that the conference title used "immigrant brides" knowing that the term "bride" was problematic and planning to raise it as an issue for discussion and debates at the conference. After heated discussion and debates, my proposal of the term "marriage migrant" was accepted. Moreover, one of the resolutions of this conference was to establish a network for marriage migrants' welfare, which was realized in 2008 when the AMM♀RE was established. Since then, the term "marriage migrants" has been promoted by AMM♀RE at all possible venues and engagements, including UN processes. Eventually, the UN also started using the term "marriage migrants" in some official documents.

Moreover, the most crucial strategic framing to help establish TAN for marriage migrants is to link it to the global issues of forced migration. Since this framing of marriage migration as part of forced migration under neoliberal globalization has been accepted, issues of marriage migrants have been gradually incorporated to the global movement for migrants and thus the TAN for marriage migrants has been developed and expanded.

One vivid example of how such "frame alignment" helps is the activities held in Berlin, 2017. Many migrant activists and advocates involved in the activities organized by Churches Witnessing with Migrants to counter the inter-governmental conference the Global Forum on Migration and Development were not aware of the issues of marriage migrants. At the rally held at the end of the activities, as the chairperson of AMMORE – which originated in AMM♀RE and was formalized in 2017 – I spoke about marriage migrant issues and shared my analyses of how marriage migration is part of forced migration. After my speech, several migrant activists told me that they did not realize they were marriage migrants themselves until they listened to my speech and that they were eager to be part of AMMORE and consequently started organizing marriage migrants in Europe.

Countering hegemonic discourse

In addition to analyzing the root causes, another important aspect of knowledge production in praxis-oriented research is to debunk the mainstream discourse of the phenomenon. As pointed out previously, the mainstream discourse had painted the so-called "foreign brides" as causes of social problems. My first step to challenge the mainstream media discourse was to publish my academic analysis of how such media discourse was constructed via problematic techniques, such as overlapping media coverage, fabricated statistics and equivocal wording, and collaboration with governmental agencies while silencing voices of the "foreign brides" and their advocates. It further analyzes the national anxiety behind these media constructions, explaining why the media constantly construct the "foreign brides" as social problems and threats to Taiwanese society (Hsia 2007).

In addition to my academic analyses, the marriage migrants organized by TASAT have also developed their critical views countering the mainstream perception about them. However, as Gupta (2004) argues, it is difficult for activists to spare time to record their work, which is crucial in the age of information. To popularize these views countering the dominant discourse and gradually changing the public discourse, I endeavored to maximize my position as a scholar to frequently write columns and articles for various newspapers. The opinions I presented in these newspaper articles are not only from my academic analyses but also from marriage migrants themselves, which were mostly ignored in the mainstream discourse. Moreover, since many NGOs and even movement organizations also shared such mainstream perceptions about marriage migration, my academic as well as popular writings also need to aim at criticizing such views from NGOs and movement organizations.

To document our critical views, especially those of the marriage migrant women themselves, I collected various writings – including those awarded in the aforementioned Writing Contest – paintings, and pictures of the marriage migrant women at rallies, and edited them into a book titled *Don't Call Me a Foreign Bride* (in Chinese) in 2005. As the first book of marriage migrant women's writings, this book successfully attracted much public attention. As the editor of this book, I noticed that the most common responses from readers was amazement over how talented marriage migrants were, and how the book made many readers so much more appreciative of multiculturalism and aware of their own prejudices.

TASAT has endeavored to change public perceptions of marriage migrant women via various methods. In addition to written publications, TASAT also published a documentary film titled *Let's Not Be Afraid!* and a music album titled *Drifting No More*, as well as several theater productions, all of which are products collectively accomplished by marriage migrants and local volunteers, including myself. All of these productions have been well received and demonstrate that making heard the voices of marriage migrants is the best way to subvert the hegemonic images of them as submissive, problematic, and incompetent.

Networking

Since the root cause of marriage migration is capitalist globalization, which is related to multi-sectoral issues including gender, class, race/ethnicity/nationality, and since "foreign brides" face difficulties of isolation, it is essential to network with different sectors of Taiwanese organizations to advocate for their rights and welfare. However, my initial networking with feminist organizations was not successful as previously mentioned. Nonetheless, I continued my work of empowering the marriage migrant women through Chinese classes, which increasingly caught the attention of various feminists and feminist organizations. Later, several of them approached me to join their organizations. However, since most organizations still perceived marriage migrants as victims and focused on issues of domestic violence and trafficking, I did not accept their invitation. At the end of 2001, the Awakening Foundation, the first feminist organization in Taiwan, invited me to join them as a board member. Since the marriage migrants from the Chinese programs had been significantly empowered and had discussed the problems they faced with laws and policies, after discussing with activists in Meinung, we concluded that it would be an opportune time to collaborate with the Awakening Foundation whose expertise is on campaigning for policies and laws concerning women's issues. Therefore, I joined the Awakening Foundation as a board member in 2002 and served on the board for two terms until 2005. During my first year, my task was to familiarize the staff and the board members, which consisted of several leading feminists, with issues of migration. I designed and facilitated a series of forums to discuss issues of women and migration under globalization, after which a series of public activities were organized, and AHRLIM was established in 2003 as a platform to campaign for policy and law changes.

Since the Awakening Foundation is the most well-known feminist organization, it often receives invitations from governmental agencies to various advisory committees and consultation meetings, which brought to my attention that the government had a hasty plan to establish a National Immigration Agency without comprehensive immigration policies. In response to the plan, as the board member responsible for designing programs for migrant women's issues, I suggested to the secretariat of the Awakening Foundation to call for meetings with various NGOs interested in migrant women's issues. After two consultation meetings, the AHRLIM was established in late 2003 (Hsia 2008b).

Through the Awakening Foundation, the networking with other organizations had successfully resulted in the formation of AHRLIM, composed of actors with diverse backgrounds, including grassroots im/migrants' organizations and domestic movement organizations of women and in the labor and human rights sectors. The reasons why AHRLIM obtains such diverse memberships include the following. First, since the immigrant movement was not developed yet, it was necessary to bring together different organizations interested in immigrant issues. Second, since marriage migrants are socially, economically, and politically disadvantaged in Taiwan, and there were no strong immigrants' networks like those in the United States, Canada, and other countries with long histories of immigration, it was necessary for local activists to provide assistance. Third, while it was necessary for local activists to take part, the legitimacy of the movement would be questioned had marriage migrants themselves not been active. Fortunately, long before AHRLIM was established, efforts had been made since 1995 to develop the subjectivity of marriage migrant women, when the Chinese Literacy Program was initiated to empower marriage migrants. Since the very first protest initiated by AHRLIM in 2003, marriage migrants organized by TASAT have always been active, including participating in internal discussion and speaking at protests and press conferences. The legitimacy of the marriage migrants' movement in Taiwan is thus founded in the active participation of marriage migrants themselves (Hsia 2009a).

In addition to networking in Taiwan, I also help networking across borders to expand the movements for marriage migrants' rights and welfare to regional and global levels. The TAN for marriage migrants originated from the International Workshop for Asian NGOs on Female Immigrants and Migrants held in Taipei, 2005, initiated by the Awakening Foundation when I served as the board member responsible to help develop programs for migrant women. To organize this workshop, I requested Asia Pacific Mission for Migrants (APMM), a regional institute for advocating migrants' rights and welfare, to recommend speakers from other Asian countries. APMM was very interested in the themes and became the co-organizer of this international workshop.

After this international workshop, APMM decided to work on the issues of "foreign brides" and invited me to serve as a board member. To establish a new program, APMM conducted a few studies on "foreign brides" in 2007. To follow up the 2005 international workshop, APMM organized the International Conference on Border Control and Empowerment of Immigrant Brides in September 2007, in collaboration with TASAT, the Awakening Foundation, and AHRLIM. One of the conference's resolutions was to establish a transnational network, with 16 organizations from nine countries pledging to join. In October 2008, several participants from the 2007 conference gathered together when the International Migrants Alliance (IMA) organized the first International Assembly of Migrants and Refugees (IAMR) in Manila. To implement the resolution of the 2007 conference, AMM♀RE was formed on October 31, 2008. After a series of consultations, exchange programs, trainings, conferences, and campaigns, AMM♀RE transformed itself from a loose network to a formal alliance with a constitution and elected officers. After the founding assembly in March 2017 held in Bangkok, AMM♀RE was renamed AMMORE, which includes members in Taiwan, South Korea, Japan, Hong Kong, Malaysia, Australia, the Philippines, Indonesia, Canada, and the United States (Hsia 2018)

According to Porta and Tarrow (2005: 237), one of the factors for the emergence of transnational social movements is the new stratum of activists, the "rooted cosmopolitans" who are "rooted in specific national contexts, but who engage in regular activities that require their involvement in transnational networks of contacts and conflict".

As the first elected chairperson of AMMORE, I can be identified as a "rooted cosmopolitan" based in Taiwan and engaged in regular activities required for the formation and operation of TANs for migrants in general, and for marriage migrants specifically. The primary source of the beginning of my transnational activism is the transnational network for Filipino migrants movement. I was one of the Taiwanese activists contacted by the Asia Pacific Mission for Migrant Filipinos (APMMF) in the late 1990s when they tried to develop networks to support Filipino migrants. APMMF was established in 1984 as a regional research, advocacy and movement building organization for Filipino migrants in the Asia Pacific and Middle East regions and Taiwan was one of their focused countries. APMMF's establishment was the result of a Filipino migrants' movement initiated in the early 1980s, as the extension of the anti-Marcos movement in the Philippines since the 1970s. As labor migration intensified, Filipino migrant activists became aware that they needed to extend their support to non-Filipino migrants, so in 2002 APMMF was changed to APMM – the Asia Pacific Mission for Migrants – to expand their work to all migrants from different nationalities in the region. Filipino migrant activists recognize the need of simultaneously dealing with both sending and receiving countries, as well as the importance of transnational networking (Hsia 2009b).

After the initial contact by APMMF in the late 1990s, I was requested to consult or assist when there were cases of migrants in need of help. I also helped organize types of activities to enrich mutual understanding of Taiwanese and Filipino activists. All these efforts of building contacts, exchanges, and collaboration contributed to the formation of AMM♀RE.

As a scholar known for marriage migrants' issues, I have access to more networks at the national, regional, and international levels, which can easily build up "social capital" for my own career. I can therefore quickly be seen as the expert who can speak "on behalf of" marriage migrants, which in turn will gradually uproot me from the grassroots level of working with the marriage migrants and national level of networking for continuous campaigns for changes in policy and law. Without the active participation of activists rooted at the local and national levels, the transnational movements run the risk of being dominated by "professional advocates" whose activism is not grounded and who only project themselves as the "spokespersons" of the movements. These ungrounded professional advocates will not only harm the normative legitimacy of the transnational movements but also the well-being of marriage migrants, because the policy recommendations they make to the supra-national institutions would be detached from the realities of marriage migrants. Therefore, while recognizing the importance of transnational activism for marriage migrants, I argue that cross-border transnationalism should not take primacy over domestic transnationalism. Activists concerned with the well-being of marriage migrants should constantly reflect on their involvement in transnational activism both within and beyond the nation-states, and make conscious efforts to balance these two types of transnational activism (Hsia 2018).

Being constantly reflexive of the roles of praxis-oriented researchers in the movements, elsewhere (Hsia 2006b) I suggest that intellectuals should see themselves as a "conscious wolf man", rather than the leader in the movement. The "conscious wolf man" is aware of his capacity to cause harm. Therefore, before the full moon, he tries every means to prevent himself from causing fatal damage. He constantly reminds people around him that he might betray them and helps them learn all his expertise so that the people can carry on with their struggles after he eventually betrays them. This metaphor of the "conscious wolf man" can also illustrates the role of the praxis-oriented researcher: while seeing themselves as part of the movement, they do not project themselves as the leaders, but instead, continuously empower more people to gain the capacities of abstraction and analyzing, avoiding the possibility of causing a vital wound to the movement upon their future betrayal.

The role of the praxis-oriented researcher in capacity building will be illustrated in the following.

Capacity and movement building

To sustain changes initiated by action research, the praxis-oriented research must gear towards movement building. To develop and advance the movements, individuals must create certain forms of institutions or organizations, which requires the capacities of operating organizations and networking.

To build the movement for marriage migrants' rights and welfare, the organizations run by marriage migrants themselves are crucial. However, it takes time for marriage migrants to develop the capacities of institution building. Without reflecting on the role of praxis-oriented researcher in the process of movement building, one can easily become the "spokesperson" of the issues, which in turn will harm the development of grassroots movements.

Shortly after I initiated the Chinese programs for marriage migrant women in 1995, a friend of mine familiar with mechanisms in the political arena gave me some friendly advice, "The way you are acting is too slow. The best way to get attention and make changes is to call a press conference with the presence of a legislator to push the governments and a 'foreign bride' sharing her story". I fully understood that the press conference could quickly push governmental agencies to respond to the needs of "foreign brides". However, I also knew that no "foreign brides" would dare to speak in front of the media at that time. Even if I could convince a "foreign bride" from the Chinese program to attend the press conference, she would only show up with her face covered with sunglasses and a mask, so that her identity would not be revealed to the public. In such a case, I would become the spokesperson on behalf of "foreign brides" in the press conference and the appearance of a timid "foreign bride" with her face covered would only reinforce the mainstream images of "foreign brides" as helpless victims.

Being inspired and reminded by many feminists of color and from Third World countries, I was very critical of the fact that many activists impose themselves as the "spokesperson" on behalf of the marginalized mass, neglecting their subjectivity in the movements. Therefore, I decided to work from the ground up: empowering the "foreign brides" to be able to speak for themselves before any campaign was initiated. That is, I believe that capacity building for the marriage migrant should be the basis for movement building for their rights and welfare.

The capacity building started by trying to fulfill the basic needs of the marriage migrants, beginning in 1995 with the Chinese language classes. As the marriage migrants became more familiar with the Chinese language, learning Chinese alone could not attract much interest, so in 2002 we started to offer classes on parenting, since most of the marriage migrants at that time had had children and they became anxious about how to educate their children properly. Their anxiety was caused by the prevalent media reports about their children's propensity for "delayed development" which would consequently deteriorate the "quality of the population", despite their being little evidence of this and the likelihood that this was just a reflection of stereotypes and discrimination against marriage migrants (Hsia 2007). In all our classes, we endeavored to create a space where marriage migrants from different nationalities could all share their feelings and discuss issues, so that a sense of collectivity could be gradually developed.

Moreover, efforts have been made to train marriage migrants as public speakers. Since I was the first scholar studying issues of marriage migration in Taiwan, I was frequently invited to give talks at various venues and interviewed by media. While it was important to make the public more aware of the issues via these talks and interviews, I was also conscious of the danger of positioning myself as the "spokesperson". Therefore, I made plans to train marriage migrants to become public speakers. At first, I invited some marriage migrants to share their own experiences for a few minutes when I was invited to give talks. Several of the marriage migrants who had experiences in these brief sharing sessions became more confident and capable of talking for longer periods. To train marriage migrants as public speakers more systematically, I proposed to TASAT to organize training programs for marriage migrants as teachers of their home country's languages and cultures, and to speak on issues of immigrants, beginning in 2004. Since more marriage migrants were trained as public speakers, when I received invitations for talks or interviews, I often recommended those who invited me to contact TASAT directly and invite marriage migrants as speakers. Since then, TASAT has frequently received invitations and marriage migrants organized by TASAT have been invited to share their knowledge about Southeast Asia and issues about marriage migrants not only in Taiwan but also abroad.

After eight years of empowering through various programs, TASAT was formally established in 2003, which led to the need of learning how to work collectively and run an organization. Since almost all marriage migrants organized by TASAT had no prior experience in running a grassroots organization and they often encountered difficulties in collaborating with people from diverse backgrounds, TASAT has consequently experienced a lot of ups and downs since its establishment. Some organizational crises were so serious that TASAT almost ceased to exist. Whenever TASAT hits the bottom, we try to transform the organizational crisis into opportunities and eventually leap forward.

To build capacities for marriage migrants to run grassroots organizations, I conducted trainings on various themes, including collective leadership, conflict resolution, planning and assessment, critique and self-critique, among others. The training modules I conducted are based on various training handbooks I have collected from different countries, as well as the trainings I experienced previously.

In addition to trainings for organizational skills, it is also important for marriage migrants to situate themselves as part of the social movements not only in Taiwan but also at the regional and international levels. To broaden their perspectives, I often arranged for TASAT leaders to be exposed to grassroots organizations in other countries. This exposure helped marriage migrants learn from other organizations and realize that they are not alone in their struggles. As Yadrung, a TASAT leader from Thailand, reflected on her learning in my previous study (Hsia 2016):

> We went to Philippines to attend the Cordillera Day, the big event of the indigenous peoples movement ... Because of the exposure and sharing with organizations abroad, we learnt that these organizations are doing similar things and they also have problems. When we visited the organizations, I asked them: What do you do when some officers' families are against what they are doing? How does the organization help overcome that? She said that this problem, though personal, should be brought to the organization and the organization is responsible to help

handle it. After hearing her reply, I immediately cried, because I was facing great tension with my family then ... The exposure helped me realize that I was not the only one having problems and learn from others about how to deal with it.

Through training and exposure to other organizations and movements, these marriage migrants gradually developed perspectives beyond their personal problems. They began to see members of the organization as part of the bigger "we" with the same goals, and the moments of feeling discontent are perceived only as temporary emotions and should not get in the way of achieving the larger goals of the organization and the movement (Hsia 2016).

To be able to situate themselves as part of the broader social movements, it is necessary for marriage migrants to transcend the politics of identity solely based on their own nationalities, ethnicities, gender, and class. To this end, I also made efforts to help marriage migrants see the link between themselves and the so-called "others". Two crucial methods of moving towards the "others" include the creation of an environment where marriage migrants develop empathy with the other disadvantaged people and build alliances with them. For instance, since TASAT is an active member of AHRLIM, which is composed of organizations from different sectors, including those of migrant workers, TASAT members are often requested to serve as interpreters to help cases of migrant workers, which in turn helps marriage migrants develop empathy with migrant workers. By joining AHRLIM, TASAT members learn about the issues that migrant workers face and thus see the commonalities between migrant workers and themselves and the importance of collaboration. As Manchi reflected on her learning in the process:

I also had stereotypes against migrant workers, feeling that it's because of them that the Taiwanese have negative images about we Vietnamese ... After I went abroad to attend activities, I realized that migrants and immigrants from different countries are facing the same problems. (Hsia 2016: 158)

In addition to encouraging marriage migrants to join activities organized by other organizations in Taiwan, I often accompanied

TASAT's delegates to participate in activities organized by AMMORE and other international networks to expose them to other issues and learn ways of transnational networking. To build their capacities of transnational networking, I helped marriage migrants navigate these international activities, including interpretation, explaining the issues and contexts, and introducing them to various organizations and networks, so that marriage migrants could gradually become more familiar with the transnational work and more active in transnational activism.

As a result, many marriage migrants organized by TASAT have gradually broadened their perspectives and begun to understand capitalist globalization as the root cause of their escape from their home countries, and to see the importance of transnational collaboration. These marriage migrants began to see themselves and TASAT as part of the broader, global movement of im/migrants and realized the importance of linking the social movements in the home countries of im/migrants. As Pei, put it:

> After I went to the Philippines and learnt about their organizations, I am very impressed ... and feel we can learn a lot from them ... I learnt that the Filipino people are fighting, including old and young ... I was inspired to see that though they are in danger and some were even murdered by the military, they are still continuing to fight bravely ... They are so united and committed, and that's why no one is afraid ... It's the feeling of solidarity that makes people not afraid ... I feel happy doing these things because I feel meaningful and therefore happy. (Hsia 2016: 159)

All the different aspects of capacity building illustrated above are based on my constant analyses, from identifying organizational problems to ways of expanding and sustaining the movements. Moreover, these analyses not only help develop various training modules and exposure, but also lead to knowledge production grounded in the movements, such as academic work on subjectivation (Hsia 2010; 2016) and transnational activism (Hsia 2009b; 2018), which can serve as references for activists and scholars interested in similar work.

Conclusion

This long-term praxis-oriented research has lasted for more than 20 years, with the aims to empower stigmatized "foreign brides" to speak for themselves and to develop social movements that can gradually change the unequal structures, which are the root cause of their suffering and precarious conditions. The beginning and core of this long process is to empower the marriage migrants to become vocal subjects, who can speak for themselves. This subjectivity of marriage migrants is the basis of the formation of the movements for marriage migrants' rights and welfare, which started with transnationalism within Taiwan, and later expanded across borders to deal with transnationalism beyond the nation-state boundaries.

As a praxis-oriented researcher, I have played three major roles in this long process, including knowledge production, networking, and movement building. While these roles are important in the movement-building process, praxis-oriented researchers must be constantly critical of the tendency to speak about the issues "on behalf of" of the marginalized people who should be the primary actors of the movements for their own rights and welfare. Therefore, I suggest that praxis-oriented researchers should see themselves as a "conscious wolf man" rather than as the leaders of the movements. In other words, they need to continuously empower people to own not only the capacities of institution building and networking, but also abstraction and analyzing, so that the movements can be sustained even if the researchers have to leave them.

Notes

1 www.ris.gov.tw/346 [Accessed June 21, 2018].

2 Hakka is an ethnic minority in Taiwan. The community in which I initiated the Chinese literacy program was a Hakka rural community.

References

Boal, A. (1979). *The Theatre of the Oppressed*. Translated by Adrian Jackson. London: Pluto Press.

Choudry, A. and Kapoor, D. (2010). *Learning from the Ground Up: Global Perspectives on Social Movements and Knowledge Production*. New York: Palgrave Macmillan.

Freire, P. (1970). *Pedagogy of the Oppressed*. New York: Continuum.

Gupta, R. (2004). From recurring themes: Southall Black Sisters 1979–2003 and still going strong. In R. Gupta (Ed.), *From Homebreakers to Jailbreakers: Southall Black Sisters*. London: Zed Books.

Hsia, H. (1997). *Selfing and Othering in the "Foreign Bride" Phenomenon: A Study of Class, Gender and Ethnicity in the Transnational Marriages between Taiwanese Men and Indonesian Women.* Dissertation, Department of Sociology, University of Florida.

Hsia, H. (2004). Internationalization of capital and the trade in Asian women: the case of "foreign brides" in Taiwan. In D. Aguilar and A. Lacsamana (Eds.), *Women and Globalization.* Amherst, NY: Humanities Press.

Hsia, H. (2006a). Empowering "foreign brides" and community through praxis-oriented research. *Societies without Borders,* 115(1): 93–111.

Hsia, H. (2006b). The making of immigrants movement: politics of differences, subjectivation and societal movement. *Taiwan: A Radical Quarterly in Social Studies,* 61: 1–71 (in Chinese).

Hsia, H. (2007). Imaged and imagined threat to the nation: the media construction of "foreign brides" phenomenon as social problems in Taiwan. *Inter-Asia Cultural Studies,* 8(1): 55–85.

Hsia, H. (2008a). Beyond victimization: the empowerment of "foreign brides" in resisting capitalist globalization. *China Journal of Social Work,* 1(2): 130–148.

Hsia, H. (2008b). The development of immigrant movement in Taiwan: the case of Alliance of Human Rights Legislation for Immigrants and Migrants. *Development and Society,* 37(2): 187–217.

Hsia, H. (2009a). Foreign brides, multiple citizenship and immigrant movement in Taiwan. *Asia and the Pacific Migration Journal,* 18(1): 17–46.

Hsia, H. (2009b). The making of a transnational grassroots migrant movement: a case study of Hong Kong's Asian Migrants' Coordinating Body. *Critical Asian Studies,* 41(1): 113–141.

Hsia, H. (Ed.). (2010). *For Better or for Worse: Comparative Research on Equity and Access for Marriage Migrants.* Hong Kong: Asia Pacific Mission for Migrants.

Hsia, H. (2015a). Action research with marginalized immigrants' coming to voice: twenty years of social movement support in Taiwan and still going. In H. Brabury (Ed.), *The Sage Handbook of Action Research,* third edition. Thousand Oaks, CA: Sage.

Hsia, H. (2015b). Reproduction crisis, illegality and migrant women under capitalist globalization: the case of Taiwan. In S. Friedman and P. Mahdavi (Eds.), *Migrant Encounters: Intimate Labor, the State and Mobility Across Asia.* Philadelphia, PA: University of Pennsylvania Press.

Hsia, H. (2016). The making of multiculturalistic subjectivity: the case of marriage migrants' empowerment in Taiwan. In K. Iwabuchi, H.M. Kim, and H. Hsia (Eds.), *Multiculturalism in East Asia: A Transnational Exploration of Japan, South Korea and Taiwan.* London: Rowman and Littlefield.

Hsia, H. (2018). Incubating grounded transnational advocacy network: the making of transnational movements for marriage migrants. (Under review).

Iwabuchi, K., Kim, H.M., and Hsia, H. (Eds.). (2016). *Multiculturalism in East Asia: A Transnational Exploration of Japan, South Korea and Taiwan.* London: Rowman and Littlefield.

Porta, D. and Tarrow, S. (2005). *Transnational Protest and Global Activism.* Lanham, MD: Rowman and Littlefield.

INDEX

easo4 csv

free labor, 113
free-prior informed consent, 166
Freire: coding/decoding, 23, 233, 235, 271; critical consciousness, 24, 55, 233 (*see also* conscientization); generative themes, 112–113, 235–236; popular education, 21, 87, 92–94, 97, 113; problem-posing, 112, 129
funded research, 100–102, 105–106

genetically modified organisms, 34
global war on terror, 213, 214, 215, 225
going out into society, 21, 190
gradual self-eviction, 114, 116
Grameen Bank, 18, 138–139
Gramscian Marxism, 93
grassroots organization, 45, 138, 265
grassroots-oriented research: alliance with indigenous methodology, 158; and militarization, 158; as political engagement, 156–157
green revolution, 31, 117, 142, 229
guerrilla history, 5, 6, 204, 206

history: continuity, 2, 127; dialectical materialism, 39; learning, 18, 102; official, 197; oral-history-based museum, 240, 243, real, 242, relations with land, 102; resilience, 118; social historians, 190; traditional history, 28, 244
human trafficking, 253
hygienic enclosure, 21, 185

incarceration, 113, 171
indebted servitude, 9
India: Adivasi-Dalit social movement, 88; Bhopal disaster, 23, 230, 239; caste politics, 93, 100, 102, 105; development-displaced persons, 88; government forest, 101; Hindu fundamentalism, 97, 104, 228 (*see also* saffron groups); Land Acquisition Act, 10; Maoist, 97, 104; *panchayat*, 96; passive revolution, 229; Scheduled Areas Act, 90, 96; Union Carbide India Limited, 228

Indigenous: knowledge, 17, 19, 142–143, 158, 167; methodologies, 158
Indonesia: land and forest concession, 120, 123; Marga Serampas, 112, 116, 118, 119; Salim Group, 120, 123; Suharto authoritarian regime, 120, 125; Village Government Law, 112
informant, 102, 164
informational learning, 103, 122
ININNAWA, 110, 112
insurgent research, 2, 19, 159; *see also* grassroots-oriented research
internationalism, 40, 136
inter-village organizing, 95

Karsa, 111, 121, 124, 125
knowledge dissemination, 98, 100, 130
knowledge production: in academic, 98; 106, 224; criticisms, 5; cultural criticism, 5; emancipatory knowledge, 5, 99; epistemological radicalism, 6; for the movement, 15, 16, 41, 47; no neutrality, 15, 38, 54, 67; our ways, 92, 97, 119; as political engagement, 45–46, 67, 156–157

La Via Campesina, 62
labor: brokerage states, 62; exploitation, 31, 107; politics, 107, 191
land: based activism, 134; grabbing, 8, 47, 89 (*see also* dispossession); as property, 102; rights, 8, 103, 111; violence, 53; war, 11, 53
landless peasants: as research objects, 47
Landless Workers Movement: *Educação do Campo*, 54–55, 59, 65–66; fight against agribusiness, 33; Friends of the MST, 45–46, 54, 57; *garimperos*, 52; generalization of research result, 42; history of, 52–53; land occupations, 32, 38, 42, 58; research-action, 37; research dissemination, 63; research and internal strategy, 45; role for research, 35–37; Scholars' Collective, 54, 57; Sem Terrinha, 64, 65; types of research, 14, 38–39, 41; types of researchers, 41

ZED

Zed is a platform for marginalised voices across the globe.

It is the world's largest publishing collective and a world leading example of alternative, non-hierarchical business practice.

It has no CEO, no MD and no bosses and is owned and managed by its workers who are all on equal pay.

It makes its content available in as many languages as possible.

It publishes content critical of oppressive power structures and regimes.

It publishes content that changes its readers' thinking.

It publishes content that other publishers won't and that the establishment finds threatening.

It has been subject to repeated acts of censorship by states and corporations.

It fights all forms of censorship.

It is financially and ideologically independent of any party, corporation, state or individual.

Its books are shared all over the world.

www.zedbooks.net
@ZedBooks

www.ingramcontent.com/pod-product-compliance
Lightning Source LLC
Chambersburg PA
CBHW060152280326
41932CB00012B/1731